STORIES OF WOMEN WHO GREW UP IN THE CHILD WELFARE SYSTEM

OVERCOME

ANNE MAHON

GREAT PLAINS
PUBLICATIONS

Great Plains Publications gratefully acknowledges the financial support provided for its publishing program by the Government of Canada through the Canada Book Fund; the Canada Council for the Arts; the Province of Manitoba through the Book Publishing Tax Credit and the Book Publisher Marketing Assistance Program; and the Manitoba Arts Council.

Foreword © Beatrice Mosionier
Photography © Andrew Mahon
Cover image "My Tears Turn Into Something Beautiful" © Jackie Traverse
Design & Typography by Relish New Brand Experience
Printed in Canada by Friesens

Library and Archives Canada Cataloguing in Publication

Title: Overcome : stories of women who grew up in the child welfare system / Anne Mahon.
Names: Mahon, Anne, 1965- author.
Identifiers: Canadiana (print) 20220234426 | Canadiana (ebook) 20220238634 | ISBN 9781773370835 (softcover) | ISBN 9781773370842 (ebook)
Subjects: LCSH: Ex-welfare recipients—Biography. | LCSH: Ex-welfare recipients—Mental health. | LCSH: Ex-welfare recipients—Social conditions. | LCSH: Child welfare—Anecdotes. | LCSH: Poor girls—Biography. | LCSH: Poor children—Biography. | LCSH: Welfare recipients—Biography. | LCGFT: Biographies.
Classification: LCC HV715 .M34 2022 | DDC 362.7092/52—dc23

ENVIRONMENTAL BENEFITS STATEMENT

Great Plains Publications saved the following resources by printing the pages of this book on chlorine free paper made with 10% post-consumer waste.

TREES	WATER	ENERGY	SOLID WASTE	GREENHOUSE GASES
2	500	1	10	1,400
FULLY GROWN	GALLONS	MILLION BTUs	POUNDS	POUNDS

Environmental impact estimates were made using the Environmental Paper Network Paper Calculator 4.0. For more information visit www.papercalculator.org

Canadä

FSC
www.fsc.org
MIX
Paper from responsible sources
FSC® C016245

Stories are a way that we can talk to each other without having barriers between us.
Elder and author Maria Campbell, in conversation with Shelagh Rogers, November 2, 2019

What makes a tragedy bearable and unbearable is the same thing—which is that life goes on.
Miriam Toews, *Fight Night*

The author is donating all proceeds from the sale of this book to Voices: Manitoba's Youth in Care Network (www.voices.mb.ca), an organization that supports young people in and from the Child and Family Services system in Manitoba. Visit www.annemahon.ca for more information.

Individual opinions expressed in this book may not be shared by the author and other participants.

These stories are written from firsthand interviews. No records or documents have been viewed by the author.

Trigger Warning

This book is about the lives of women who were apprehended into the child welfare system, and oppressed by other systems. Each story is unique. Details may include child apprehension, abuse and neglect, suicide ideation, self-harm, physical violence, addiction, and residential school descriptions.

Table of Contents

Foreword

The founder of *Save the Children*, Eglantyne Jebb, stated, "All wars, whether just or unjust, disastrous or victorious, are waged against the child." Spoken about a hundred years ago, these words would have been true over two hundred years ago, just as they still are today.

When you grow up in the foster care system, you see the underbelly of society. Gradually, you become a part of that underbelly. Still, when the bad unspeakable things happen, as children we blame ourselves. We take on the responsibilities for those bad unspeakable things, and we think we are the bad ones. It all haunts us for a very long time.

In 1952, when I was three, my two older sisters, my older brother, and I were apprehended by the Children' Aid Society (CAS) of Winnipeg. When I was five, my sister Vivian took me to visit an auntie and uncle after a family visit at CAS. As we were going home on the bus, she told me not to tell anybody about our second visit. From that, I understood we were not supposed to go see any of our aunties and uncles.

About forty years ago, I wrote a fictional story about two sisters who, like me, grew up in foster care. Some know me best for my first novel, *In Search of April Raintree*.

As a child, as a teenager and as an adult, I had been ashamed of being *part-Indian*.

The writing of my first novel got rid of some of that shame. I am a senior now. It occurs to me that we, the First Nations people, the Inuit people, and the Métis people, were not the ones who came to Turtle Island to commit genocide and cultural genocide. I will not carry the shame of the oppressor anymore. I think it is time to let the oppressors carry their own shame.

Shortly after the signing of the first treaties, John A. Macdonald formed the first government under the Conservative party, then known as the Liberal-Conservative party. In 1876, he passed the Indian Act. It gave a name to a war against the children of the Original inhabitants. The Euro-Canadian government made residential schools compulsory as a means of assimilating Treaty Indian children. Indian agents and police went from reserve to reserve to force the removal of children from their homes, threatening parents with imprisonment.

Churches helped the government by running the residential schools, which were intentionally located far from home communities to separate the children from their families and homes. They deliberately destroyed Aboriginal languages, traditions and cultural identities. They physically, sexually and psychologically abused the students. They imposed their own languages and religions.

Métis people do not have treaty rights. However, nuns raised my mother from when she was about three years old. That was why she attended Indian residential schools until she was eighteen. Students from Métis communities had to attend church-run day schools.

Over the years, whispers of heinous criminal activities against the students by staff at the residential schools began to seep out. Through the years, the churches tried to bury their secrets. Some of the former students tried to tell of those secrets but no one in power believed them. However some Euro-Canadians with moral courage did hear those whispers and they helped force the closures of residential and day schools. The secrets are now being unburied.

In 1951, instead of helping families of the residential school system heal, the federal

> I will not carry the shame of the oppressor anymore. I think it is time to let the oppressors carry their own shame.

government absolved itself from the shame of their residential schools by giving provinces jurisdiction over Indigenous child welfare, a system that would continue what the residential schools had started. Thus the war against the child continued.

The residential schools became the foundation of the child welfare system that continues institutionalized racism, also known as systemic racism. Some of the former foster children of this book have experienced forced assimilation, which is so subtle no one is aware they are living it. This system throws them off and intentionally keeps them off balance. The first casualty is Trust, followed by Forgiveness. Some have had good foster homes and some have not been as fortunate. I believe balance was lost when parents were lost. Many who told of their experiences are thoughtful thinkers, and have processed their thoughts in a way that will help set lives back in balance.

Our hope is that our traditions can see us through the negative experiences of our childhoods. We have strengths that come to us through our parents. When I was seven, I was without any Indigenous human guidance. I was taking Catechism, preparing for our first sacraments. One day, a knowledge came to me that I had three animal guides who would help me through my life. That traditional knowledge was like a gift that came to me because of my parents. I can read my Catechism book, but this knowledge was not written down, and it became a part of me. This gift meant that I would do something special in my life. Over time, this knowledge became a part of my spirituality.

We began our lives with innocence, and trust, and joy and curiosity. We are supposed to grow from that: to bond with our parents and our siblings; and with our spouses or partners; and with our children; and with our communities.

I believe that the people of Turtle Island, whether they know it or not, have a traditional knowledge of the Haudenosaunee's Great Law of Peace. What we do today will affect the people seven generations in the

> The residential schools became the foundation of the child welfare system that continues institutionalized racism, also known as systemic racism.

future. This is why we should always do our best for ourselves and for others. I believe this knowledge will return to us and the more that people become aware of this knowledge, the more we will challenge ourselves to take on the responsibilities of doing better for not just the land and the waters and the animals, but also for ourselves. It will be up to us to end this war against our children.

Anne Mahon has a unique ability to inspire trust and confidence and gratitude. Most importantly, she gives the participants the freedom to tell their stories. Talking about traumatic times can be so difficult for some but with her compassion, Anne inspires them to find their courage.

Beatrice Mosionier, June 1, 2022

Some Numbers

- Manitoba has the highest rate of children in care among Canadian provinces.[1]

- There are over 11,000 children in care in Manitoba and this number has been steadily rising.[2]

- Almost 90% of the children in care in Manitoba are Indigenous.[3]

- For children who enter care at less than one year of age, over one quarter (26%) stay at least 12 years in care.[4]

- Less than 10% of youth in permanent care graduate from high school.[5]

- Less than 5% of youth in permanent care go into post-secondary education studies.[6]

- 51.5% of people experiencing homelessness have been in the care of CFS at one point in their lives.[7]

- One study of youth who had aged out of the child welfare system found that depression and/or depressive symptoms/treatment was experienced by 48% of participants.[8]

Jackie

I thought a lot about how I'd begin to tell my story, and figured it's by telling the first memory I have of my mom. It's not going to reflect good on her, but I think it explains a lot.

I had to have been about four. Me and my mom lived in a house on Logan. We were really poor. I don't remember even eating in that house. We had a bed with one sheet. I was sitting on the bed with my mom when she just stood up, walked out the front door, onto the porch, and down the stairs to the street. I ran out after her and saw her walk to the curb and stick out her thumb. I had never seen this before, and I didn't know what was going on. It didn't take a minute and a car picked her up. And I remember standing there on the steps in a T-shirt, watching her get into that car, and yelling, "Mommy!"

I knew enough to push the chair up to the door and lock it. Not the next day, but the next day after that, my auntie and uncle came there looking for my mom and saw that I was all alone. They were young, just teenagers. They were surprised my mom had left me. But they didn't know any better, so they left me too.

Again that night, I stayed alone. My mom was gone for three days. She finally came home, drunk, and she brought a party home with her. That's all I remember. So I guess you could say that my first memory was of her abandoning me. Leaving me to drink. Most of my memories of my mom are centered around alcohol. I don't really have a memory

ANDREW MAHON

of her sober. She was always drinking. I still think about that first memory and cry about it. It's not me crying for myself now, it's me crying for that little girl. Like how could somebody do that?

My mom was fifteen when she had me. I have two sisters and a brother. I'm the oldest. My one sister is three years younger than me and the other one is five years younger. And then my brother was born in 1975, because I was six or seven when he was taken. I saw him just once. My mom had been so happy she finally had her boy after she had three girls. I remember her bringing him to visit at my dad's house where I lived. I didn't know whose baby it was because he was brand new and my mom was never around much. She was breastfeeding him. He was the only one that she breastfed. But Children's Aid took him from her as a newborn and adopted him out in the Seventies Scoop.

I never met my biological father. My mom had an arrangement with this man named Joe. He had a relationship with my mom and thought I was going to be his child, but I came out another man's child. I was dark and had big eyes. I didn't look anything like Joe. I came out a Portuguese instead of a Hungarian! But

it didn't matter to him. Joe loved me and he raised me. I called him dad. He was an amazing man—not only from what he did for me, but what he did for other people.

Ever since I was about ten, my dad had a restaurant on Main Street. There's a lot of homeless and a lot of street people down there. He cared for them. Every day my dad gave them a free meal, let them sit in the restaurant and talk and drink coffee. They'd get their bags of tobacco with rolling papers too. You could tell that some of them were mentally ill. I'd get mad sometimes because they'd ask to borrow five bucks from my dad, and I would've just saw the same guy borrow five bucks the last week. I'd say, "Dad, he never pays you back. Why do you keep giving him five bucks?"

"Jackie, you might not know this, but God sees everything, and if I say *I don't have five bucks* but I have an extra five bucks in my pocket, God knows. And if I already have what I need, and the other guy doesn't have what he needs…" That's the way my dad thought.

When my dad would tell his stories he would get so excited he would laugh-cry. It was just the beautifulest thing. He said, "You know, Jackie, you ask me why I do things for others? It feels good. That's why." I'll never forget that. He's right; it feels good. Joe died in June 2018. He was ninety. I miss him.

My dad cared for me from the time I was born. Fed me, changed my diapers, everything. He fell in love with me, I guess. He was just a very good man. He knew my mom had a drinking problem, and he didn't want her to lose me. I lived with my dad most of the time. He was amazed by the drawings I did. I started drawing when I was about four. I knew already at that age I was going to be an artist. He bought me art supplies and put me in art classes at the Winnipeg Art Gallery when I was in Grade 3. He's the reason I'm here—the reason I'm alive and the reason I'm an artist.

But I also remember that drawing was like my babysitter. I remember, when I was about four, my dad setting everything up on the couch and putting the black, rotary-dial phone on the pillow, then putting out the number to the Hungarian Village. "You phone me here if you need to talk to Daddy. If anything happens, if you need me, if you're scared." He showed me how to work the phone. He gave me my colouring books, my paper. I had the smelly markers and this big box of crayons that had so many colours.

"Okay, Daddy."

"You draw me nice pictures and Daddy will look at them when he comes home, okay?"

I wanted to make my dad proud. I didn't realize that drawing was my babysitter. There was nobody else to watch me I guess. My dad needed a break too. But it's kind of sad. Even thinking about that hurts.

My mom was out drinking. Doing her thing. There'd be times where I could be living with my dad and I was so happy. But my mom would come back and take me from him. I think she was trying to make him mad. Who knows? Maybe she was trying to hurt him because she could see how much he loved me.

There was this one time where my mom had me, took me away from my dad. She and I must have been at one of those old hotels on Main Street, because I remember the old glass windows you could open, up high above the door. My mom and her friends were locked out of their room. I don't know how many times I was pushed over those open windows and dropped into the room so I could open the door for them. I must have been young, man. She was with her friends, there must have been five or six of them, and they were drunk. There wasn't very much light in there. I don't know why. I went in the bedroom and my mom told me to go to sleep. They had their chairs in a little circle. I could hear them outside my room crying and I didn't know what the heck was going on. I opened the door and that's when I could see they were all cutting their arms—slashing up. I remember I could see red even though it was so dark. That red, it shined. It scared the shit out of me. I closed my door. I don't remember what I thought, because I was so little. I went back to sleep. But the colour—that vibrant red—is still in my mind. And I remember the suffering and the crying and the moaning. They were all doing it at the same time. I remember wondering why they were so sad.

My mom and dad would fight, and then I'd end up in care. I don't even really know how old I was the first time I went to care. I was in about Grade 1. My dad had said, "Don't go to your grandma's place." He'd never, ever said that to me before. But my friend called on me, and we went to my granny's anyway. My mom had left the babies (my two younger sisters) there with my two uncles who were sniffers. My uncles were lying on the couch under blankets, sniffing.

I said, "Where are my sisters?" I went to the room and the babies jumped up in their cribs. Nobody had fed them. The window was smashed and there was snow on the floor. It was freezing in there. The uncles had the only blankets and they wouldn't give them to us. The babies were in diapers. My youngest sister's diaper was hanging down to her knees and she had lollipop stuck all over her hands. (When the babies cried, they'd give them lollipops just to shut them up.) She was jumping up and down in her crib just so happy to see somebody.

I said, "Well, we can't leave them here." I was not even in Grade 2, but I knew I couldn't leave them there like that. There were no clothes for them—we had looked. No winter jackets. So we took our coats off and wrapped the babies in them and carried them to my dad's place. The babies were heavy. We walked eleven blocks with them. Nobody drove by in a car and said, *Hey man, look at those kids in the dead of winter with no jackets, carrying babies.* They're lucky, those babies, that they didn't freeze their feet off because they were hanging out of the bottom of the jackets. But we got them there to my dad's place.

My dad was very happy because we had rescued the babies and he loved children. But he gave me shit. He was mad. Later, I could hear him on the phone saying, "I'm going to lose my job. I can't lose it." And then I heard him say, "I need help. No, I don't know where she is." I found out that he'd been talking to the Children's Aid and I guess they had asked, "Where's the mother?"

And next thing you know, there was a knock on the door and I heard my dad saying, "No, no, not Jackie, not Jackie." He was telling them to take my sisters. The Children's Aid workers didn't listen. They took us all. So that was my first memory of being taken into care.

I'm not sure if I was in care before. Maybe as a baby, a toddler, I don't know. It's nothing that was ever talked about, but I remember always hiding from Children's Aid. My mom was always at the window watching. My aunt knew what to do. She'd pick me up and whisper to be quiet and then hide me under the sink in the bathroom. So I have a feeling that maybe I was taken away at some point as a baby. Nobody's ever talked about it.

Yeah, Children's Aid...those were bad words in our house. I knew those words probably right after I learned the words mom and dad. The Children's Aid was just as bad as the police. When you heard *Children's Aid*, you knew they weren't there to aid you. They were there to take you.

When I was five or six my cat had kittens. They all came out pure white. I loved them and I'd play with them all the time. Then one day I came home and went straight for my kittens. They were gone. I asked my auntie, "Where's my kittens?" And she said, "Children's Aid took them away." And it made sense to me. That night I cried and I pictured them, each of my six little kitties in those kind of hospital beds with green bedding. They were being put to bed all in a row, kind of like in a dormitory, tucked in by white women. And the kittens didn't look happy. They didn't look anything. Emotionless. I learned to fear Children's Aid at a very young age.

That first time, I was put in a white family. It was not good. They were very mean to me. I remember the mom and dad saying, "Stay in the room, don't come out." I didn't listen very well, and I got curious. So I went and poked my head out and walked down the hall. In the 70s they used to have a photographer that'd come to your house, put up a backdrop, then the family stands in front of it, and they'd take the family photo. The family was standing in front of some beautiful mountain landscape and the father was holding the son and the mother had the daughter. A perfect white family. I was standing there watching that and thinking, *I could never be in this picture. Who's that little brown girl in the photograph? That's why I had to be in my room, because I am not a part of this family.* I learned right then and there that I didn't belong.

They would say things about my family, about Indians, about my mom in front of me. How my mom was an alcoholic and she didn't love me. That she didn't even care, she'd rather drink. That was a form of mental abuse that I got in my first foster home. So I learned to keep my mouth shut while they talked bad about me and bad about my family. I had no control over any of that. There were a few times that I did speak up, but I got my mouth hit pretty hard,

sometimes got my lip split open. I was hit in pretty much every foster family I ever had. I had no good experience in any foster home. I always felt like an inconvenience. I knew these foster people didn't want me there. Everywhere I went. My whole fucking life.

My dad fought to get me back and he did. My dad was a millwright and he worked on the Jenpeg Hydro Dam (before he had the diner) until I was ten. So sometimes when he was away working, he would pay people to look after me because he was scared to lose me to Children's Aid. I was always a problem for my dad. "What am I gonna do with Jackie? I have to work." I would hear him say that and then he'd put me somewhere with one of his friends, and I'd just want to be with my mom. Sometimes my mom took me back but then I would end up in care because she was too sick. That was a messed-up time.

I'm not sure how many foster families I lived with. There's confusion because I was a little girl, and I don't remember which homes were my dad's friends. But altogether I think I was in about seven foster homes. I ended up in another foster home in Transcona. I think

> I learned right then and there that I didn't belong.

I was in Grade 2. And that's where I was abused and sexually molested. I was touched by the father all the time, even in front of his family. I was abused not just at that home, but at multiple homes, too. But that one home in Transcona was the worst.

Then when that father was out, his wife would show me pornography and say, "We're doing this tonight, me, you, and Martin." And I'd cry, "No. I'm scared. No, I don't want to." That's when they would give me whisky to knock me out. They blacked me out and did whatever they wanted to me. I'd wake up naked on the floor. I felt such shame when I'd wake up, because they could see me naked. Grade 2! This happened for a couple of months. All I remember is being touched, molested by them. I don't remember how it felt physically.

I'm glad I don't remember anything because I don't know how I would be able to handle those memories. I might not even be here still, because on top of everything else, that'd be fucking way too much. I thought they were allowed to do whatever they wanted to me because it wasn't my home, and who was I to say things because I'm a kid? Sometimes if I disobeyed they'd also withhold food. One time they made me sleep outside on the steps all night. It was a spring thaw, but it was cold.

That's when I began to steal. On my way to school there was a drugstore I would go to. I'd open my lunchbox up and I'd pack it with chocolate bars. They never watched me. Then I'd go outside and eat like twenty chocolate bars before I got to school. Then when I had to go back home I would steal twenty more. I'd eat them at the bus shack before I had to go back in that house.

I'd been doing that for a couple months and then, finally, somebody at the drugstore saw me. They told me not to come back no more. They never took what was in my lunchbox, but they must have known. I'd been going there every day, twice a day for two months, right? I used to think, *Why did I do that?* But that's how I coped. I know that now. Food's been a way to cope since. Eating those chocolate bars made me think less about what I had to go through once I got back into that house. It was a treat for me, I guess.

After that, I started to collect paper. I remember one time walking home from school and seeing a bunch of books on the ground. There was loose leaf and plain sheets of paper. I was just so thrilled. It's like that paper was put there for me, you know? *No more chocolate bars? Here, draw.* So I took that paper. But I could never have anything in that house for myself, so I had to hide the paper outside. I'd say, "Can I go play?" Then I'd go to the hiding spot and I would draw. Then it rained and everything got ruined. But I did have that paper for a while.

I was in that house almost a year. I left because of my mom. I got visits from my mom and my dad sometimes. One day at a visit my mom was giving me that talk about how nobody should touch me here or there, and if somebody did, I should tell her right away. I said, "Mom that happens to me every day." And my mom lost it. She freaked out and started crying. (I think my mom was abused too. I don't know for sure the issues my mom went through, but I think that's why she drank so much. I know a lot of people use drugs and alcohol for coping mechanisms.) So my mom told someone, and I never went back to that home.

But then Children's Aid put me in the next home and it happened again. And then they put me in the next home and it happened again. I used to tell my dad about all this, but he thought I was lying so I could come home. He never believed me. I think about that, even to this day. It was like he was in denial; he'd look away, or change the subject. I don't know. Maybe he was abused. Or maybe because he would never ever harm a child, he just didn't believe that men would do that kind of stuff. He was too kind.

I think it was at the third foster home when I talked to my dad's friend on the phone and I told her what was happening. She came there and they took me to the police station, but the cops didn't believe me so nothing ever came of it. At that point I learned that authorities don't give a shit and they don't believe you. So after that when things happened, I never told anybody anything.

Abuse even happened while I was visiting family. A cousin of mine tried to force my legs open and have sex with me. I was in Grade 3! He was a man already. My other two cousins knew what he was going to do to me and they went along with it. But I cried out and, with all my strength, I kept my legs closed. I kept pushing him and I said, "I'll tell. I'll tell." So he got off me. It didn't stop him from groping me or feeling me up whenever he had the opportunity, but he didn't rape me. Thank God for that.

There would be times my mom would take me, but she always fucked up and lost me. I guess she wanted to love her first baby, but like, why take me? She had nothing to offer. My mom would sniff, and I started doing that too. I sniffed glue and solvents with her from the age of five, maybe even four. I remember she'd squeeze the glue in a plastic bag and give it to me. And I'd just go and sniff and black out.

My family didn't know that was bad. They thought sniffing was just a normal thing. But then, this one time we were sniffing and I got really sick. I was limp and my granny was rocking me and crying. I remember my granny talking in Saulteaux and yelling at them, telling them no more. She took me to the hospital. She didn't tell the doctors that I sniffed, but they looked me over and when they looked at my eyes they could tell that I'd been sniffing because my pupils were degenerating. They were being burnt away from the solvents. So I was apprehended right there, which was good. I could have gone blind, or I could have had no brain left at all.

I went to so many different schools. I never had the chance to actually learn anything. I remember in Grade 1 I didn't know how to read. I just looked at pictures and made up my own stories, did what other kids were doing, you know? I didn't want to let on that I didn't know how to read.

One day the teacher said, "Tomorrow we're sitting around in a circle and everybody's going to read a paragraph from this book, *Mr. Mugs*." And oh my God, talk about stress. My mind was racing: *How am I going to pull this one off? How am I going to read when I don't know how?* I couldn't sleep that night. *Where would I sit? How do I know what part is my part to read?*

So the next day I sat there and everybody read their section and then it came to me. I put my head down. "Jackie, it's your turn. Jackie. Jackie?" the teacher said. I kept my head down and she came around to me. She went down to my level and talked to me. "What's wrong, Jackie?" I started crying and said, "I don't know how to read."

That teacher took a good interest in me. She took me alone and taught me to read. I picked it up so fast. She was amazed that I could actually read these big words from the Britannica Encyclopedia. I didn't know what they meant, but I was pronouncing and reading them. My dad cried he was so happy when he saw that I could read. He had come from Hungary in 1956 and he had to learn English. He always had a very hard time spelling and reading English.

That teacher was so proud of me after I learned to read that she gave me a little hardcover book about Leonardo da Vinci. I looked at those pictures—the Mona Lisa, and his easel—over and over. That's where I first saw what a painter was.

I remember that teacher being kind, but most of them just didn't pay attention to us. I always got put to the back of the class. *There's nothing significant about you.* That's how you're made to feel. All the white, well-to-do pretty little girls and boys were in the front rows. The undesirables were at the back looking at each other. *You know why you're here? Yeah, me too.* Got those feelings.

In one foster home, I went to Catholic school. They were so mean to me there. They did not like me. I was the only Native kid and they knew I was in a foster home. One time I found seven dollars on the floor. I guess you were supposed to go turn money in. I didn't know that. I was thinking, *I'm gonna go buy candies and I'll share them with my friends after school.* I put the money in my jacket

pocket. The principal came in and went straight to my jacket and found the money. He pulled me out right away. I didn't know what I had done wrong because I didn't understand. He pulled my pants down in his office and put me over his lap. He pulled out a big, long wooden ruler and he said, "Now you're gonna get a strap for every dollar you stole." I got seven slaps on the ass. Hard too, like whips, eh? I cried and I couldn't sit right for a couple weeks.

I remember being called awful names in foster care, in schools—"wagon burner" and "dirty little Indian." They'd say *Indian* like it was a bad thing, but I was like Teflon, man. That just bounced off because not once in my life can I say that I ever felt shame for being Indigenous.

One day when I was twelve, my uncle came to see me and my dad. When he walked through the door he brought in sadness with him and I knew something was wrong. After he left, my dad came and talked to me. He said, "Jackie, your mom's sick."

I said, "I don't understand. Is she dying?"

"I think she's just sick. You have to go to Vancouver to see your mom. You're gonna go with your Auntie Maude."

As soon as we got to Vancouver, we went to the hospital and my other auntie was there. (Not a real auntie, but in my culture we call adult women aunties.) She said, "Your mom doesn't recognize nobody. She hasn't been able to talk. She just stares into the air so she probably won't recognize you, Jackie. Don't feel sad." I was thinking, *My mom won't recognize me?* I knew she would. We walked in to her room and she had breathing tubes and she was jaundiced and swollen really big.

I looked at her and said, "Mom." She said my name and I was so happy that she recognized me. She found the strength, even with those things in her mouth. I went to hug her and she hit me. I ran out of the hospital room.

Auntie Maude's sitting out there and she said, "What happened?"

I said, "She hit me."

She said, "Maybe because you've been a bad girl all your life. She never got the chance to spank you and she's finally giving you what you deserve."

I thought, *I'm a bad kid?* I took that in and for a long time I carried that.

It wasn't until I was fifteen and talked to a staff person at Marymound who I got really close with, that I thought differently about

ANDREW MAHON

what happened. I told her that story and she said, "Your mom wasn't hitting you, she just couldn't breathe." Which makes more sense, right? "Jackie, you were blocking her breathing tubes." (I was a big kid.) I didn't know

I was blocking her breathing. I know this now, but I took it the wrong way back then because I was a kid. My mom wasn't hitting me; my mom loved me. I choose to believe that instead. That comment lifted a thousand pounds off me. I didn't have to carry that guilt around no more. It had been three years of guilt. But then I resented my auntie for her comment. Why would she say that to a kid?

That same night when I left the hospital, we went to my Auntie Shirley's for the night. I had a cousin named Claudia there. She was just beautiful; I really looked up to her. The next day she said, "I have a softball game, come watch me play."

I said, "No, I should go to hospital to see my mom."

She said, "Your mom's gonna be okay. Don't worry about your mom."

I've always done things I never wanted to, just to please other people. I didn't want to go to the game, but I went. I was sitting there trying to watch her play, but I wasn't watching, I was just sad and thinking about my mom.

When we returned to my auntie's I saw my mom's bags in the living room. I recognized them from the hospital room. I shouted,

"No. No." and ran upstairs and cried. But I stopped because I thought, *No she's not dead.* I imagined my mom on vacation. I thought, *I'll see her when she comes back. My mom didn't die. No.* That's a twelve-year-old child's denial, right?

My dad came out to Vancouver to try and see my mom, so he was with me. We got stuck in Vancouver because we couldn't afford the airfare back to Winnipeg. My grandma and I ended up getting bus vouchers from the welfare office and we bussed it back to Winnipeg. My dad stayed in Vancouver because he didn't want to take a bus. He wanted to take a plane but didn't have the cash.

I was still in denial on that bus ride home. At first, I was trying to assist my granny and help her carry my mom's belongings. Everything was in garbage bags. We had to switch buses. My granny had just lost her baby and was taking it out on me. She hit me and told me to leave her alone. From Calgary on, we didn't sit together no more, and I didn't try to help her with the bags. She wanted to do that on her own.

When I got to Winnipeg, I didn't say goodbye to her. I just walked from the bus depot to the bus stop, and I got to my dad's in East Kildonan. Twelve years old and I had to go home alone after losing my mom. I got to his place, and I opened the door and that's when I remembered my goldfish. I ran to see it, and it was floating on top of the water in the fishbowl, just a carcass. That gave me the teaching about death and that's when I understood that my mom really was dead. I broke down. My mom died at age twenty-seven. I didn't see my dad for another four or five days. I was alone by myself at the house dealing with the loss of my mother. That was a lot.

Somebody phoned and told me my mom's funeral was gonna be at Lake St. Martin First Nation where my mom was from. My father still hadn't returned from Vancouver, and I had to get to the funeral. Nobody was coming to get me. I went down Main Street and I bummed change for the bus trip to the funeral. I always remembered when my mom was drunk she would say, "I want white roses at my funeral." So I told people I needed to buy flowers too. I couldn't buy a dozen white roses. I didn't have enough money to buy them and the bus ticket too. But I got her six white roses. Then I caught a bus to my mom's funeral. There was a black dress that had been left at my house by a Hungarian lady

and it fit me. I knew you had to wear black if you're mourning, so I took that dress and wore it. I went to my granny's for the funeral and then my dad made it out there too. I never held a grudge against my granny.

After my mom died, I swear it must've been just a month, my uncle came in from the reserve. He brought some people into my dad's restaurant. My uncle said, "Joe, I brought you a girlfriend." I guess my dad didn't want to be alone. He was fifty-seven. So now he's got a chance to be with a twenty-one-year-old woman, Lorraine, and she was beautiful. I could tell right away that she was after my dad's money. She came home with my dad that night, and I walked in on them and saw what I didn't want to see. That told me what kind of woman she was. My whole life was changed after my dad met Lorraine. I was no longer a priority. I was tossed aside, and I knew I wasn't welcome there.

I broke my wrist in school and couldn't call my dad at Lorraine's because our phone was cut off. I was living alone at my dad's and he was living at Lorraine's. I was trying to go to school, trying to write and I knew there was something wrong because my wrist was very painful. I started digging in the couch, and I found enough money for bus fare. I took myself to Health Science Centre hospital. They gave me an X-ray and said my wrist was broken. They didn't ask me a single question. Not where my parents were, not nothing. But at twelve I was a big kid. I was 172 pounds. Maybe they thought I was older, or my parents were in the waiting room. I don't know. The doctor put my wrist in a cast. I had enough bus fare to get back home. I just looked after myself.

I had a beautiful green diary that my mom had bought me when she went to Dawson's Creek. It was in a wooden box and you could put a lock on it. She had said, "You can write down things in here and nobody will ever see them." I started writing in that diary after my mom died. But Lorraine broke it open. She started writing bad stuff in there about the things I wrote, about my feelings. I had a crush on somebody named Gary and she had a brother named Gary. She wrote in there, "You ugly fat pig, my brother would never go out with you." But it wasn't her brother Gary; it was somebody at school.

Lorraine had two other boyfriends while she was with my dad. She ended up having six kids. My dad took in all her kids. He loved those kids even though they weren't his. He could never just let kids go without.

That's when I started to run away. She was too wicked for me to stay in their house. I remember how mean and vindictive that woman was. I know that hurt people, hurt people. I went to stay with friends. I stayed wherever I could, with whoever would put me up. Some people put me up for a couple days and then I'd hear, "She can't stay here no more." I never had to sleep outside though. My friends would feel sorry for me and they'd say, "I'll sneak you in, I don't care." That's how I got by. Fuck, I starved because everybody was so poor. This was in the North End and there'd be hardly enough food to go around for them, let alone for one of their kid's friends. I went from being obese, wearing a size-36 jean, to a size 26 in less than a year.

When I did go home, it was to change clothes and eat something or maybe because I was just hoping it would be better. But it never was. When I was around, my dad beat on me. I think Lorraine was telling him to, because he wasn't a mean person. She was telling my dad stuff about me—like that I was a prostitute (which I wasn't). Growing up my dad would smack the back of my head—he had old-fashioned ways of teaching me—but never before did he beat me. But when I was thirteen, I started fighting back. I was sick and tired of being hit. I fought him back, and he never hit me again.

I finally found a stable place when my best friend, Helen, convinced her mom, Irene, to take me in. I stayed probably a few months, but then the cops came and took me away. My father had phoned them when I ran away. Irene was crying. Helen was crying. The cops took me to Seven Oaks.

Seven Oaks used to be a place where they'd hold youth that were "runners" until they could find them a placement in a group home or foster home, whatever. But I liked it there. I made friends and got close to the staff. I loved the place. The staff loved me. They were caring. I felt safe because the place was locked. All my friends were there. Social workers would place me in a foster home, but nothing else compared to Seven Oaks, so I'd run away and end up back again. I was put in there sixteen different times, I think. Finally they got fed up. They knew I wanted to stay there but I couldn't, I had no choice.

Seven Oaks wasn't a place to live, it was a holding place.

When I was thirteen, I was back living with my dad for a while. I had this teacher, Joe McLellan, who was always kind, always soft-spoken. I've never ever seen Joe mad, or heard him raise his voice for anything. Joe got me playing basketball. I had never been interested in sports. I was always teased and picked last for teams. But Joe told me the team needed girls, needed me. I couldn't say no to Joe because he loved us all and he was the best teacher in the school. Joe's always been there for me. I saw him all the time until he passed away in 2021.

One day in class he said, "Hey guys, get your pencil crayons, your markers, whatever you have and get your stuff ready. We're going on a field trip today." I was just so excited wondering where the hell we were going. We ended up at the Wah-Sa Gallery. It was an Indigenous art gallery. Oh my god—the colours, the images. I stepped into a new world once I passed through those doors. Before then, I didn't even know there were Indigenous artists or painters. I didn't know what Indigenous art was. I had never been exposed to it. I didn't know there were different genres of art. But I knew I wanted to be an artist.

Joe told us to pick a piece of art, sit down in front of it and try to duplicate it. Of course, I picked the hardest one by the great painter Cyril Assiniboine. It was a challenge to do this piece. The picture was of a warrior with a shield. I ended up using three pieces of paper taped together to finish it because it was a big piece. When I finished, everybody's like "Holy smokes, look what Jackie did." People were just amazed. It's hard to stay humble when everybody's bragging about your stuff, but I was really, really happy with it. I used pencil crayon and marker. I looked at the picture so closely and I saw different textures. I wondered what it would be like to use paint. That experience was really life changing. It helped to influence my life path and the way I thought. My dream was con-firmed. I could see myself as a Native artist. I didn't know then that one day I would have my first solo show at the Wah-Sa Gallery. Joe would be the first person to walk through the doors there and the first to buy a painting at that show. But so many things got in the way.

When I'd run away from those group homes they'd threaten me saying, "If you fuck up one more time tonight, you're going to Marymound." We were scared of Marymound because we heard all these horror stories. Marymound was a place for bad girls. Delinquent girls. That place was for girls that were pregnant and unwed, or cast aside by their families, or without family, and probably girls with mental health problems too.

When I was fifteen they put me in Marymound. I stayed there six months, and then I went to a co-ed group home. I lasted three weeks. They even put me back in Seven Oaks once. Yeah! I was happy. But I had a feeling it would be short-lived. One day this social worker came to see me at Seven Oaks and said, "Guess where you're going?" There was this big marble ashtray on the table. I locked the door to the room we were in, picked up that ashtray and knocked him over the head with it. Broke his glasses and cut his head open. I said, "There's no fucking way I'm going back to Marymound." He could have charged me, but he didn't. I was taken back to Marymound. I had nightmares about being taken to Marymound until I was in my forties.

I remember this one day—I'd been there for a while—I was *spinning out*. That's when you don't listen and they have to restrain you. I'm not one of those people that spins out very often. There were some kids that spinned out three times a week, or sometimes three times a day. But I was just not listening that day. The staff gave me a direct order to go to my room until I calmed down, but I kept mouthing them off. Then they said, "We'll take your privileges away."

"Fuck you."

Then they said, "We will force you into your room." Two of them came and they started removing me and then I started fighting them. The staff restrained me and put me in the back room, but I kept kicking at the door and I was disturbing the whole unit. They came and dragged me down the stairs and put me in this other big room. They just shoved me in there and locked the door behind.

There was a bed and a chair and four big windows. I sat on that bed and started crying. I looked at that chair and I looked at the windows and I saw that there were chains on the windows at the top so that you could only open them up a bit. I took my bra off and tied it around my neck. I pushed that chair up to the window and I reached up to the chain and tied my bra to it. Then, I jumped.

I thought death was instant when you hung yourself. Like, *Boom* you're dead. I didn't know you had to suffocate and suffer. I was hanging, but I could still touch a bit. My toes were just grazing the ground. I thought, *Fuck, this is suffering.* I looked at the door. I was thinking, *Oh my god, if they see me like this, they're gonna send me to Selkirk Mental Hospital.* (First you get threatened to go to Marymound, and from Marymound you get threatened with Selkirk.) And I didn't want to die; it hurt to die. My bra was so taut, but I got my fingers in there, reached up, and I pulled it over my head. The bra went up with the chain. I was breathing again, and I just started crying.

I sat on the bed, and thought, *You can't even kill yourself!* I looked at my bra, and I looked at the door. *If they see my bra up there, I'm going to Selkirk.* I climbed back up on the chair, but the bra was pulled so tight. I kept looking at the door and pulling at my bra. Finally, I got it loose and I came back down. The bra was all stretched out. I put it back on and wrapped it around me twice. They never knew.

After my last bit in Marymound, I was sent to my last short-term placement, a receiving home. An Indian guy with long hair came to the door with a file folder under his arm. He was my cousin Mervin Traverse. He said, "I'm from Anishinaabe Child & Family Services (ACFS). Here's my paperwork, I've come to get Jackie Traverse. We are now taking her under our care." They told me to go get my stuff. I thought, *Yes, finally somebody's come to get me*. I was sixteen.

ACFS tried putting me in this place on Ross Avenue where you got your own little room. It was all young women, and ACFS was trying to help us live on our own. It just felt so "ghetto" to me and I didn't like it. I took the keys, but I never spent a night there. As soon as they left me there, I phoned my friend Helen. She was going with her uncle and his two teenage kids to Gimli, to live there, and I wanted to go with them. Her uncle said yes, so they came and picked me up and I went with them. They're Native people from Saskatchewan. They became my second family and I'm still really close to all of them. But, eventually I had to come back because Helen's uncle couldn't afford to look after me and all of us.

The ACFS workers were looking for me. They found out I didn't stay at that place on Ross. I went through five workers with that organization. The last worker I had was Adolph. He said, "You know what, Jackie? I think they've just been moving you around too much. How about you think about getting your own place? Isn't it time?" I said yes. By then I was seventeen. I remember my age because I was pregnant.

Love at first sight does exist. I met my first baby's father in Seven Oaks when I was thirteen or fourteen. We looked at each other, and *Boom*. We were together on and off for nine years. He treated me like shit—cheated on me with multiple women while I was pregnant, hit me, abandoned me when I went into labour. But that's how I thought it was supposed to be because I'd been treated like that my whole life. I had my oldest daughter when I was eighteen.

I decided to go to a program intended for young single mothers because I wanted to learn how to be a mother and look after my baby. At that program you go daily for programming and they teach you how to look after your child. But they didn't accept me into the program. I had gone for an interview; I was well spoken and had dreams. My baby was clean. I wasn't broken enough for them. I guess from the outside it looked like I had my shit together. My baby was only a month old then. Again, let down by another agency when seeking help. Just think if I'd been given those life skills.

My extended family loves babies—my great-aunt's children, my cousins. First they started saying, "Can we see the baby? We'll take her, give you a break." Then "We'll keep her overnight," and then, "We might as well take her for the weekend." I started going out with my friends. I got caught back up in my old lifestyle. I think my family knew that I would. My family is known to foster.

I didn't want to go on welfare because I didn't want to be a young welfare mom. So I got a job with The Ex (Red River Exhibition). They have rides and entertainment and food. I had heard you could make lots of money if you travelled with them, and I thought that if I did that I'd come back and pay my rent. So I asked my family and they watched my baby while I worked. I started travelling with the Ex, but it didn't work out. I wasn't gone even three weeks when my family said, "Come

back, your baby needs you." So, I came back to be with her.

A couple of weeks later, it was a hot summer day and my friend was babysitting my baby. She put the fan in front of the baby and the dust got in her eyes and she ended up getting an infection. I was scared so I called my family and they came and got her and took her to the hospital. I guess at that point they decided I was unfit and that they would be better off raising my baby. They just never brought her back. They said, "We'll keep her until you're more stable, Jackie." Then a week later I got served with papers saying that they were taking my baby from me.

I went to see my lawyer, but he was a criminal lawyer. (I didn't know to get a family lawyer.) He'd been my lawyer since I was thirteen. I'd had maybe three hundred youth charges—everything from assault to theft. He said, "Jackie, being your lawyer for all this time and knowing you, I think the best thing you can do is let this baby go so she can be raised properly. I'll sign these papers for you, and I'll put it in there that you have open visitation so you can see her whenever you want. You're not ready for a baby, Jackie. You'd probably lose her to someone else or they'll take her from you. This is the best thing for her." I never got to bond with her, eh? I believed him. I think she was three months when they took her for good. Looking back now, I think it was the best thing for my first-born.

I went for visits. I was happy with the way she was being raised. I could tell she was being loved. She was a little character and she was happy there. Her father never forgave me, but he was never there anyways. Things turned out. My oldest daughter doing good. She went to Red River College and is a youth care worker. She works with kids in the poorest areas of the city. She's been a foster parent since 2016.

I had my second daughter when I was twenty-three. I was in a really abusive relationship with her dad for almost five years. He would beat me, always below the face so that no one could see the marks. Almost killed me. I was thinking that I deserved that. I had all those feelings inside me that I NEVER spoke about. I believe she felt all that.

I did try to do my art a bit during that time. I tried to teach myself how to paint. My work was pretty good for someone who was self-taught. But when I was living with my

baby's dad, he broke my paintbrushes and threw my paints out. He told me I was no good, I was just copying, and that I'd never be an artist. He felt my art was a threat to his control of me.

When I was twenty-nine, I had my third daughter. I was already raising my second daughter on my own. She was six. It was so hard. We were always alone. Nobody gave a shit about us. I thought, *I can't put another child through this shit. I want this child to have a better life.* When you see what's happened in your own family, you think you're not supposed to have kids either. *My mom couldn't keep us, so I can't keep them. I'm a fuck-up, I'm no good.* So after I had my youngest daughter, I gave her to the sister of the woman raising my oldest daughter (I call her my cousin). Today my youngest is in university, and she's going to become a lawyer.

When my middle daughter was ten I was with the love of my life, a good man, Richard. I never let any man around her. I protected her because I didn't want her to get abused. But by ten I thought she was old enough to tell me if something happened to her. And I knew Richard wasn't that type of person anyway. I talked to her about that kind of stuff. So I introduced her and told her he was coming to live with us. We got engaged. We were together for four years.

My middle daughter was going through a hard time and had become rebellious. She felt all alone and she wanted her mom back. My daughter said to me one day, "Mom, it's him or me."

And that was the easiest decision, you know? I wanted to keep my child. Yah, I loved him, and it nearly broke my heart, but it would have broken my heart to lose my child. So I had a talk with him and I told him he had to leave. I'm proud of myself that I had the strength to do that. All three of my girls grew up safely. If there was one thing I learned from my mother it was to stand up for my girls. She was the only one who listened to me when I was abused.

In a twelve-year span from the age of eighteen to thirty, I accumulated ninety-seven adult charges. Assault, drug possession, robbery, theft. I took ten charges that weren't mine. You can't rat people out or you'll get beat up on the streets. I was convicted on thirty-nine of the charges. They knew me really well in the Remand Center.

I was a booster, a hustler for sixteen years. That's a professional thief. I'd steal and re-sell. I even had clients who would give me a list of things they wanted me to steal for them. I could make $500 off clients easily. Problem solved. It fed my addiction, fed my kid, and put clothes on our backs. I'd get a charge; go to jail and after jail I'd go back to boosting. I was an addict then. I remember one time I got out and went right to the mall, did a load (a boost), sold the shit, and went and got high. It kept me in the same place for sixteen fucking years. Stagnant. I had nothing to look forward to. It's *ennui*. A place of sorrow, despair or nothingness. No today, no tomorrow. Writer Richard Wagamese wrote an article on it.

I didn't get caught often. Twice, I was in the Portage Jail. I did four months once and then six months the next time. I hated jail. That was the worst thing. I had my champagne birthday (I turned 30 on the 30th) in the Portage Correctional. That's the last time I was in jail.

While I was there, I met another girl and, man, was she ever a good artist. We'd sit there and draw and we'd talk. She was so smart, and she told me I was good too. The thing I am most proud of is that I went back to drawing while I was in jail. I hadn't drawn for nine years, not since I was twenty-one and my middle daughter's dad ripped up all my canvases and broke my brushes. I never painted or drew after that until I was in prison when I was thirty.

Everybody loved my drawings and I started selling them in jail. The women that were moms would ask me to make cards for their kids' birthdays because you can't buy cards inside. They'd part with their little bits of money and pay me $3 for each card. That's when I knew that if I could sell my artwork *there*, imagine what I could do when I was on the outs. I was making good money in jail, buying my tobacco and my canteen. I had what I needed, eh? I also had a job in the kitchen making desserts there as well because I didn't like to slack off. I worked and I drew, which kept my mind off things.

Much later, when I got out, I'd see that girl from jail who I used to draw with. I saw her at an art program I was referred to by the E-Fry (Elizabeth Fry) Society. We got to talking and she told me she was in Fine Arts at university. I was so jealous. I was always waiting, wondering, like when's that going to happen for me? She was really good at drawing, better than me. But I said to myself, *Man, if she can do it, I can do it too.* After my last time in jail, I didn't want that life no more. I gave it up. I wanted to change my life too.

It was one of my best customers, one of the people I'd shop for who planted a seed in my head about going back to my art. For some reason her words stuck to me. She was a single mom, a doctor. She'd buy everything. I'd name my price and she paid it. She had the money. Then, one day she said, "Girl, why're you doing this? You're very, very good at what you do, Jackie. I bet you could be good at something else." It's just the way she said it, that it never left my mind. "I bet you could be really good at something else too, if you wanted to." And I told myself, *I am really good at something else. I'm good at drawing and I'm an artist. What the fuck am I doing?* It took me a while to decide to change though.

Another time, she came by my place to pick up her stuff. It was four o'clock in the afternoon, and I was still sleeping, eh? I woke up, answered the door, my hair's all messy. She looked at me and said, "Are you just waking up now?"

"Yeah," I said,

"Girl, life is going to pass you by and the next thing you know, you're dead." The shit this woman said to me. But she was right. *Do something you're really good at. Do something that's gonna make you happy. And live your life because it's short.* Those two encounters with that woman are part of what changed my life.

I don't know why what she said got to me. I had tried to change my life so many other times. My dad used to say, "Jackie, you're supposed to be an artist. You say you're going to do it and you don't. What's wrong with you?" But I was addicted back then. I couldn't explain that to my dad. He didn't understand.

I started partying at thirteen, but I didn't like drinking then. I always thought I wouldn't be an alcoholic because my mom was one and that would never happen to me. I tried coke at twenty-one. I tried it three times and I didn't get nothing from it. No high. I thought, *What's the big deal?* On the fourth try I felt it and I loved it. I thought *holy shit this is what it is.* I was hooked and I did it for years. When I was on coke, I forgot about all the shit that happened to me. Everything that hurt me before was gone. Being high numbed down that pain. I used coke as a medicine, every day. I never knew that what I was doing was self-medicating. I just thought it was normal, like fuck, everybody does it.

My daughter saved me back then. When she was ten she told my family I was doing coke. It hurt me that she knew and was upset. I felt it was time to change. CFS put her at my cousin's while I went for treatment at a facility in Brandon. I was in there twenty-seven days. And I had to take parenting classes before I could get her back. Those words that my client said to me about being good at something else had stayed in my head. Shortly after that I met that guy I fell in love with—Richard. He was going to university. I had five years of total sobriety from ages thirty-four to thirty-nine when I went to art school. I became an alcoholic at forty. After art school I started making money. I'd never had that before. And it wasn't until then that I liked the taste of alcohol. But by that time, I had already gone through the whole spectrum of addictions: crack, coke. Alcohol was just another addiction to pick up. When I was forty-three, I realized I felt empty and lost. It just wasn't worth it, you know? That's self-punishment and I ended up thinking,

Why are you doing this to yourself? Do you not love yourself?

I'm starting to love me, so drinking is not important to me anymore. I was using alcohol to cope, and to socialize (I prefer to be alone). I had to have a balance. So I put my career first.

I'm not gonna lie. I've had relapses. I don't live a completely sober life. But I haven't had a relapse since my dad died in 2018. I do go out from time to time. But I also know it takes me away from my work and my art. If I end up having too many drinks, I can't touch my paints. Learning to say no has been the hardest part, not drinking for other people just because they enjoy my company. But I chose to do art. This is my destiny. Without art, I don't know where I'd be. I'm thankful I've got art, or else I'd still be stuck in addictions—or I'd be dead.

In 2004 I got accepted into university. I took Fine Arts at the University of Manitoba. I went as a mature student. At that time I was engaged to the love of my life, Richard. What attracted me to him was the paint all over his clothes. He was in year two of Fine Arts and he was a muralist. Richard helped me put my portfolio together when I applied. I got sponsored by my band. They paid for my tuition and gave me a monthly living allowance. But it was only after seven tries that the band agreed to support me. That seventh time, I had twenty letters of support from different organizations in the community that knew my work. People started to see that I had talent.

Richard coulda easily drove me to school on the first day, but I took the bus. Going to university was something I wanted to do by myself, and I wanted to do it *for* myself. When I got there and I got off the bus I thought, *I shoulda let him drive me.* I was fucking scared. I didn't even know where to go. I was lost. I just stood there, and then I heard the drum, the big drum. My culture. I thought, *I'm gonna follow that drum.* So I followed the song of that drum and then I saw fancy shawl dancers dancing in a circle in front of the Fitzgerald Building where I had to go to art school. I heard my people singing, heard the beat of the drum and I knew I was where I was meant to be.

University wasn't always beautiful. I was told by three white male professors I'd never graduate. One, I believe, was using reverse psychology. But the other two really meant it.

I was told, "Look, Jackie, most First Nations students that come to university only make it to year two and then they drop out. You probably won't even graduate." I just took their words in and never voiced my opinion. I wanted to tell them, *I know exactly what you are doing. You're trying to make me doubt myself, You're trying to set me up for failure with your words.*

I graduated in 2009. I was very proud. But to be honest, I didn't like the graduation ceremony. Everybody got a degree, but I got a diploma. I was the only one graduating fine arts that year that didn't have a coloured sash. I just had the black robe and a cap. Again, I felt like I didn't belong with this group of students. I had voluntarily withdrawn from the Fine Arts degree program in my first year and switched to the diploma instead because of my art history course. The professor told our class that if we couldn't write an essay we should walk out. I couldn't write an essay. I had like maybe a Grade 7 education, so I left.

But the best part of graduating was that the artist Wanda Koop was there getting her honorary doctorate and she told the story in her speech that she had only graduated with a diploma. And look at her now! I felt that if she could do it, I could do it too. I had met Wanda Koop when I got to go to her studio for a field trip when I was younger. I had never been to an artist's studio and I was just in awe. So to end up graduating at the same time that she was getting her honorary doctorate was amazing. I only remember Wanda Koop's speech. I didn't even stay for the whole ceremony. I hated sitting through the boring speeches. I had told my family, "After I get my diploma, meet me at the side and let's dip out." We took pictures outside and went for East Indian food. I went to my graduation for my kids.

I was proud to graduate though, because all my life I've started things and never completed them. I would start programs but I didn't like to follow the rules, so I'd sabotage myself and quit. I never finished anything but I did finish university. It took me a little longer (five years) to get my diploma because I had my middle daughter. It was hard being a single mom doing it, but I graduated with a 4.0 grade point average.

I'm a very curious person. If I want to learn something, I'll learn it. I teach myself. I don't like anybody thinking or saying I can't do anything. My whole life I was told that

I'd be nothing. And then that carried on into my adulthood. Now I know that the only limits are the ones that I set for myself. And I always tell myself—I say this to myself out loud—*You can do whatever you fucking wanna do.*

I never had a plan before in my whole life, but after graduating I told myself, *I'm gonna be an artist.* The day after graduation, my family gave me $1000 in Artist Emporium gift cards and there was my future! I bought canvases, paints, brushes, everything I needed to start out.

I remember one day a couple of weeks after I graduated, we were at home and there wasn't much food in the fridge. At that time my two oldest daughters lived with me plus we had a friend of my girls' staying with us. (My oldest was rebelling and had left my cousin's because they were strict. She stayed with us about two years.) We had just enough food for that day. I said, "You guys leave me alone, don't bug me. I'm going to my room and I'm gonna paint and take care of this." So I painted until about 6:00 in the morning, and I had six paintings. After I had a few hours of sleep while my paints dried, I said to my kids, "Okay, you guys wait by the phone.

Mom's gonna go sell these paintings and then I'll phone you, and you have to come and help me with the groceries." There was no doubt in my mind, right?

So I went to some offices downtown. Nobody knew who I was. I knocked on the doors and said, "Hi. I'm Jackie Traverse, I'm a visual artist and I have paintings. I want to sell them. Would you want to look at them?"

Some would say, "I'm sorry, we're not interested in art." or "We don't look at art." That just made me mad. But you know what? You can't let that get to you. I thought, *People have walls; people need art. How are people going to know me if I don't introduce myself, right?* It was do or die. I wasn't living a life of crime where it would've been so easy to earn fast money. Then, finally, one person said, "Well sure, come in. Set 'em out. Let me get the other staff in."

That very first place that let me set up my paintings was the Canadian Centre for Policy Alternatives. They're watchdogs for human rights, for people that are marginalized and living in poverty and prison. They're really good people. They bought my work. All six pieces! I've done the art for a few of their report covers over the years.

There was another time when it was three days before the rent was due. I had two apartments in the same building—one where I painted and one where I lived. My rent was 800 bucks, $395 per unit. I was so stressed because I had not made a sale for days. I had no way to get the rent. I was crying and asking myself, *What the fuck am I gonna do?* All of a sudden I got a phone call and it was from the First Nations Child and Family Caring Society, which works with children that are in foster care and with adoptees—Cindy Blackstock. (She's an Indigenous children's rights activist.) They wanted me to do the cover for their annual general report.

They asked what I would charge them. I said $800 (because that was what I needed to pay the rent). They said okay. It was a beautiful painting. I should've got more, but I got the copyrights so I've sold a lot of prints of it since then. I painted my little brother wearing a sky-blue jumper with a white collar. It's called *On Eagles Wings* because the eagle represents love. My sky blue and white colours are in there. The boy is transforming from the clouds into the eagle. He's holding a braid of sweetgrass.

After that, I never really stressed about making the rent. I always know that something is gonna show up because I know that if I put forth good, it'll come back. I do have a good heart. I've never worked for anybody but myself since then, but that's not an easy thing to do. A lot of people that went to art school are working at other jobs and art's something they are doing on the side. I don't have that option. And I'm thankful I don't. If I couldn't do my art, what would I do? I honestly don't know. I don't even want to think about that 'cause it scares me. I'm proud that I've never had to take a penny from welfare. I've been able to make my living for ten years.

I've been honoured and gifted so many times, like when I go to schools. Children even study my art in schools now. A teacher messaged me on Instagram and said, "Our Grade 5 class chose you as our artist to study because we're studying Indigenous artists. I'd like to show you our students' work." She sent some pictures and they brought me to tears. The students copied one of my recent paintings called *Water Woman*. I remembered back to when I was a kid in school and did exactly that. I thought, *Now they're doing that to me.* I told the teacher I wanted to

ANDREW MAHON

this artwork? Apply that to everything you do in life and you will succeed." It felt really good to say that because I believe it—If you're going to do something, give it your all.

I guess that teacher told her principal about me. When that principal moved from that school to the middle school next door he hired me to come work with some of his kids. We ended up doing the Seven Teachings because it worked so well. When I was leaving there after two weeks, I told all the kids I loved them because I do. I left there crying.

When I first saw that craze for adult colouring books all over the place I thought that the books were nice, but I wanted to see images of my people, my culture, the celebrations of our life, and the goodness and greatness of my ancestors. I went online and did some research. I saw that some Indigenous men in BC had made colouring books, but they were in that West Coast style. My work is more soft, feminine, and flowy. I thought, *Wouldn't it be nice to have my work in a colouring book?*

I'd always wanted to see images of myself, my people, in the mainstream. How come I don't see our people on TV or in

come meet them. The kids didn't know I was coming and I surprised them.

I just walked in the class, eh, and they all ran up and surrounded me. The students hugged me and I hugged them. I said, "Let's see this artwork, you guys." And I told them how super impressed I was. I said, "See how much hard work and dedication you put into commercials? When I was in the foster home in Transcona, I had paper dolls. There was a white doll and a black doll, but I only played with the black doll. I felt that one was the closest to me. I never saw myself anywhere. I remember putting up the Christmas tree and there'd be a little blond-haired angel on top of the tree and I'd say, "How come there's no Indian angels ever?" I remember seeing Buffy Sainte-Marie for the first time on TV and thinking, *Oh my god. There's my people. I'm just like her.* I was so happy. I could see us in the mainstream. So when I realized that no Indigenous woman had made a colouring book, I wanted to be the first one to do that.

I have a friend whose partner owns Fernwood Publishing. I asked him about doing a colouring book, but he said they didn't do colouring books. But I didn't give up. On the fifth time, he finally said yes. He said, "You know why I said yes? Because we shouldn't say no to things just because we haven't done them before. We don't grow if we do that and you're right, Jackie. We should make a colouring book to celebrate your culture and to celebrate women and life givers." We made the book and had the launch. That was 2016. A lot of people came out. Two of

my daughters and my granddaughter were there too. The publisher called me up a year later and asked me about doing a second book. The first had become a bestseller.

Now, I'm helping out a few artists that are trying to make it. There is an artist, a young girl, that I saw sitting in a downtown bar close to my studio. I started talking to her. Her boyfriend was pretending that it was his artwork because nobody will buy a woman's painting. She signs her paintings with a man's name so they can sell. I've given her some canvas and a whole bucket of paint. She's come to my studio and I've given her advice about her work. They're black and white drawings on scrap frame paper. Her work is good. If she were given the right tools and the right materials she could become a full-time artist. I try to be...I don't know, a mentor, I guess, for her just so that she can get herself out of the bar and then the value of her work would go up.

That's the type of support I was given by another artist, Louis Ogamah, when he first met me. We were all artists in a residency at the Martha Street Studios with Urban Shaman Gallery. Louis said, "Whatever you do Jackie, do it with your heart." That's the best advice. He said, "If it doesn't feel good in your heart, don't do it." I pass that advice on to other artists too.

I feel so fucking lucky. I get to live at my own place and I have a studio. It's filled with paints. I don't have much money, but when I make a decent sale I'll message an artist and buy something from them. Sometimes they undersell themselves, and I'll give them more because I have more. When I have the wealth, I share the wealth.

In 2016 a doctor wouldn't give me pills to sleep and instead sent me to a psychiatrist, who diagnosed me with Bipolar types 1 and 2. That was a breakthrough, which I am thankful for. Now I understand why I am like I am. For years I never understood and I'd hate myself. I wondered what the hell was wrong with me. Why I was so mad all the time? I would have been happy just ten minutes before.

When I got the diagnosis, I told my daughter—she was twenty-four at that time. She said, "Mom, I always knew. There was never no middle ground with you." That hurt.

I said, "What do you mean, no middle ground?"

She said, "I was always coming home thinking, *What's mom going to be like today? Is she gonna be mad? Is she gonna be happy? Is she gonna be sad?* I had to walk on eggshells."

Poor kid, the shit I put her through. I blamed myself for the longest time, but you know what? Why should I blame myself for something I didn't know about? Had I been diagnosed earlier, I would've dealt with it. I really think that the bipolar could have started when my mom died.

I told a very good friend of mine about the bipolar. He paid for me to see a therapist. I only had six sessions, but I did learn lots. The therapist said, "You know, you have a right to say no, Jackie. When you were a kid, you didn't. What happened to you, what was done to you, you couldn't say no. But you're a woman now. You have the right to say no and make your own decisions." I needed to hear that. Otherwise, who knew how long I would have been trying to please other people. Fucking up my career, my life, my relationships. Art is the one thing I have, the one thing I'm good at and I'm not going to let alcohol and addictions take that from me. I just made up my mind.

A lot of the things that have happened to me, I don't see as happening *to me*. I'm me, but it's like I'm above, in a room, looking down at what's happening to this little girl, and I'm crying. I know it seems like I'm crying for myself, but I'm not. I'm crying for that little child. I feel so bad and I want to help her. I'm an empath and I hate what they're doing to her. I talked to my therapist about this and she said that's a coping mechanism called *floating*. I never knew that. But I was just a kid, and I guess that's how your brain tells you to survive, right? I still remember most things but thanks to floating, it's not as if they are happening to me.

I forgive, because I realized that people gotta forgive me too for a lot of the shit I did. I don't blame my mom for her alcoholism or the choices she made. She was sick. I've been sick too, and I've made bad choices. You know? I forgive myself, and I forgive my mother.

There's so many people that haven't forgiven me. They've got a big bag of shit that they're carrying around with them everywhere they go for like thirty years. That must be heavy. I don't want to carry a heavy bag of shit with me no more. You know? It weighs me down and I've got other things to do. I feel freer now.

I used to worry so much about what people thought of me because I was always the new kid in the school. I went to sixteen or more different schools (I'm not sure). But I know there's people that have had it way worse. I have a friend who was in 144 placements. How the heck do you expect to build a healthy strong person if you move them that many times? They never get to plant roots anywhere. They never feel a connection. By doing that, by keeping families apart, by breaking us up continually, we never connect with anyone again. But my friend is good. She got sick, she almost died and then just changed her life around four years ago.

Until probably the past couple years, whenever somebody was telling me something, I always thought they were lying, bullshitting me. I've thought that ever since I was little because I learned not to trust people. Now, I would say to my younger self, *You might not know it now but you're here for a purpose. If there's nobody to love you now, there'll be people that will love you later. You might not feel love (because I didn't, I felt all alone) but there are people you can trust, people that will love you.*

When I was about fifty, I started growing into my own skin and having the power to say no and to set boundaries. Before, I didn't know I had that right. There's just this resilience inside me. Even though I didn't deal with all my trauma, I knew what I wanted and I went for it. I have to say I think that comes from my ancestors and my grandmothers. It's already been planned out by Creator. I was blessed with the ability to be a creative person, to see and feel so much more, but to be strong too. I'm happy I know about my bipolar. I see it now as a gift. It makes me more understanding of other people.

I have my daily routine. I smudge and I pray. I talk to Creator. First of all, I always say how thankful I am. I never pray for things. There's nothing that I'm attached to. Creator told me my life here is to create works that will uplift our people, make them remember, instill pride and give them hope.

I never had any exposure to my culture or teachings. But, I remember being five or six, and we would go to the reserve and my mom would take me to see my Nookoo—my great-grandma. She had a little tiny house. It was probably ten feet by ten feet, with a wood stove, her bed and an old table. She was ninety-eight, completely blind. I didn't know she had cataracts, so I always thought she had silver eyes. Her hair was pure white. She had leathery skin, and her wrinkles were deep. Her cheekbones were so pronounced because her blood hadn't been mixed. She was pure Ojibwe. She must have had arthritis. You could see her big bones, and her big hands. I'd always have to go stand in front of her, and she'd feel my face because she couldn't see. Then they'd talk in Saulteaux or Ojibwe. I'd stand there and just look at her. She didn't speak English so I never got to talk to her, but I was mesmerized. *Who is this woman?* I wondered.

The last time we went to visit, my Nookoo pulled out a leather bag that had beadwork on it. It was rolled up. I found out later it was a sacred bundle. I thought she was going to give it to me. To be given a sacred bundle is like my Nookoo passing on all her knowledge to me. From there, I would have got training and been taught about the medicines from the Midewewin (medicine people). My mom was ashamed to be Indian, because it was a bad thing back then. (She could pass for Chinese, and so she'd pretend not to be Indian.) It could have been different for me if my mom was proud of her culture. I never got to see that bundle. My mom never gave it to me. Had it been given to me, my life probably would have been very different. I don't know.

Whatever teachings I do know, I've just picked up along the way or I just know instinctively. My culture also just kind of came to me through dreams. When I've had these dreams I've asked Elders about them after, and I was right about what I guessed. I have a few cousins that I'm close with. One cousin said to me, "How do you know all this Indian stuff? We weren't raised like this." I looked at her and I said, "I wasn't raised with you guys. I raised myself." They don't know my story. My cousins had the blessing of having both parents and a huge family with siblings and everything else. I didn't have that.

When I was around thirty, I had a ceremony with a medicine man at my house to see why there were spirits in the place. I could feel them, and sometimes see them. Two old women watching me. When I looked, they would hide from me. When the medicine man was done, we turned the lights on and he said,

> Whatever teachings I do know, I've just picked up along the way or I just know instinctively.

"Jackie, your gut instinct is right about there being something sent here. You know when you see those two women looking around, that's your grandmothers." He told me that they're protecting me. They're with me all the time. I can sense them. This means I have no fear. I don't even really fear death. I know that where I'm going all my family's there. I'll see them again.

The medicine man also told me he was given my spirit name and my colours. He said, "Your name is *The Sounds of Thunderbirds Approaching*. And your colours are sky blue and white."

Right then, I remembered a time when my mom tried to be sober. I think I was four. She told my dad to buy paint and tape. She painted the whole house, and she put that tape across the wall. She painted sky blue on the top and white on the bottom.

Standing with the medicine man, right there, I knew my mom would know that I remembered when she painted our house. She was telling me, *You remember that time I painted the house sky blue and white? I'm here and I'm listening to what's going on. I'm watching you, and I know you'll remember these colours. You'll remember that time, and you'll remember me.* I don't doubt it no more. I know my mom was talking to me through colour. I felt like my mother was looking after me spiritually.

When I was a girl in foster care, at school, they had a big box of crayons and all the crayons were in there. Every day I would go to that box and I'd steal that sky blue crayon. I carried it in my pocket. Before school was out, I would go put it back. Then, the next day when school started, I'd run to the crayon box and see if my crayon was still there and then I'd get it, and I kept that crayon with me. I did it every day.

I have learned that my name is about the thunder before we have a thunderstorm. Those are called thunderbirds in our culture. That noise is to tell us that they're flying in the sky and they're here to cleanse the earth. It's the sounds that they make when they come. My name is about being loud, being a voice, and not being scared to say what you're supposed to say. I take that personally to mean I have a voice, and I'm meant to use it.

I used my voice in 2016 to start a taxi boycott after an Indigenous woman was threatened by a cab driver. (I've had all kinds of things happen with taxi drivers—been stabbed, been thrown out of a moving taxi.) I thought we needed an alternative, so I created IKWE Safe Rides (Women Helping Women). It was kind of like a taxi service with women posting on Facebook when they could give rides to other women. Facebook said it was the first time it was used in this way. We had fifty female drivers. Over 70,000 safe rides have been given to our women, children, and elders. It is still in existence, but I no longer run it.

I've made three videos about hard times in my life. They are part of my art. I didn't know how to deal with these things, so I made art. *Two Scoops* is about when we wrapped my sisters in our winter jackets. *Empty* is the story of my mom dying. And *Butterfly* is about our murdered and missing women.

The week I turned eighteen I looked up the post-adoption registry in the phone book, and I went and signed up to find my siblings. That was on my mind ever since I was a little girl and they were taken. I thought if I sign up, I'll get them back. It's been thirty-two years though. I know where my youngest sister is. She's here in Winnipeg. A family member took her in. We're both grandmas. Could I sit and talk to her today? Probably not. We can't connect because of that separation that was forced on us.

My younger sister, who is half-Chinese and half-Ojibwe, was just the most adorable, cutest button you could imagine when she was a baby. After she went to Children's Aid, she was adopted right away to people in Ontario. I found her through a confidential friend that worked in a government agency. She wasn't supposed to, but she ran a search for my younger sister. I wrote that sister a letter and tried to meet her, but she doesn't want to know me. That was really hard at first, 'cause I love her. I'm sure my sisters' memories are different than mine. I hope they don't remember the times we had with my mom in care, the bad times. I remember everything though.

When I was about twenty-five I found out what happened to my brother. I talked to some people at the First Nations Repatriation Office. He was adopted out to a single white man in Pennsylvania. My brother was part of the Seventies Scoop. He was a newborn and those get picked right away. His adoption fee was $1000. It boggles my mind to think that anybody could think that a baby would be better off with a single white male in Pennsylvania than being with his own mother who was breastfeeding him. It disgusts me that people could even think that's okay.

I always worried about my brother. I just prayed that he was sent to a good home, not with a pedophile, and that he's still alive and loved. He was taken from our family but I love him still. The repatriation office told me that they couldn't do anything to help me find my brother, because he's never reached out to find his siblings. Who knows, he could be dead, or in jail.

Sometimes I think about what my life would have been like if I had been adopted too. Then I thank God I wasn't. I wouldn't be me. I would've been molded and shaped into somebody else. I know it. I wouldn't be an artist, or my art wouldn't be as strong.

The lines of communication with my daughters are not as they would have been had I been raised in a loving environment and been taught how to love back. That's part of this. I think it's important to say that the breakup of my own family meant I didn't know how to function and led to my dysfunction with my own children. I lost my sisters and brother, and lost my own kids. They're the third generation. I should be fucking distraught, but I think *It fucking happens. It's always going to be like that.* That's what the government wanted, and they succeeded. It's the breakdown of family. Divide us and we're weaker. I wish it could be different.

Even though I raised my middle daughter and she has had trauma from me, she is the most compassionate and caring person. She'd give someone her last ten dollars, push an elder down the street in their wheelchair, share her meal, whatever. She has the kindest heart. That's the type of person she is. Yeah, I've done wrong and I said some wrong things but I did my best raising her. She is doing her best too. A few years ago she gave me a granddaughter. When she was born I got her a drum and painted it for her. We sing together. I am rich in culture and that is what I can give her.

I was given the ability to be strong and the ability to create as a gift, because I had nothing else. Everything else was taken from me. This gift was given to me.

For a long time I use to split my life up into categories. I referred to my life as before I was twelve when my mom was still alive, and then after I was twelve, when my mom was dead. That was when my world changed. And there's my life before I was twenty-one and after twenty-one when I got hooked on coke.

After art school I stopped splitting my life up into categories, because now I see it as all just one story. Going to art school I finally felt like I was where I was supposed to be. I found that passion and drive to do something more. I was given the ability to be strong and the ability to create as a gift, because I had nothing else. Everything else was taken from me. This gift was given to me.

I am telling my story for this book because I want my daughters to know about my life. I want people to know that even though all this shit happened, I rose above it. They can too. Everything I've been put through in life was for me to create art and share my story, to show others, teach others, and build others up. I don't regret nothing, you know?

Without that life I would not have all these ideas, understanding and empathy for others. And without those things happening to me, I wouldn't feel what I feel, and create what I create. I am not a woman of words; the paint says everything for me.

Jackie was the first participant I interviewed for this book. Her former junior high school teacher, the late Joe McLellan, was a mutual friend and introduced me to her. At lunch together, Jackie was outspoken and fierce (the good kind). But she showed her soft side as we were leaving when she gave me a big hug.

Jackie is a very generous person. Jackie told me a story about her art and her ex—the guy who beat her, broke her brushes and canvases and told her she was no good. That same guy called her years later asking for a donation of art for a fundraiser. Jackie said, "I had a choice to make. Do I hold onto that grudge?" Jackie gave him not one piece of her art, but two.

Jackie painted the book's cover art which is titled My Tears Turn Into Something Beautiful. *The minute I saw this evocative painting I knew it would be an amazing* cover. This is what Jackie says about her piece: "Everybody knows I love butterflies. I remember reading a quote of something Chief Dan George said to his granddaughter. She was going through her teenage years and didn't feel she was pretty. He told her, 'Right now you are a caterpillar, but one day you will come out of that cocoon and be a beautiful woman.' In 2019 I was going through a hard time and painted this picture of a woman with butterflies for tears." To view Jackie's art visit jackietraverse.com.*

Mary

I've been called an expert in the child welfare system, but I describe myself as a helper. Michael Redhead Champagne, the co-founder of our organization, Fearless R2W, calls me a *super granny*. I have claimed Michael as my brother, even though we are not biological siblings, and I've come to accept his term super granny because I have successfully stopped many, many CFS apprehensions. I stood my ground with CFS when I was a teenager and didn't want to stay in foster care anymore, I fought the system to keep custody of each of my own children, and I have gained guardianship of three of my grandchildren. I have helped many people either keep their children or get their children back from care. I've helped hundreds of families with their dealings with CFS.

I am proud of myself for having been able to help many families and my community. I don't need to be given recognition to know the good that I do. I see it every day when I see a neighbour I've helped to get her kids back, and she's prospering. She's got her kids, and a great place and doesn't need help anymore. I see how happy she and her children are. That's my reward.

In addition to being a helper and a super granny, I describe myself as *crazy* because I have so many things on the go. I'm constantly busy, running around the house like a chicken with my head cut off. My mom used to say *idle hands are the devil's playground,* so I try to keep busy. I spend most of my waking time volunteering or working in some way. I'm always looking for more things to do in this community to help our families. Community means everything to me. We've got to try and make our community as healthy as possible so that our children can be raised in a healthy way.

When I get tired, and I do, then I look into the eyes of my grandchildren and see how happy and healthy they are going to be when they grow up. There are children in some of these homes in my housing development who are starving, who don't have a bed to sleep in, and who have parents who are negligent or have issues, and they need help. That's what keeps me going.

I have three adult children. I was seventeen when I had my first child, eighteen when I had my second, and twenty-one when I had my last. I was a single mom raising them on my own until my youngest was eighteen. I was with their fathers for periods of time, but most often, they were not taking on any responsibility for their children. I was the one raising my kids, financially supporting them, the one they went to when they were hurt. Their dads were never there for them. I literally grew up with my children. I didn't get married to my husband, John, until after my youngest child was nineteen.

I have four grandchildren and total custody of three of them. They are young, so there is chaos with the kids everywhere. The children's energy, their need to be loud and exuberant and their need to be heard fuel my soul. Without them, I'd be a pretty boring person. They help me live my life, and I think, in a way, I live vicariously through them. My grandkids know that I love them dearly and that I would do anything for them. I'm the reason they didn't get lost in the foster care system. I refuse to let my grandchildren go into the system, not when I'm healthy and able to look after them. My husband and I had my grandchildren by what CFS calls "kinship care" until 2017. Then on September 7th, 2017, we got sole guardianship of those three grandchildren.

My stepson also lives with me and my husband. Space was one of our biggest issues. We were all tripping over each other because we lived in a very small three-bedroom rowhouse in Manitoba Housing. In the winter of 2021 our family was able to move into a bigger four-bedroom unit.

I work part-time as the Executive Director of Fearless R2W, the organization Michael Redhead Champagne and I started in 2014. We see ourselves as a circle of support for parents in our community (those trying to keep their kids from being apprehended, those who have got their kids back from CFS but need support, even those who want to learn how to be better parents). I also work part-time for North End Community Renewal Corporation (NECRC) as a housing advocate. I used to volunteer for and be on the board of NECRC, but once I got employed with them, I had to get off the board. It's supposed to be forty hours a week for these jobs (twenty and twenty), but I end up doing a total of about eighty hours of work a week. And then for my community volunteering, I'm doing about another thirty hours. I'm on the board of my granddaughter's daycare and Winnipeg Boldness Initiative. I'm also part of an international board called International Parents Advocacy Network (IPAN). They have members from all over the world. Fearless R2W is the Canadian representative for their board, which was formed in 2019. I try to be a good multi-tasker—and it helps that I'm ADHD.

I was born in Winnipeg in 1970. (Actually, I was born in the Rural Municipality of St. Boniface because St. Boniface didn't become a part of Winnipeg until March of 1971.) I have six siblings—three older and three younger. Two brothers and four sisters. We were the ones who got the brunt of the abuse growing up. I have a right to talk about my story, but not about theirs. My story is different from their stories, and their stories will be different from each other's. All my siblings have issues in their lives and they are learning to be issue-free.

My first childhood memory is from when I was five. My sister took me to the park and we ended up going on this really big teeter totter. I was up at the top and my sister was on the bottom. I was a big child, but she was bigger. I got scared so I wrapped my legs underneath the teeter-totter. My sister jumped off and I didn't pull my legs out so I broke one in thirteen places, my mom said.

My sister was trying to carry me home, but she couldn't because I was too big. She got so tired that she left me in some bushes and told me to stay there and be quiet. She ran home and tried to get the attention of one of our parents. Nobody was really paying any attention to her because they were partying, except for my cousin, who was a lot older than us. He came with her to where I was and he carried me home.

The home I grew up in was volatile. It was because of Ernest—I can't even call him Dad, so I call him by his first name. He was an alcoholic and a womanizer and a drug addict. I think back now to my life when I was a kid, and I wonder how he could do the things that he did to my family.

I remember that when we came home from the park that day, Ernest was so angry because he had to take me to the hospital that he beat the living shit out of me. And then he beat the living shit out of my sister, for me getting hurt. When we got to the hospital, they asked about the bruises on me and Ernest said, "Oh, I don't know how those happened. She came home like that." I had to make up a story saying that I was beat up by some kids in the park.

Life at home was very traumatic. Growing up we never had enough food, and the electricity and water were often shut off. And we always had to move. Every time we made friends in the neighborhood, Ernest would uproot us and move us again. I never understood why we moved so much until I was older. When I was a teenager in foster care, I realized we moved so much because he couldn't hold a job and also because he was probably afraid he'd get caught with what he was doing to my siblings and me.

Ernest was raping us, nightly. Like every night. He would take turns on us older children. There were six of us at that point, including the two younger than me. (My younger sister wasn't born until after Ernest was already put in jail.) He had no preference on gender when it came to abusing us. One of my sisters caught him doing it to me one day. She had enough, so she told her friend's mom what he was doing. That was back in April of 1980. I was ten years old. He was arrested and we were all apprehended. I haven't spoken to my dad since then. He spent fifteen years in jail for the abuse.

Because of Ernest, my mom went to her grave being called a child abuser by CFS (back then I think it was called Children's Aid), but she wasn't. My mother never laid a hand on us, unless we deserved it. The CFS agency said that she could have done more to protect us from our father. But he was giving her sleeping pills at night so she wouldn't wake up when we were crying and screaming. I tried to say this to the lawyers for CFS, but nobody believed me. CFS brainwashed me into believing that my mom was a bad person and because she was an alcoholic, she didn't want to have anything to do with us. This only changed for me later, when I went back to live with her at fourteen. It's true, my mother was an alcoholic, but she did fight to get us kids back. (She didn't quit drinking until she found out she was a diabetic. By then, I was already an adult with my own kids.)

When we were apprehended, we were all sent to different foster homes. I was alone without any of my siblings. It was fucking terrible. On the day we were taken by CFS, I sat in the police station for thirteen hours, and it must've been around 11:00 or 12:00 in the evening that I got to the foster home. The foster parents were as white as white can be and they kept calling me a "dirty Indian." Even though it was late at night, they made me have a bath, and they cut my hair before I got into bed. I had really long, thick, black hair, but the foster parents just put a bowl on my head and cut my hair off. They said it was because I had lice, but I didn't. In the past if I ever had lice, my mother would painstakingly pick everything out of my hair. She then put stuff on my hair and a bag on my head, and made me sleep with it. I never had lice at that foster home. The foster parents just used that as an excuse to cut my hair. I didn't know what the hell was going on or why they were doing anything that they were doing.

There were six of us foster kids at that house, including me. The others were all Native and they were all older than me. It was scary. The parents told me that if I stole anything, they would break my fingers. I had to clean the entire house and do everything a certain way. I was the new kid, so they made me cook too. But I couldn't sit at the table and eat with the family. I had to wait till everybody was done eating and I would get the leftovers, which I ate alone in the kitchen. When I first moved in, they forced me to wear diapers because I had developed a bedwetting problem. I never had one before. It lasted until I was about twelve or thirteen.

Back in the 80s, CFS didn't do a very good job of checking on children. I think I saw my social worker about three or four times in eight years. It was a very different time. When I did try to say something, I was chewed out by the CFS worker and told I was lying.

The foster parents were older, so when they retired and left, the agency had to get a new set of foster parents to come in. (The difference between a group home and a foster home is a group home has rotating staff. A foster home has one set of people looking after you 24/7.) I had several different foster parents in that time. The next foster parents were very religious, and so overbearing. The mom was a younger lady, and her husband was a gospel singer. He had a couple of records out. They had one or two of their own children, I think.

I could not handle it. I started spending a lot of time at the Unicity Mall after school. I wouldn't go back to the home until I absolutely had to. I ended up starting to steal. I was shoplifting because I had nothing better to do. I was really, really good at it. I shoplifted for almost two years but was never caught. All of these stores knew me by name, but they would just leave me alone in the store to do whatever the heck I pleased. I finally let them catch me, because I wanted to stop. I would have continued on stealing and I didn't want that. I actually looked for a Loss Prevention Officer at the store and when I saw they were looking at me, I put things into my bag.

They took me back to the foster home. The foster mom came into my bedroom and started hitting me because I was stealing. She wanted to make me cry but I wouldn't. I told her, "You can hit me as much as you want, but I'm not going to cry. I don't care how much you hit me. I've been beat down by better people than you and I didn't cry when they did it."

I refused to let that woman see me cry, not because I couldn't cry, but because I chose who I cried in front of. Nobody else decided for me. I cried when I was by myself. There was this really nice manmade pond by that foster home. That's where I'd sit and cry.

Because I was having a hard time, I was taken to a psychiatrist. The psychiatrist said I had a very well-developed sense of

> I refused to let that woman see me cry, not because I couldn't cry, but because I chose who I cried in front of.

unworthiness and a well-developed feeling of being unlovable. That was true back then. I did not feel worthy of anything or of being loved by anyone. I know the difference now. In those therapy sessions the psychiatrist kept telling me not to internalize the things that were happening to me, because I did not ask for any of it. Those words kept replaying in my head, and finally a light went on. He was right. I did not ask for any of that.

So I didn't blame myself. I know that a lot of times when children have been abused, they will internalize it because they think it's their fault. I never did that. What I know now, that I didn't know then, is that I was a strong and independent child. It wasn't the first time and it wasn't going to be the last time I had been molested. I did not deserve the abuse. But you know, it is what it is, and it happened. CFS was not aware of many things that had happened to me because I didn't tell them. If I'd said anything, they wouldn't have believed me anyway.

CFS does a five-level ranking system on the special needs of children. Level one would be a child with no issues. Level five is a child who is psychotic and always trying to hurt people and is probably on all kinds of medication. I was always considered a level five because CFS thought I was psychotic. They thought I wanted to hurt people because I was angry. But I was angry because I had been torn away from my mother and my siblings, I didn't get to be in an environment that I knew, and I had trauma.

When I went into care I was in Grade 3. I couldn't read or write. According to the Winnipeg School Division I was *a retard*. In school I was not taught how to read or write; I was only taught how to play. I had ADHD, but no one knew that back then. Because I had no diagnosis, I was put into special remedial classes until I went into care. CFS thought there was something wrong with me. When I was apprehended, they had me go see all these doctors and put me on all these different kinds of medications. The more medication I was on, the more money the foster parents got because I was seen as having higher needs.

For a lot of years, I was messed up. I was physically messed up and I was damaged emotionally. A lot of times I had no say in how or why that damage was done to me. I was twelve when I started drinking. And by the time I was thirteen, I was an alcoholic.

Eventually my mom found out. She came looking for me and dragged me home to her house. It was a relief to be caught. I was so lost in addiction that it felt like nobody gave a shit about me. My mom actually proved to me that she cared. She called the agency and told them that she wasn't sending me back.

The agency sent a social worker and the police to see me at my mom's house. I looked at the police officer and said, "I don't give a fuck how many cops you have with you. I'm not leaving. I'm not leaving my mom. You want me to go back to the foster home? I'm not doing it." I said, "If you make me go back, I'm just going to run away again. And I'm going to keep running. And maybe you'll never find me this next time." The social worker let me stay. My older siblings were already living at home too. My younger siblings were still in care.

I stayed with my mom until I was eighteen but I was still under the care of CFS. I was a permanent ward. Like I said earlier, CFS never checked in on me. They gave my mom a cheque every month for me though. Technically they put me on independent living at age fourteen and they paid my mom to look after me.

After I started living with my mom, she put me into treatment. It was free. There's no way my mother would have been able to afford it. I did residential rehab, living there the first three months. I went to school as part of the requirement. After school I would go to the program and then I would go to Alcoholics Anonymous (AA) meetings. Once the first part was over, I returned to live with my family. I was still doing out-patient rehab every day. When I got out of treatment I still smoked weed but I didn't drink. I was invested in getting out of my addiction. I stayed clean for two years.

About six or seven months after I left foster care, my younger siblings came home too. My mom had also fought the foster care system for my three younger siblings and got them back. My mom got a job at Ma Mawi Wi Chi Itata Centre in 1984. I started to stay home to help my younger siblings. I made sure they had breakfast and lunch and got off to school in the morning. I was home at 3:30 when they got home. My older siblings didn't want to take on that responsibility. They thought it was my mom's job. But my mom needed to work to support all of us, so someone had to stay home to look after the kids. I did this because I didn't want any of us to go back into foster care. I eventually quit school because I was busy taking care of everyone, and school just wasn't a priority. I was looking after the younger kids and doing my rehab. I did that until I left home.

Shortly after I finished treatment, I met my daughter's dad. I was about sixteen. He was my next-door neighbour. He was a drinker and he smoked weed. Almost immediately, I started smoking weed and drinking again. Then I found out I was pregnant with my daughter and I quit all substances because my doctor told me I should. It was the hardest nine months of my life because I didn't drink and smoke weed. And boy did I want to! I was going through withdrawals like you wouldn't believe. But I stuck to my guns because I wanted my child to have a good start in life. That's what kept me motivated. I wanted her to be healthy and I wanted her to be strong.

My daughter was born in August of 1988. Because I was a child in care, there was an immediate birth alert for her. I didn't know anything about it back then. (That's one of the reasons I ended up getting into foster care advocacy—I noticed I wasn't the only one who didn't know what was going on with

ANDREW MAHON

their children.) The CFS worker I had at the time came to see me just a couple months before my daughter was born. He told me that CFS was going to apprehend. I said, "Over my dead body you're going to get your hands on my child. You're not the one who's carrying this kid."

He said, "Well, we don't think you can parent." CFS wanted me to go to live at Villa Rosa. They said I had to do something or they would apprehend my baby.

I said, "Don't even go there. I don't want to deal with this right now." I was seven months pregnant and we were going through a really crazy heat wave. I was hormonal, I was cranky and I was fucking hungry all the time. Constantly. I said, "We'll talk about it when I'm in a better frame of mind."

In the case of birth alerts back in the 80s, the government would fill out a form and send it to all the hospitals in Manitoba. Now they send those forms all across Canada. So even if a person decides to go have her baby in a small, humble, fuck-nowhere town, she would still have her child apprehended.

CFS wanted to apprehend my first child right from the hospital. I told them, "You guys cannot take this child from me. You have absolutely no reason to apprehend her. I don't have any addictions. I don't have anybody around who is going to hurt her." The fear of losing my daughter is what motivated me to find the strength to speak so strongly. I didn't want my child to go into foster care and live the life that I had lived.

What I didn't know then is that they wanted to apprehend my daughter because of my mother. We were going to be living with my mom. The way it was with CFS back then, and the way it still is now, is that it's *always the mother's fault*. (The mother didn't take good care of the kids; she didn't stop the abuse from happening…) As soon as CFS found out that once I was eighteen, I was looking to get my own place and move out, they didn't apprehend my baby. But they opened a file for my daughter because I was a minor and a child in care.

My baby's father and I were on and off again for most of our relationship. When my baby was born, we were not together. I lived in my family's house with my mom and whichever siblings were around. Five months after I had my daughter, I turned eighteen and I got my own apartment and furnished it. CFS came to see me once at my apartment and then told me they were closing my file because they didn't see any need for it to be open.

When I had my baby I breastfed her for about six months. While I was breastfeeding, I still wasn't smoking weed or drinking alcohol. But as soon as I was done breastfeeding, boy did I go back to alcohol, hardcore. I had issues with being a mom at such a young age. I didn't want to admit it back then. My issues weren't the day-to-day tasks of parenting; I knew how to do all those things from taking care of my younger siblings. My problems were with the stresses of being a young mom in poverty: coping with financial and relationship issues and finding a decent place to live.

I was back with my baby's dad, and I ended up getting pregnant a second time quickly. With my second pregnancy, I again didn't drink or smoke weed right up until I was done breastfeeding. That was the one thing I held really close and dear: my children were going to be born healthy and strong.

Two weeks before my nineteenth birthday, my second daughter was born. Before I went into the hospital to give birth, my doctor told me there was another birth alert. My second daughter was born six weeks premature and immediately the agency thought that it was because I was drinking again. The reason she was six weeks early was because my water broke. My older daughter was really overweight. I had picked her up while we were on the bus, which caused my water to rupture. I was in the hospital and went into labour a week later. When I was giving birth, her cord was wrapped around her throat three times, and every time I had a contraction it would tighten. I was supposed to go for a C-section, but the resident that was on call decided I was perfectly fine to have a vaginal birth. That almost killed my daughter. She was born at 3:30 a.m., and that same morning the CFS agency came to tell me they were going to apprehend once my daughter was released.

The doctor had sedated me so that I could sleep, and the nurse woke me up and said, "I'm so sorry, these people are demanding to see you and there is a birth alert." I had to literally bring myself out of that sleep.

I said, "Yeah, I know about the birth alert."

When the social worker came in I was grumpy and tired and emotional. My daughter had almost died. A nurse said to the CFS agents, "You know what? Leave her alone. Let her sleep. This baby isn't going to be released for at least two weeks because she's too small. Let the mom comprehend what the hell you guys are saying to her." She said, "You can't just come barging in here and expect these women who are having babies to know what you're talking about. I don't want to see you back here until this woman's had at least two or three days rest."

After they left, that nurse told me she remembered when I was born. She said, "You gave your mother such a hard time when you were coming out, too." I thought *What the fuck?* She said, "I know you. I remember your mom. I was the one who caught you when you were coming out." I was like, "Oh, wow." That nurse's name was Mary.

I was breastfeeding my daughter, so I was at the hospital every day. I ended up sleeping at the hospital with my older daughter in a room that was next to the NICU because it was just getting too much to go back and forth from home. Mary worked it out with the hospital. So I was there constantly with my daughter. The nurses were keeping a tab on what I was doing so that they could fight for me with the agency. It was Mary who convinced CFS not to take my daughter. She told them that I had done so well with my first child, that they should give me a chance to do it with my second child.

She didn't know me personally and hadn't been involved in my life at all, but she was very anti-CFS. She was a give-the-moms-a-chance type of person. She was a blonde-haired, blue-eyed white lady. I call people like that our allies: people who stick up for us, who fight alongside us. Mary was an ally. She fought on my behalf for me to keep my baby. My daughter had to stay in the hospital for two weeks after she was born because she was only four pounds. She needed to weigh five pounds before she could get out.

On the last day my baby was there, I was kind of scared to take her because I didn't know what the agency was going to do. That nurse said, "Don't worry about it, Mary. If CFS bothers you, we've got loads of reports on how good you are with your children. Not just your baby, but your other daughter as well."

When I brought my daughter home I was living with my ex. I spent five years in a very abusive relationship with my daughters' father, just so they would know who their dad was. I was physically abused by him daily. At that time in my life, I had very little self-esteem. He beat me down so badly, he made me feel like I would never find anybody to be with me. He always said he was the only one that would ever want me. I stayed with him because I believed him. He nearly killed me twice.

The last time he nearly killed me, I said enough is enough. I called the police on him. My brother-in-law, who lived close to us, happened to be walking by and he heard me screaming. He came in and got my ex off me and took him outside. Just at that moment the cops were coming and my brother-in-law said I needed medical attention immediately, and that my ex needed to be arrested.

I kicked my ex out of my house and got the balls to charge him with domestic assault. I was twenty years old when I got out of that relationship. For a year after that, he was stalking me. Every time I moved from one place to another, he would find me. He would tell me to drop the charges and would threaten to kill me if I didn't. But I didn't drop the charges and when we finally went to court, his lawyer tried to make a plea bargain with me but I refused. It turned out that the judge said there wasn't enough evidence, so my ex got just a slap on the wrist and probation.

And then to add insult to injury, his probation officer would call me every two weeks and she'd tell me, "I know it's only a matter of time before you take him back. You might as well just take him back now and get it over and done with." I was starting to develop a really big backbone. I called this woman's supervisor and complained about what she was doing. I found out later that the probation officer was actually having sex with my ex. She got fired.

I was not bothered by CFS again until my son was born. I was twenty-one, turning twenty-two. My baby's dad was never in his life. Again, during the pregnancy, I stayed away from alcohol and weed and my baby was born healthy. But I was placed on the birth alert again. I had been a child in care, so therefore it was assumed that I was a bad parent. But CFS didn't get my son. They just did not have a leg to stand on to take my child away. They didn't open a file on me. They couldn't justify it.

As soon as I was done breastfeeding my son, I went right back to drinking again. It baffles me that I did that after each of my kids were born. I was such a dummy back then. But when I think back on it, all of my friends drank and did drugs. That was how I would socialize. If I'd go to the bar with my friends, I'd get totally shit-faced, come home and pass out. It got to the point that I was leaving my kids with a sitter on a Friday and

I wouldn't be back until Sunday. I never saw my kids on the weekends; I was always drunk. I went from being a daily drinker to being a binge drinker.

In '93, I went back to finish my high school. I went to RB Russell School because it was close to where I was living and it was free for me to go there. I had decided that I wanted to get my Grade 12 education so that I could make something of myself and not be dependent on the system for the rest of my life. I had tried to go a few times before, but I just never thought I was strong enough or ready enough. When I went back to school, I kept my drinking to binging on the weekends so I could separate school and drinking.

I drank while my kids were young but at the time, I didn't think my kids ever suffered. I didn't see any issues with my drinking, because I thought they always had everything they needed. We had a roof over our heads, food in the cupboard, and the kids had cable TV and all the entertainment things. The kids had everything they could want, except, I realize now, for their mother. I never saw a problem with my behaviour because I was raised basically without a mother when I was growing up. That was due to a combination of my experience with CFS and foster care, and my mom being an alcoholic. I own my shit. I was a bad mother back then. That's because I didn't know any other way.

I remember this one day early in 1994. My oldest daughter was six. I must've been blacked out because I came out of the blackout and she was leaning on my lap and she said, "Mommy, you drink too much." I started bawling. I had twenty-four beers sitting on a table next to me. I took them to the kitchen counter and I dumped every one of those bottles down the drain.

I decided that I wanted to be better. I knew that the reason I was drinking and smoking weed was to drown out feelings of inadequacy, of not being good enough. I was scared shitless because I didn't know the first thing about being sober and dealing with my issues. But I was finally ready to quit drinking. I went to my doctor and told him I needed to talk to somebody because I didn't want to be that way anymore. They have counsellors at the clinic where my doctor is. That was when I started my counselling journey.

I graduated from high school in 1995 when my son was three. I had two teachers there who never gave up on me: Jay Willman and Helen Strock. I'll never forget those two. They got me into drama at the school. It was called the Community Action Program. They got me into acting and kept me busy. I loved acting because I could step out of my own head and be somebody else for a little while.

My teachers told me that I was worth more than I thought I was. They said that they saw I had a lot of potential to be something better than what I was (not that I wasn't worth anything). They kept telling me that I could be so many different things if I just set my mind to it. They literally saved my life and helped me stay sober. I will never forget them. I'm still in contact with them, but I haven't seen them since the pandemic started.

When those two teachers told me these things, at first I was very resistant. I was like, "Fuck off you guys. You don't know what you're talking about." But then there were also a few times when my mother actually told me she was proud of me. She told me I was a good mom and doing everything that I needed to do for my kids. That meant a lot to me, because the times my mom would say that she was proud of someone were very few and far between. I understand why. It was because of the way she was treated growing

up. She had gone to residential day school on her reserve—Norway House. She was terrorized there. My mom had also had a lot of abuse from her siblings growing up.

I started to think, *Hey, wait, there's got to be something people are seeing that I'm not seeing.*

One of my turning points came when I graduated high school. I was the first one in my family to graduate from high school. I learned that I was smart enough, strong enough, and resilient enough to do something that nobody else in my family had done.

After I graduated, I started living with this guy. I had known him for about ten or fifteen years. I spent six years with him, on and off from '96 to 2002. I was very much blinded by my inability to be alone. I was afraid to be alone. He was good at manipulating me and making me feel like shit. I had started to do good in my life, but I was marred by how he treated me.

He was a big alcoholic and a big drug addict. I didn't realize at that time that I could not be around that type of lifestyle because I was very much an alcoholic. I still thought, *I can handle this, I can do this.* Yeah, right. I was trying to be sober, but being with him and the exposure to that lifestyle was really hard. I did have periods where I was slipping up and would relapse. I was messed up and wasn't always thinking clearly. I would relapse and then go back to being sober. Then I'd go back with him and I'd start drinking again. When we were on, I was drinking, when we were off, I was sober.

This guy was abusive too. The abuse started about a year after we were together. I got tired of being pushed around and treated like I was nothing, and I was tired of being the victim, so I became an abuser. I never abused anybody sexually but I started to physically abuse him. I had met with an Elder who told me I had to stop abusing myself and others. I didn't want to hurt people. So I talked to my counsellor about this. I had to realize that the pain I was inflicting on my partner was the exact same kind of pain that had been inflicted on me for years. I had to understand that what I was doing wasn't right. No one deserves that, man or woman. Once I could get that into my head, then I was able to stop abusing, but that took a while.

While I was working with that counsellor, one day she asked me, "When you *really* look at yourself in the mirror what do you see?"

I said, "I see somebody who is trying to make everything work in a healthy way."

She said, "That doesn't sound like a victim to me." That was when I realized I had stopped thinking of myself as a victim and started thinking of myself as a survivor.

I had been a victim to external sources, but I learned that if I internalize that, then I made myself a victim. I learned not to internalize all that pain. If I take those feelings of fear and anger and rejection and sadness and blame others, then I am a victim. But if I learn how to use those feelings to the best of my ability, I am no longer a victim. Instead of letting those feelings fester and grow, I turn them from a negative to a positive. Those feelings now give me energy to do my work. It's kind of like a fire has been lit under my ass. I didn't ask for any of the bullshit that happened to me, and I won't take it on as my own. I won't allow somebody else's fears and anger and power-hungry selves to impede me and my spirit. I am a very strong and resilient individual. This was another turning point for me.

I eventually kicked that guy out. That was when I realized I couldn't be around people who drank or did drugs, because I'm forever going to be recovering. I knew that in order for me to be successful at being sober, I had to be away from people who would live that lifestyle. I decided that I was going to throw myself into university. I was going to do whatever I could to make my life successful for myself and my children. I was in my late twenties, early thirties. But university didn't feel right for me at that time.

I had cravings. I still have cravings. But every time I had a craving for alcohol, I would just go do something with my kids. I replaced my addiction with activities with my children. We'd go to the park, or I'd go take them shopping or I'd go do something that was fun with them. I would also take the kids out to community events and then I would get to know people in the community. I started volunteering and that's also how I got involved in my community.

I realize that as far back as before I was apprehended by CFS, I felt different from all my siblings. I love my siblings to death, but they were not the caregiver-type like I was. I felt like I didn't belong. In foster care I turned inward into myself—into my mind and my heart—as a way to protect myself and keep my strength and resilience alive because I had been beaten down so much. It is only as I got older and felt safer that I've been able to come out of myself and turn outwards to the community.

I'm still doing those things to this day. Working with the community gives me a sense of purpose. Especially when my children got older, as teenagers, and then became adults and moved out. My work in the community gave me a sense of purpose, a sense of belonging. I was doing something where I was needed. All my life, I've wanted to feel I was needed.

Around 1999, when I was in my late twenties and my kids were elementary school age, two of my sisters became sex-trade workers. I was looking for them, but I couldn't find them. So the next best thing for me to do was to take care of the ones that I could find. I started taking in these women off the streets and into my home. Every night, I had no less than six or seven women sleeping in my house. I would feed them, clothe them, let them take a shower. They had a safe place to sleep. They were never allowed to do drugs or drink in my home because by that time I had quit drinking and drugging.

In the back of my mind, I always hoped that someone was being that good to my sisters. I opened my home to those women because I wanted them to feel like there was a safe place they could go to and that somebody gave a shit. And I did give a shit. I always told the girls, "I'm looking for my sisters. If you see them, let them know I'm looking for them. Tell them I'm here if they need somewhere safe to be." And finally, I found my sisters because of a woman that I was helping. I think I did that for about four years until I found my sisters.

Three years after I found my sisters my mom died of complications to diabetes. I was thirty-three. About four or five years before she died, my mother got diagnosed with diabetes and she also had heart problems. The doctor told her that she had to quit drinking or she was going to die. So she quit drinking and went back to the church. She was trying to make things better. I got closer with my mom after she stopped drinking. She became my best friend.

We had very rough times as we were growing up. (I say *we* because my mom was growing up then too.) She was a very angry woman, but I didn't realize all of the shit she went through in her life. She had a lot of hurt her whole life.

We had it out really good one day when I was eighteen. It was after I had my first child. A few weeks before that, I had decided to move to Ontario with my partner. My mom didn't like the idea of me leaving the province with my daughter. She told me that if I left, she would disown me. I figured it was my life and my daughter. I wanted to go somewhere where it was going to be a better life for us, so I left. But lo and behold it wasn't a better life. My mother was right. I came back home to Winnipeg two weeks later. I hadn't spoken to my mom while I was gone. Then we bumped into to each other on the street and got talking. We went back to her house to have coffee and we had this big-ass screaming match.

After that fight, we had this long very revealing conversation. That's when my mom first told me about some of the things she had been through. We actually talked about her history and her time in residential day school. My mom told me more about her life. She went through a whole lot of bullshit: the abuse from her siblings, and Ernest physically abused her too. I did not know the extent of what had happened to her before that day.

I also told my mom that I had been molested by Ernest. She did not know that. She cried and called herself a bad parent. And she apologized to me for what had happened. I told her she had nothing to apologize for. She said that she initially internalized all of the shit when she found out what my dad did to us kids. She made it all about her, and that it was her fault. I had to explain to her that it wasn't her fault.

That's when things started to change with me and my mom. That was when I realized that not only did I go through a lot of trauma and bullshit, but so did she. She did the best she could with us, with what she knew. That was a turning point for me and my mom. It wasn't hard to forgive her because I always knew it wasn't her fault. She didn't know what was going on.

My mom had a heart of gold, she was very generous. When she started working at Ma Mawi and had more money, she would always help people. No matter what situation. She probably needed the money, but she shared it. She was very caring, giving, and loyal.

My mom also had a backbone. She could stand up for herself. If somebody was trying to hurt one of us kids, or hurt her, or anyone

she cared about, that's when she would step up and protect people. (I think one of the reasons she started drinking was because she couldn't handle the truth about Ernest.) I developed my backbone from my mom. I don't let people walk all over me.

Shortly after I graduated high school, I went to a ceremony and this gentleman came up to me and told me that I had very beautiful eyes. I said, "Yeah, fuck, whatever. Get lost." An Elder came up to me and told me that I should never, ever say anything to anybody when they're giving me a compliment.

He said, "When someone gives you a compliment, the only thing that should ever come out of your mouth is thank you."

I said, "Well, why? I don't believe these people are saying these things just out of the goodness of their heart."

He said, "If somebody says something nice to you, and you say anything other than 'thank you,' you're taking away their ability to give you a piece of themselves." He said, "From now on, Mary, I want to hear you say only thank you when someone gives you a compliment." I've kept that advice in my head all these years because it's a reminder to me that I'm not the only one who sees me, other people see me as well. I think people see strengths in me that I don't see in myself. I sometimes get taken aback because other people see me as someone who has knowledge.

I still have a really hard time accepting compliments. When someone says something nice to me, it's hard to zip my lip and say thank you. I walk away because I get so embarrassed. But I've had Elders tell me that's humility, because I'm a very humble person. I try to be! But there are some days when I'm like *Fuck yeah, I'm the shit*! I have successfully run the organization Fearless R2W since 2014 on zero-dollar budget. It's hard to be humble about that!

In 2008 I started volunteering at Ndinawe Youth Resource Centre and then I worked there for a couple of years. But I had personality clashes with some of the management, and I didn't feel like I fit in there anymore so I left. I married John around then, near the end of 2011. I didn't have work, so we went on social assistance and then became homeless. We stayed at his mom's house in a tent in her backyard. We didn't have any of our kids or grandkids with us yet. I had a really great opportunity to go to school at Red River College for the child and youth care certificate program (to be a child and youth care worker). It was through Ndinawe, weirdly enough. The program is free and you can either continue on in your studies or get a job.

My grandsons got apprehended just after I started that program (our granddaughter was not born yet). They were taken into CFS custody at the beginning of 2012. My daughter signed a voluntary placement agreement (VPA) for three months. As part of that agreement, my husband and I moved in with my daughter to try and teach her how to parent. After the three months, CFS returned my grandsons back to the sole care of their mother, and my husband and I moved out. I stopped that Red River College program because I had just secured employment at Spence Neighbourhood Association as their rental safety coordinator. So we got our own two-bedroom apartment.

In November of 2012, the boys were apprehended again. And that was when I took them for good. My daughter had gone out drinking one night, and I couldn't babysit because I had an early appointment the next day. So she took her kids to somebody else's place to be babysat. I guess my daughter paid the sitter in advance, because that person started drinking and drugging while they had the children. The sitter passed out with a pot of something cooking on the stove and that started an apartment fire. My grandsons were caught in the apartment during this fire.

My daughter got kicked out of the bar she was at, so she just decided to go and check on her children. She couldn't get into the apartment. She heard the alarm going off and her boys crying. She ran and got the security guard for the apartment building. He got the door open, and they called 911. The kids were taken to the hospital. She got to the hospital and they arrested her at the hospital and took her to the drunk tank. My daughter called me that morning and told me what had happened. She said, "CFS is on their way." I stopped my appointment and I went to the children's hospital. When I got to the hospital there was this lady sitting outside the room.

I asked her, "Do you work for the hospital or do you work for CFS?" She wouldn't tell me right away, so I got angry and I said, "Listen, I need to fucking know who you work for, and I need to know right now. These are my grandchildren and I don't trust you to be sitting here and watching my grandchild." So she told me she worked for CFS.

I gave her my business card with my cell number on it and said, "Give this to your supervisor. I want my grandchildren." I asked her where CFS had taken one of my grand-kids, because he was not at the hospital. She gave me the hotel name and the room number. I thought she must be new because the CFS workers are not supposed to tell those kinds of things. My other grandson was going to be staying in a hospital overnight because he got the most damage from the smoke.

That afternoon, I got a call from the social worker saying she was confused because she had my business card with my cell number, but the woman who was at the hospital outside my grandson's room had said I didn't want my grandkids. I said, "Well, that woman is a fucking idiot. Why would I give you my business card with my cell number on it if I didn't want my grandchildren?"

Once I filled out all the paperwork, it took me about a month to get them. They were only in a foster home for a very short time. They don't even remember it. The boys have been with me since January of 2012. I also have had my granddaughter, who was born in 2016, since she was three days old. My daughter comes to visit whenever she can. My grandkids rock! They are doing amazing. They are flourishing and doing well in school. I am so proud of them!

Back in 2012 or '13, Michael (Redhead Champagne) was getting yelled at by the grandmothers in our community here in the North End. He was in charge of the Friday night community meetings called Meet Me at the Bell Tower. These meetings were about stopping violence and finding solutions to the violence that was happening in our community. One Friday, the grandmothers said to him, "If you're all about stopping violence, why aren't you stopping the violence that CFS is inflicting on us every time they take our children?" For three or four weeks in a row he kept getting yelled at by grandmothers.

So Michael said, "Okay, let's find a solution." And Fearless R2W was born. At first the only thing that happened was that a Twitter account was created, but it was never monitored, so the grandmothers complained again. Michael contacted me and asked me

for help. I've known Michael since he was eighteen years old and we used to work together at Ndinawe. He knew that I'd been advocating against unfair practices by CFS since I was seventeen. I learned the hard way how to deal with the agencies. Michael also knew all about how I had just got custody of two of my grandkids.

So Michael and I sat down to talk about Fearless R2W. I said, "Okay, enough with having these damn meetings. Let's just get a space and do it. Make sure you have food for people, bus tickets, and also make sure that you're there." He said okay, and told me he was expecting me to be there with him. I said okay.

I can tell you about the name Fearless R2W. The predominate postal code of Winnipeg's North End is R2W, and the reason we chose the word *Fearless* is that we want people to *be* fearless. We don't want people to be afraid of CFS, we want them to be educated. You fear something you don't know, but once you learn about it and know it, you no longer fear it. One big problem is that the apprehension rates of Indigenous kids by CFS has been ridiculously high. Back in 2014 when we first started out, the CFS apprehension stats were that about one in six families in our R2W zone were being affected daily by CFS.

I've spoken out against a lot of CFS practices, but I'm not saying we don't need CFS, because we do. There are children who are being horribly treated by their families. I was one of those children who was being horribly treated by one of my parents. We needed to be removed from that abusive situation. So there are cases when CFS provides the services that are needed, and I have had some positive interactions with the agencies. I had a really good working relationship with the agency I dealt with in the Northern Authority when I got custody of my grandchildren.

Me and Michael started hosting a community meeting once every two weeks, to talk about our hopes and dreams for Fearless. At our first meetings we had a ton of food and bus tickets, but it was just me and him. No one else came. We had to carry on to prove to the community that we were not going to stop in six weeks if nobody showed up. But after about six months, we started getting more people coming. We never turn anyone away. If someone needs our support we will give it, or we'll find them what they need.

We do CFS advocacy, housing advocacy, and we educate the community on system literacy. We bounced around from organization to organization, wherever we could use their space for free. It wasn't until 2016 that we got our forever home at Turtle Island Neighbourhood Centre (on King Street) and we have stayed there, still doing our work for free on a zero budget. It wasn't until about three years ago, in 2018, that we started getting small grants to help out with the food and bus tickets and honorarium for speakers.

In 2020 Fearless R2W became an actual organization. We registered our name and we're in the process of developing policies so that we can actually have funding and hire people. Right now I'm the only paid staff at Fearless. We have six volunteer staff. My big dream is to have actual advocates who get paid to do the work that I do. I am giving myself five years to get Fearless up and running and to be what I envision it to be: a wraparound service in the community.

One big problem is that the apprehension rates of Indigenous kids by CFS has been ridiculously high.

In 2021 I switched to working part-time for three months for Fearless so I could work full-time as the coordinator for the Community Helper Initiative at Ma Mawi. It's a mobile crisis line for people who want to get help. That help could be anything from mental health issues to CFS issues to disability issues. Fearless got the funding for it, but we knew it wasn't enough money to be sustainable, so we partnered with McDonald Youth Services, Ma Mawi, and St. Amant Centre as well. St. Amant Centre has a lot of specialized services to help people who are on the spectrum (autism for example). St. Amant gave us free training so we could better understand our clients' needs and help them get the appropriate services. The initiative had gone through two coordinators in a year and nothing had been done, so I took that three-month leave from Fearless and got the Community Helper Initiative up and running.

Fearless R2W meets every Wednesday night. Some days we have thirty to forty people, and some days we have five. We meet regardless of how many come. The kind of people that come to the meetings varies too. Sometimes we'll get parents who are in the middle of a custody fight with CFS and they're trying to learn more about the system. We'll get people who are community members trying to be allies and learning about the system so that they can help their friends and family. Sometimes we'll even get government officials. They'll come because they're new to being government officials and want to learn about the system, or they just want to learn more about Fearless. Everybody's always curious as to how we went for seven to eight years with no funding and were still able to produce the number of programs and supports that we've produced.

At our Wednesday meetings we always have an "Ask Mary Anything" question period. I am an encyclopedia of CFS information. I read legislation religiously. I've become a legislation geek! I love learning new things. Any time there's a change to the legislation, I read it and I memorize it because we need more people who understand legislation. CFS legislation is always changing. If we know what the legislation says, then we can explain it in layman's terms and we can educate the families and the community. I've even been reading Pennsylvania laws on child welfare. A parent in Pennsylvania contacted me about their foster care battle. I forwarded the email to IPAN so they could find somebody in Pennsylvania who could help them, but it made me curious. So I started reading Pennsylvania CPS (Child Protective Services) laws.

Another issue we have with CFS is that the money they pay for kinship care is less than half of what they would pay a stranger to look after the children. When I was a kinship home for my two grandsons, I was getting $1,300 a month in total for the two boys. Once I became a licensed foster parent, I started getting over $3,000 a month. Now that they're not in care and I have custody of them, I get no money for them, other than the child tax.

From my work over the past couple of decades, I believe that approximately 85% of all apprehensions are the result of poverty. They don't have to happen. If CFS gave the same amount of money to a single mom on EIA that they give the foster parents, there would be fewer apprehensions due to poverty. EIA gives you not even one-third of what the agency will give a foster parent.

There are not enough foster and group homes and there are not enough people who are able to get licensed to be foster parents.

Some of the agencies' expectations of foster parents are pretty high, as they should be, because these people are taking care of children. So it's really hard for people, especially Indigenous people, to get that certification to be foster parents. I've gone through the licensing to become a foster parent. The paperwork was thick and CFS asked some very invasive questions. They ask you about your sex life. I've met non-Indigenous foster parents who say that they've never been asked that question. There's many other cases where there's a difference in what's asked of Indigenous people. I answered every last one of the questions. My husband had to fill out a booklet too. He's white, and his booklet didn't have the same questions as mine. I know because I helped him with it.

There are some good safeguards that are in place now, that weren't there when I was a kid. For example, a social worker has to have a face-to-face meeting with each child at least once a month, and they have to take pictures of the child. CFS workers have been getting a lot more education on abuse, what happens with children who have been abused and how they present. If those two things had been in place back in the 80s when I was in care, it would have been a different story. Although some things are better now than when I was a kid, there are still huge systemic issues with so many Indigenous kids in care.

I understand that social workers are overworked and underpaid. There's only one of them to like fifty or sixty kids. It's hard for social workers to keep up. The system that we have right now has not changed much since 1948. The CFS Act (as it is known today) has been around since then, and it is outdated.

The system is very much broken, but it's working exactly the way the government intended it to. With the residential school system, the government removed Indigenous children from their families. With 11,000 kids in care in Manitoba, and 90% of those kids being Indigenous when we only represent 18% of the population, child welfare is the new residential school. It screams racism. It screams *taking the Indian out of the child*, taking the Indigenous children away from their families, their culture, their teachings, their language. What we are working towards at Fearless R2W is that more families stay together.

Social workers need to be trained and educated with a strength-based approach, focusing first on what the parents are doing well. They need to be taught to keep their biases out of what they are observing. A lot of times, not every time, apprehensions are mistakenly done. (Poverty is at the root of many apprehensions.) Social workers and CFS workers need to go in with a strength-based approach, and let the family know the things that are being done well, along with focusing on the areas that need support.

Let's say there's a poverty issue and the parent is having trouble making ends meet. They can't pay the bills, buy groceries, and get kids proper clothing for the seasons. Instead of CFS saying, "You're not doing what you need to do, I'm taking the kids," they could say, "Okay, you're doing really great by keeping up on your bills, but here's the issue of the clothing and the food. What can we do to help you? How can we fix this? Do you need some budgeting courses? Do you need some short-term help with money? Can we help you find a job? Can we help you find childcare?" If they went in with a strength-based approach, there would be fewer children in care. Instead of traumatizing the children by taking them away from their family and siblings, put resources in the home. Help the family.

In cases where there's a single parent and they have an addiction, CFS has to figure out what the family is doing right. Addiction can impair the parent, but if they can get help for their addiction they can be a good parent. Does the parent with the addiction need residential treatment or outpatient treatment? If it's residential treatment, then take the parent out, leave the children in the home, and put a temporary foster parent in the home while the parent is in treatment.

Unfortunately, nothing could have been done differently for my apprehension as a child. It was right that my siblings and I were removed from our home. But the following year when Ernest finally went to jail, CFS could have put us back in our home with our mom. They didn't because CFS judged my mother and blamed her for what happened to us kids. CFS took total guardianship of us children away from our mother because of this. In 2021 I read my CFS file. It says it all there in black and white. That makes me so angry.

Another thing, aging out of the foster care system at eighteen is terrible. It's really hard because once children turn eighteen the agency has no legal rights because they have

become adults. Kids that age out of care will go back to their families if they are able. If they know where their family is. The ones that don't have the luxury of going home to a family end up homeless. (In the 2018 Winnipeg Street Census, 51.1% of Winnipeg's homeless population said they were former children in care.) Most of the time, the foster parents will bag up the foster kid's clothes in garbage bags and the CFS worker will come and get those kids and drop them off at Sally Ann's (Salvation Army) at Main and Higgins. There are other shelters, but it's the biggest one. Ninety percent of the youth get dropped off there.

The shelter will help them get on EIA. The young adults don't know how to budget, or how to look after themselves. They don't know how to look after a home, because they're not taught these things when they are in care. The shelter is where they meet the drug dealers and the street workers, so they end up being homeless, addicted, exploited and usually caught up in the justice system. It's all because they were not taught how to properly look after themselves. I've not met one child who's aged out that got any type of budgeting courses or learned how to clean their home or buy their food or how to pay their bills. Nothing.

My first experience of Indigenous ceremony or cultural traditions was an eye-opener. I was fifteen and in drug treatment when I got introduced to my culture. It was amazing. My culture is so beautiful, and our traditions and teachings are so ingrained in the Earth and all about protecting it. I became very involved. Although I was baptized Roman Catholic, I was never Christian. I was always atheist because I didn't know any different. Then when I started learning about my culture and my traditions, I started believing in a higher power and a spiritual way of being. I now try to live that way. Whenever I get a chance to go to ceremony, I take my grandkids with me because I want them to have some knowledge of their culture. My Indigenous spirituality and culture have been a big part of my healing, and they still are.

My spirit name is Red Sky Woman. It was given to me by Elder Stella Blackwood when I was in my twenties. She has passed on. She told me that I have two parts to my spirit name. I have sky spirits and I have water spirits that have given me my name.

To me, Red Sky Woman means that I am a helper. I have the wisdom of the beaver and the compassion of the sky spirits. Together, that compassion and wisdom make a perfect ball that is constantly spinning, constantly intertwining, and constantly helping. I feel that I was given this name by these spirits because of who I am and what I do.

Michael has been at me for many, many years to write a book about my life, but I just don't have the time, the energy or the inclination to do it. I'm really glad that I was able to be part of this book because I think that it's worthwhile. I am very proud to say that the author's not getting any money for this. It's going to the organization Voices. I know it's going to a worthy cause. This book helps me get my story out. It's kind of therapeutic. I have no problem speaking of my past, because I've dealt with it and I understand it now. I am happy I am able to speak about it and not feel ashamed.

Looking back on my worst days as a kid, I realize I was very hard on myself. I had nothing good to say to myself. I didn't think that anyone gave a shit about me or that I was worthy of anyone loving me. Everywhere I turned, I was facing racism, prejudice, stupidity. I was tired. There were a couple of times I contemplated suicide. Back then if you'd asked me why I didn't go through with it, I'd say that I was a coward. If you ask me today, I'd say it was because I was stronger than I recognized at the time. I was able to think of how many people would miss me, how much heartache it would have cost my mother, my sisters and brothers. The first time I thought of killing myself I was only nine. I was living at home and things were really bad. Today I would say to that little girl, *It gets better.* I am living proof it does get better.

And now I no longer have a problem crying because Creator gave us our tears for a reason. They're healing and they help us become stronger. When you hold your emotions and your tears in, you can make yourself physically sick. Those tears were given to us for healing purposes. We cry to heal.

One day while we were talking on the phone, Mary proudly read to me a message she'd recently received from her former teacher Helen Strock who had read about Mary in a newspaper article. Helen wrote that she remembered Mary being a young student who was "smart and vivacious." She also described Mary today as "charming, smart, brave and having a strong understanding of the community." I so valued hearing Helen's description of Mary.

Mary agreed to be part of the book during the pandemic. All of our interviews were done on Zoom, so I did not meet her face to face until the very end. It turns out we are both huggers, so we put our masks on and had a huge hug.

Sarah

I'm really into the character of Phoebe on the TV show *Friends*. When Phoebe was fourteen she lived on the streets. When she moved in with her friends she brought all these boxes labeled "From the Streets."

In the early seasons of the show she is in her twenties and very cavalier about her personal story. In one of her songs in the coffee house, she sings, "I made a man with eyes of snow and a smile so bewitching. How was I supposed to know that my mom was dead in the kitchen? Lalalalala." Everyone in the audience is looking on in horror, but this was her life. I can relate to that so hard. I found it hilarious. Everyone's like, "Oh, Phoebe's so kooky." But as the show goes on, you see her forge an identity outside of those things. That is inspiring for me. I had to go through those same kinds of stages, and I can also be cavalier talking about my time in care because to

me it's just normal. But sometimes that makes people super uncomfortable because it is some really heavy shit I'm talking about.

My birth parents had four kids: me, my sister, and my two brothers. We're all a year apart. I'm the oldest and I was born in Winnipeg in 1985. My mom was eighteen when she had me, and my dad was around ten years older. I remember there was an Extra Foods store and a parking lot on one side of my house, and the Transcona Library on the other. I remember spending time at the library looking at books and being on my own a lot. I don't remember my parents at all. I had to

ANDREW MAHON

take care of my younger siblings. My baby brother would always climb out of his crib and so my sister and I would have to wake up and move stuff around so he couldn't get out of his crib. Keep in mind I was four or younger, and my sister was a year younger than me. So we were pretty young to be doing that stuff.

When I was around five, the four of us got put into foster care. The night we got apprehended I was out riding my trike and I got hit by a car. It wasn't serious—just a scraped knee. The driver took me home and found no parents and three other little kids alone so he phoned the police. I don't remember my parents coming home while we were being apprehended, but my sister seems to remember my mom putting her in a car. The police took us that night. My sister and I went to one foster home in Richer, Manitoba; my two brothers went to another one in St. Anne's. It was incredible that we weren't all split up to four different homes.

Shortly after we went into foster care, there was a hearing or something to see what the plan was with my biological parents. Were we going back to be with my parents or were we becoming permanent wards? My birth parents already hadn't shown up for a few court dates. This had been a regular issue. On this last court date, my birth dad showed up and said, "You know what? Screw you guys, we'll just start another family," and stormed out of the court. My biological parents moved to BC and we were made permanent wards. By then I was six. I don't know when it happened, but my birth parents had four more kids, and gave them the same names they'd given us first four. At some point later, my birth parents had two more kids.

Yeah. Yup.

I found this out from my adoptive parents later on. That story's been well documented and corroborated by social workers and therapists. My sister and I did make contact with my grandmother—my mom's mom. We saw her a couple of times. My aunts and that same grandmother gave some baby pictures and early childhood pictures to the social workers. That was cool.

I do remember the day my foster parents had to sit down and try to explain to us that our parents weren't coming back and we were going up for adoption. I had no idea what any of that meant. I just remember crying a lot and asking, *Did they die? What do you mean my parents don't want me?* I definitely feel for those foster parents having to break that kind of news to a six-year-old. My sister and brother have no memory of being told about our parents not coming back, and my youngest brother was only like eight months old when he went into care.

We stayed at that foster home until I was seven, and then this other couple in Winnipeg, the people I call my parents, adopted all four of us. Basically, CFS told them if they didn't take all four kids, they would be black-balled from every adoption list and would not be allowed to adopt. (That's a whole other bag of crazy.) So they took all four of us. It was October of '92 when we were adopted. I don't remember seeing my two brothers all that much when we were in foster care, because when we moved in together again, I couldn't remember which brother was which.

I've always been really over-sensitive and emotional. In elementary school, there were lots of kids who were not allowed to play with me because I was from foster care. I cried easily so it was really easy to pick on me. I got bullied a lot in junior high too. It makes sense that I was having a ton of anxiety

and panic. I started getting kicked out of school—mostly for acting out. I was getting in fights with my teachers and running away from home.

The guidance counsellor at school suggested I see a psychiatrist. My parents sent me to see one I don't even remember meeting. I literally sat in a waiting room at Manitoba Adolescent Treatment Centre (MATC) and the counsellor came out with a prescription for Paxil. I remember being angry that I didn't get a chance to talk to the psychiatrist. Everything changed when I started taking the Paxil. It was supposed to be an antidepressant that helped with anxiety. Instead, I just became really violent. I was violent towards others. I was also violent towards myself; that was the beginning of me constantly trying to kill myself. That became a lot for my parents to handle, so ultimately I ended up back in care. But at the time I really hated my parents so I was like, *Screw you guys, it'll be way better anywhere else anyways.*

My adoptive parents also had a kid when I was ten. Around the time that first son was born, our adoption sort of started to fall apart. One at a time, we all ended up back in care again. One of my brothers was the first one to go. I still don't really know why or what actually happened but he ended up going to a group home. It was fairly close by so we got to see him a decent amount. I was the next to go. I think I was in Grade 8. I was thirteen.

I stay in touch with my (adoptive) parents now. We got back in touch when I was twenty-three, I think. Long after we were all gone, they had another child. So there's six of us kids in total. All of us siblings are in touch now and we all have regular contact with our adoptive parents. We all consider them to be our parents.

When I left my adoptive parents' care, it was just before Christmas. I went into an emergency foster home right away. The foster parent was a sixty-five-year-old alcoholic who I saw maybe twice the entire time. It was me and a fourteen-year-old boy. I was there for about a month and at one point, the boy tried to sexually assault me, but I threw him off me. I told my guidance counsellor what had happened the next day because I was really freaked out and upset (as I think is completely justified). The foster mom basically made it

known that bitches like me start drama and it was my fault for being a slut. I was thirteen; I had never had any sort of exposure to that kind of thing before, so I thought, *Maybe this is my fault. What was I doing that made him want me?*

I got kicked out of that foster home and I went to an all-girls group home where I was the only white person. I got picked on all the time because I had had a very different life than a lot of these girls I was living with. At home I had gone to school, there were rules, my parents weren't alcoholics, they were good parents. Mine was just a very different experience. These girls in the group home were all my age but they had already had boyfriends, knew what drugs were, and had next to no supervision. I had no idea what was going on. I didn't understand that some parents just weren't there for their kids. You'd think I would have, given the first five years of my life, but I was so confused. I would think, *What do you mean you just skip school and no one makes you go back? What do you mean you never got grounded for mouthing off?* I thought that was just how it was in

> I didn't understand that some parents just weren't there for their kids.

every family. I think there must have been another emergency group home placement though because I was only there for a few months.

Then I got put in a foster home where the foster mom greeted me with, "Oh my god, this girl Crystal that lives here is going to kick your ass. She is going to have so much fun with you because you are so stupid and naïve. Crystal is going to eat you for breakfast."

And so she did.

Crystal was always giving me digs, calling me names. She'd steal stuff from the foster family and blame me. It seems little now, but it was constant. Everyone thought it was hilarious when I would get upset or try to run away. That foster mom coined the term Psycho Sarah for me. I'm only starting to escape that name now.

One day I started screaming at Crystal and calling her a bitch and telling her to leave me alone. My foster mom was laughing at me and calling me Psycho Sarah for supposedly starting all this drama. I got mad and found the closest object to me, which happened to be a picture, and threw it towards my foster mom. It was just in her general vicinity, it wasn't even at her. So she had me charged

with assault with a deadly weapon. She called the cops. Yup. I had been at that foster home for about six months.

At that point, I was only fourteen years old. I had been kicked out of the entire River East School Division. Again, I can't remember why, but I was not welcome back. So I kind of bounced around a few schools in Saint Boniface. Mostly I just didn't bother going. All through elementary school, I loved school because it was my escape from all the crap at home. I hated the part where I had to interact with classmates, but I loved learning. I've always loved reading; maybe it was a comfort for me from when I used to escape to the library when I was four. I remember I loved band class. I played flute and piccolo and I loved being in French Immersion. That was Grade 7 and 8, so when I got kicked out of school, my CFS social worker tried to find a school that had band and French but most schools didn't want me. It was really hard to join junior high in the middle of the school year when all of the groups were already established.

I took up shoplifting and I was really good at it, so I would skip school to go shoplift and sell whatever I got. I also took up drinking and smoking. Then, I started smoking pot and being promiscuous. I got arrested several times because that's what happens when you break the law; eventually, it catches up with you. So I went to the Manitoba Youth Center a few times. I think after the third time, I was not welcome back at that foster home where Crystal lived.

So I sat in juvie until a bed opened at Knowles Center. At the time—this is like 1999—Knowles was a lockdown facility for youth with behavioural issues. So they wanted to lock me up there to keep me safe and get me all sorts of treatment for all my mental health issues. The first thing they did was to up my medication because it clearly wasn't working. But more meds just made me angrier and crazier.

I was released from the Manitoba Youth Centre with a bunch of different conditions— I had to go to school, I had to go to therapy, I couldn't disturb the peace, couldn't use substances. I was fourteen when I went to Knowles and I didn't get out until I was eighteen. So that's how I started at John G. Stewart School. That school and Knowles are on the same property. Everyone who lives at Knowles goes there. They put me in a Grade 8 classroom. They would group classrooms loosely around grade but it was more like approximate age than grade. So they stuck me in that classroom for a couple of months to wait until the next semester started when I could start Grade 9. In Grade 8 I learned how to cross stitch and play crib. I had been out of school for a while by the time I got there. I told everyone I was too cool for school, so I was pissed off about going. I thought it was bullshit that they were telling me what to do. I didn't want to be there.

In Grade 9, they actually taught classes that were worth credits. For the most part, they put only smarter students or ones with slightly less behavioural problems in that classroom. I liked it. I liked woodworking. I liked taking Futures in Business. That was my favourite class. At one point, I know me and Trevor—Trevor Holroyd, my Grade 9 teacher—sold potato chips in the hallway for that class.

Trevor is the principal now. That happened long after I left but you know what? I always say that he deserved to be named principal after having to deal with me for four years. Trevor had the patience of a saint. I remember at one point I threw a desk at him. I can't remember why. I'm sure it seemed perfectly reasonable to me at the time! It had to be so challenging to teach under those kinds of conditions. Trevor and I got along well though. I really liked him, and I felt he liked me.

I was back to liking school but I hated Knowles Centre. I hated the staff. It sucked so bad being there. The Knowles staff hated me and couldn't handle me. But school was really cool because they liked me there. I was smart, I enjoyed what I was learning, I liked feeling useful. I was reading a lot. They had computers with the internet, which was super cool. That was brand new to me.

At one point, I ended up going back to the Youth Center because I was "disturbing the peace." I got pissed off at some of the group home staff. They took my guitar, stripped my bed, and searched my room. They must have suspected I had something—I can't remember. Anyone could go to the staff and say "So and so says they have cigarettes in their room" and that would trigger a search. I started screaming at them, and they called the cops. The Knowles staff said I was disturbing the peace, so I got carted off to the Youth Center again because it was really that easy for the staff to arrange.

I can't remember how long I was there, but basically I didn't come back until after I had been sentenced for all my shoplifting charges. I also had that charge of assault with a deadly weapon from my foster home with Crystal. (Eventually, they negotiated that one down to assault because even the judge thought that charge was ridiculous.) So I appeared in court for all of those charges. My time in juvie was considered time served, but I also had an additional two years of probation. During that time I couldn't drink, had to go to therapy, and had to go to school. By the time I got off probation, I'd be sixteen. I wouldn't have a record once I turned eighteen, and that'd be a good thing. That's something that a lot of people in foster care can't say. This would be really good later on, because I couldn't have worked in tech security if I'd had a criminal record. And having a criminal record would have also made navigating things at eighteen even harder than they were.

So I went back to Knowles and John G. Stewart School. I was actually really good during that time. I didn't run away, I wasn't drinking or smoking weed (I didn't even have access to it anyway). Lots of kids had family or siblings that would come visit them. I didn't. My siblings weren't allowed to see me and, at that point, my parents couldn't handle it and they had stopped all communication. I know at the time I felt angry all the time but I think, in looking back, I also felt alone.

I was being picked on for being white. Most of the kids at Knowles were Indigenous. I remember there being one other non-Indigenous person the entire time I was there and she was gone by the time I got back from the Youth Center. To be fair to the other kids, I couldn't relate. I grew up in a neighbourhood so white that I thought Native people were fictional. That was how innocent I was. I grew up thinking that Native people were like Pocahontas and they were fake. I'm pretty sure that for a lot of the Indigenous kids, they thought all white people were like white people on TV.

Knowles had an on-call psychiatrist that came once every two weeks (it might have been once a week). He saw all of the patients there. So we'd go and see the psychiatrist who then told the staff what medication we needed and wrote a prescription. Knowles also had their own doctor that all the youth were required to see. This doctor didn't talk to us at all, just did all the prescription refills.

Basically, he just did whatever the staff said. It seems ridiculous that any staff could make an assessment, even just a respite worker driving me to an appointment. They were not qualified. They needed to speak to a supervisor. There needed to be checks and balances. The staff would come in and they'd say, "She's mouthy." The doctor would say, "Okay, well, we'll just write her another prescription."

The good news was that it took them bumping up my Paxil once before they realized it was bad for me. The bad news is that the doctor said the antidepressants made me extremely manic; therefore, I must have bipolar disorder. So the psychiatrist gave me rispirodol. That's an antipsychotic drug. It actually worked really well, except it made me lactate, like when you're breastfeeding a child. I had never been pregnant in my life, but I was literally leaking. It was so gross. I really could not understand what was going on. Apparently, that's also a common side effect. So I begged this doctor to give me something else. After several arguments, he did finally give me some sort of mood stabilizer. When that medication didn't work, the doctor would up the dose or add something else.

By the time I left Knowles at eighteen, I was on twenty different pills a day. I took clonazepam and Ativan three times a day. Those are anti-anxiety medications. They are benzodiazepines, which are extremely addictive and normally not prescribed for everyday use. I was also taking valproic acid and lithium. They're both mood stabilizers usually used for bipolar disorder. I think those two aren't supposed to be taken together, but I don't know for sure. The doctors had doubled up on these medications because I had already been prescribed the max dose, so they gave me two different ones at the same time. I took an antipsychotic—I can't remember if it was Seroquel or Topamax. I tried both, because the antipsychotic meds didn't agree with me. I also took Wellbutrin, which is an antidepressant. Then I took a sleeping pill to get to sleep at night. I was on a fuck-ton of medication.

My two go-tos were being angry or attempting suicide. I was a very angry teenager. Of course, the care workers' jobs were made harder because of that, so they tried to find a way to make their jobs easier.

During that time at Knowles, I was basically locked in a room all the time with nothing to do.

Over-medicating people in your care to the point of complete complacency makes it easier. I think that attitude just comes with the job eventually. If it says in your chart that there are behavioural issues, then the next time they see the doctor it'll be like, "Oh, we can up their medication and that should take care of it," or something like that. I really don't think youth care workers are terrible people. Looking back, I think they were extremely underpaid and incredibly overworked. A lot were students. A worker might be dealing with ten kids on a unit, all with behavioural issues.

During that time at Knowles, I was basically locked in a room all the time with nothing to do. I remember at one point reading the DSM from cover to cover. That's the manual that they use to diagnose mental illnesses. I can't remember why it was there. At one point the psychiatrist decided to start me off on 900 milligrams of lithium. I said, "Well, according to this manual, that is three times the maximum adult dose." They put me in containment until I agreed to take that amount of medication.

The containment unit was literally a windowless room that you could not get out of. It's basically like the padded rubber rooms you see in movies, except there was no padding. Kids only went into the room if they were at risk of harm to themselves or to others. The province did have laws on how long someone could be kept in there. After an hour, there had to be approval from the supervisor. The supervisors often weren't in the same location and did not want to come and check on the situation. I definitely thought those laws were there to protect me, but there was always some way they'd work around them. So if the staff opened the door and came and checked on me, then that timer would start over again. I know that I was in there for days at a time. If I was in there for more than four or five hours, staff had to put a bucket in there so I could go to the washroom. I slept on the floor a couple of times. There was no pillow or blanket because that could be used for self-harm. It's kind of insane when you think about it.

Years later, Trevor told me I was definitely the toughest kid they ever had to deal with at John G. Stewart School because I was right about a lot of stuff and staff couldn't say anything because then they would lose control. To be completely blunt, I was smarter than most of the people taking care of me. Staff at Knowles would make it sound like I was crazy or they'd up my medication. There were two staff members who were sleeping with each other, and they weren't exactly discreet about it. I had said something to their boss and the couple got super pissed off. They told the boss and everyone that I was making shit up, and it was complete allegations. Their boss had me go and stand up in front of everyone and apologize for lying and making things up. No one said shit when that couple got married three months later because she was pregnant. I was pissed. I'm still pissed about that.

I knew what some of our rights were according to the United Nations Convention on the Rights of the Child. I'm not sure where I learned that, maybe from a poster or a brochure in a waiting room (I spent a lot of time in waiting rooms). But from my reading I knew that those UN rights had been ratified. Which meant that our caregivers were responsible for adhering to those, and they would get super pissed off if I reminded them of that. A lot of staff had this opinion that the kids in their care were just stupid fuck-ups and that it didn't really matter because nobody cared. So someone that challenged that for them made it difficult.

But some of the staff at Knowles were good. One guy, Brad, was awesome. He had a biker vibe to him, but he was really sensitive and patient and liked spending time with me. He would bring his guitar in and teach me stuff on it. He wasn't power tripping like a lot of the others. Then this other guy, Rob, had a PhD in psychology. Most of the people who work as youth care workers have gone through Red River College's Child and Youth Care program and that is their level of education. And so it was really cool to meet someone who had taken a different path.

At that time, these were the things I knew to be true about myself: I was very sensitive, I had a lot of mood swings, and I was definitely angry all the time. I thought I was perfectly justified in my anger and frustration. I was a human being locked in a cage and every single time I questioned anything I would get my medication upped or I'd get locked in the containment unit. Something that used to make me feel sad was that I was simultaneously ten steps behind everyone my age and ten steps ahead.

At the time I thought it all seemed fairly reasonable. If bipolar is diagnosed because of ups and downs (which was basically my understanding of it) then I guess that matched my behaviour. The more frustrating thing was that in my psychiatrist's notes it said "bipolar disorder but actually more likely borderline personality disorder." They don't like to diagnose borderline personality disorder (BPD) until someone's an adult because the argument is that your brain's not fully formed yet and your personality can change. I get that and know that kind of change does happen.

I'm angry that as a teenager I was purposely misdiagnosed. I did have a severe mental illness that could have been helped, but it wasn't, because of their refusal to give me a proper diagnosis. That got in the way of me getting help for a really long time. BPD is marked by lots of suicide attempts and difficulty in managing emotions. The only proven treatment for that disorder is Cognitive Behavioural Therapy (CBT). Even if I didn't have BPD, having that kind of therapy to deal with anger and mood swings would've also benefited me if I had bipolar disorder. There were literally no negative consequences to trying CBT, even if there was a mistake with the diagnosis. But BPD takes a lot more effort to treat than something that requires medication. The argument was, "We can't diagnose that so we can't treat that." I don't know if it was known back in those days that CBT had been proven to be effective for treating pretty much all the mental illnesses with varying degrees of effectiveness. Most people with BPT who get the proper treatment can make a full recovery.

A lot of the really, really shitty things in my life could have been avoided had I had a proper diagnosis and access to proper treatment. So I'm angry because although they weren't completely wrong—I mean, yes, there was definitely a severe mental illness—it was their fault that I didn't get treated for it properly to begin with.

I thought that my foster mom was onto something calling me Psycho Sarah. She thought it, the people who lived in the group home with me thought it, and the Knowles staff thought it. Even when I made what I thought were really logical arguments, they'd lock me up or they'd up my medication or ground me.

I spent my entire time in care with youth care workers and psychiatrists telling me that I was very mentally ill and would never be normal. They told me I needed to take huge amounts of medication for the rest of my life. (Turns out, that wasn't true.) I was on so much medication that I was sleeping twenty hours a day. I was missing a lot of school because I couldn't physically get out of bed. I was devastated when I was told that this was going to be the rest of my life. That was just not a life I wanted. And to tell me I was so sick that I'd never do anything other than sit around on welfare—that was awful.

From the time I was twelve or thirteen until I was in university, I constantly thought about killing myself. There was almost no time when killing myself actually left my mind. There were some times when I had more energy to try. I actually tried about once a week for probably about ten years. I think saying I made at least 250 attempts is a very conservative estimate. (I want to stress that it's no longer something I struggle with.) I went to almost all the bridges in the city, climbed over and thought of jumping. I tried suffocating myself with a plastic bag, and lying on train tracks. I tried overdosing on whatever medication I could get my hands on—I tried that a lot. I cut myself to kill myself, but it didn't work. One time, I even tried to make my own chloroform.

I never managed to accomplish it, partly because I'm terrified of pain. Also for a long time I was such a high suicide risk that I didn't have access to enough drugs at once, so that's why my attempts to overdose didn't work. There were also a few times when I worried about who would find me. That kind of thing messes someone up for life. I'm very well aware of that. And so I would feel immense guilt about putting someone in that situation and that's what stopped me. I didn't always care, though, there were definitely times when I was just like, "Fuck it." But there were definitely those times when the thought of someone finding me would go through my mind and cause me to pull back from doing what I'd set out to do.

The scariest time was when I was actually really close to dying. At the last second, I woke up because I had this scarf with me that was a gift from my boyfriend at the time. I thought he would be really angry if he found me with that scarf. I still have that scarf. It literally saved my life. That time was

definitely the closest I came to being successful. After that, there weren't a lot of really serious attempts, although I know that all attempts are serious in a way.

Sometimes what saved me was knowing that people cared about me. But a lot of times, I just felt numb, so I couldn't really care much about anything. It was just like nothing mattered to me. I had very, very good justifications for wanting to end my life. As much as I don't want to kill myself now, and I haven't wanted to in a really long time, I understand my earlier justifications for attempting suicide. A lot of that was medication related, but I also think some of it was that things got so painful I just had to shut the pain out. You can only sustain that much agony for so long.

Every time I tried to go get help, I was basically described as attention seeking and not serious. I was hospitalized a couple of times when it was really bad, but for the most part, the attitude I got was, "You'll be fine in an hour with all your mood swings." That was really frustrating. To me this was the end of the world. I did want to kill myself. My life was always some sort of struggle where I was feeling really stuck and completely powerless.

I am glad that none of the people I love had to find me or mourn my loss.

Now I have this amazing life that's absolutely incredible. I love my life. When people found out that I once wanted to end it all, they'd be kind of like smug and say, "Aren't you glad now you didn't end your life?" I'd say, "Well, I wouldn't have known the difference." My life would have ended there and that would've been it. I know that I'm supposed to say, "Oh, I'm so grateful none of those attempts worked out" but there were a lot of really painful experiences that I could have done without. And had I been successful, I wouldn't have had to live through a lot of that. So I don't know. Yeah. But since that's not what happened, I'm very happy with what's happening now.

In 2003 I turned eighteen. That's when kids age out of the system. CFS started to transition me into independent living. They tried to force me to sign something that said I accepted I was unfit and couldn't take care of myself because of my mental health. That would have left me in their care until I was twenty-one. They told me how much they'd be giving me for living allowance through CFS, but when I looked at what I would be getting on welfare and disability, it was more than I'd be getting from them, so I said I was not signing. Then they cut off all my support, which was to be expected, I guess. I was eighteen, no longer their problem.

It was around that time that I got involved with an organization called Voices, a youth-in-care network. It consists of youth who are in and from foster care. They provide a lot of advocacy, teaching youth about their rights, providing activities, opportunities, and scholarships. My sister knew about it and invited me to come along. She said, "Come on, we're going to go somewhere. They're looking for opinions on how to change the foster care system." I didn't really feel like going out. I was depressed and having a really hard time, but she said, "We're going. They have pizza."

I said, "Fine, I'll go."

And when I went there, I heard all these stories that were similar to my own and for the first time, I didn't feel completely alone. There was some legitimate fucked-up shit going on in their lives. All my life I had care-givers telling me that I was crazy. It was really nice to meet people who had been through the same things and knew that I wasn't crazy. Some had also been overmedicated as kids. Everyone wants to feel special, but there's something really, really nice in finding out I was not unique. That was probably one of the most important discoveries in my life, and it made the rest so much easier. I realized that there wasn't anything wrong with me. And then when I went through a lot of really hard times and shitty relationships and homelessness, my Voices family was there whether things were good or bad.

I had my own apartment for a little while, but it became rat infested and I'm really scared of them, so I didn't want to be there anymore. I found another place to live. I can't remember why I left that apartment. I don't even remember where I went next.

When I was twenty, I had a boyfriend who convinced me to go off all my medication. That was six months to a year of withdrawals. Getting off the meds sucked. I had hallucinations. I remember hiding out because I had people in positions of authority trying to put me in the hospital, which makes sense because I really wasn't okay. I had a community mental health worker and a welfare social worker. Every time any of them would hear that I was making changes to my medication, they would question whether I was able to take care of myself. There had been times in the past when I had tried to reduce my medication and the response had been to put me in the hospital until I agreed to go back on all my medication.

I begged my sister not to tell anyone where I was. I said, "You have to trust me on this one. I know that this is really terrifying and really scary. I'm on so much medication that nobody knows what to adjust and it's not getting better. Just give me a few months once the withdrawals are done, if I'm still not okay, then we can go and get some medication, and we can start from scratch. Just don't tell anyone where I am and don't let them put me in the hospital." And luckily, she agreed, and it did get better, but stopping that many drugs at once, of course it was a bad time. Yeah.

I moved around a lot for the next few years and at some point ended up at the Salvation Army. I was basically homeless. Then from there, I moved to the St. Regis Hotel. There, I met a guy. He was a karaoke host at the hotel and he paid attention to me, thought that I was pretty and wonderful. No one'd ever thought this about me before. Well, it turns out he was an abusive fuck. He lied to me about being single and I was young enough that I believed him. He had a fiancée. When I found out, I broke up with him and started dating another guy, who I eventually moved in with. The first guy had threatened to kill my new boyfriend, so I'd break up with the new one and move back in with the first one and host karaoke with him. Even though he was abusive, I'd stay.

Eventually it became too much and I left him again. He started telling everyone that I was crazy. At the same time I was trying to move on but he'd show up at my work and threaten me or other staff or customers, and I'd get fired. This happened repeatedly at different places I worked. That way I'd be back to being dependent on him, and if I didn't live with him, I would have been homeless.

This went on for about five years. I didn't meet a lot of people because of how little I was allowed to go out. When I did try to leave him, I had nowhere to go, and so I lived with my friends. I went back and forth a lot. I felt really stuck. In my mind, I could picture myself in charge of a business—having more in my life. I could see it clearly, and I wanted it so badly, but I couldn't figure out how to get there, to that future: making my own money, being independent and strong, having flexibility. I didn't know how I was going to go from where I was, to where I wanted to be. This was what I was trying to figure out every time I tried getting out of these situations with abusive guys. I'd think, *Well, fuck, I guess this wasn't the right way out.*

While I was back living with that second guy, I went to broadcasting school in 2007. I moved out to Dauphin to do my practicum. I was so excited because I was finally getting away from both those abusive relationships. I was going to do my practicum and get a real job. It was going to be awesome. I actually did get a job in Dauphin, but then I ended up getting fired a couple months later.

I was an on-air DJ and late one Friday night this guy called in bragging about being super drunk and on his phone while driving. He was bragging about all of that and screaming into the phone, "Play 'Copperhead Road'." I said, "I'm not talking to you" and I hung up on him. He kept on calling and I'm like, this dude is drunk and on his cellphone while driving on the highway. So I keep on hanging up on him. It turns out he was buddies with the boss. So I was fired because I hung up on a listener. I still stand by my decision, but that was like, well, shit. I never worked in the industry again. I kept on trying to find jobs but that boss talked smack about me.

I went back to Winnipeg, and ended up back in the same shitty relationship with the first guy, because, shit, what else was I going to do? I didn't know. To get out of that shitty relationship, I moved to Saskatchewan with a friend. I lived there two years. After that I returned to Dauphin, and then came back to Winnipeg with my friend. We lived together.

Voices asked me to do an hour-long talk show called *System Kids* once a week on CKUW. I got to use my radio experience, so that was cool. We'd talk about the issues surrounding youth in and from care. It was really good, but it was a volunteer position. I was working a crappy part-time retail job for minimum wage and trying to make ends meet. It wasn't happening. My coworkers asked me about where to get some weed. So I got some from my brother and sold it to them.

In 2013 I went to Comic Con to sell some more weed. There, I happened to meet these two people who were computer programmers and we ended up becoming friends. I dated one of them. It was a terrible relationship but it was a really important one because it sparked my interest in technology and computers. I was fascinated with the internet when that became a thing, but it wasn't something I ever thought I could work at. For me, I didn't even have my own laptop until I started university. Everyone I knew who was doing tech for a living had, from a young age, always had access to technology.

I was still hosting the radio show for Voices. One day, I had these foster kids come on the show and they were talking about how they weren't allowed to have any sort of social media or cellphones unless they handed their passwords over to their social workers or youth care workers. I thought that sounded ridiculous, especially because in the United Nations Convention of the Rights of the Child, the right to privacy is one of those rights. So I asked youth care workers and social workers I knew about what their stance was on those kinds of rules. At that point I was older, I'd been out of the system for a while, and a lot of them were willing to talk to me like human beings, not as authority figures. I found that when it came to their own kids, these people generally didn't ask their kids for passwords except when they thought that something bad would happen to them. But with foster kids the stance changed because the workers were concerned that the kids were doing something bad. Right away I thought, *I don't think that they're doing this for the safety of these kids*.

That interview got me thinking about technology and security issues for kids in care. Computer security is a privilege. This affects foster kids: they can't afford internet access so need public computers and public Wi-Fi, they can easily have a cellphone stolen, they are constantly changing phone numbers and being unable to receive communication, and CFS staff often take a kid's phone away or gain access to their password.

Vulnerable people like youth in care are also most at risk of having their IDs stolen. A lot of people have access to their personal information, enough to open bank accounts in their names. I know for me there were people in and out of my room all the time, being really intrusive and going through all my stuff. And then records aren't necessarily very well kept. When I was in Knowles, there were handwritten charts that weren't hard to steal. I don't know if that's different now, but I do know that the Province of Manitoba has

only recently started to digitize their foster care information, so there must still be a lot of paper files, which are easier to copy and easier to alter.

People who are poor may say they have no money for others to steal, but it's still possible to steal their identity. Kids in care should also know how to check their credit reports. It's free and it gives you a good indication if somebody has stolen your identity. As far as trying to prevent identity theft, the best thing is to have a safe place where you can keep your ID, which is not easy if you're a child in care.

Another security issue is that, for some reason, when you go into CFS your name's added to some sort of registry. This is a huge privacy issue. You are on that registry for life. And I don't know how to get access to that registry. I don't think it's publicly available, but I think if you're involved in the CFS system in some way, you can go and check that registry. Someone at Voices said that when it came time for her Red River College practicum, her name came up on this registry and she nearly didn't get a practicum placement because of it. She was over the age of eighteen. This is a case of discrimination.

Around the same time I had those foster kids on the radio show talking about the problems with their access to technology, I also had on a guest from an organization that's really well known in the community for sex education and sex positivity. I was asking the basics: How do you have safe sex? How do you deal with abusive relationships? One of the questions I asked—which I really didn't think was unreasonable given the fact that it was 2012 or 2013—was what advice they'd give to young people for being safe in digital relationships? The person said, "We tell them don't do that."

I said, "So you can be positive about everything else but you tell people not to do that? Coming from your organization, you, if anybody, should know that's not how things work." I realized I needed to find someone who knew more. So again, I went to my tech friends. They referred me to this guy who worked in cyber security. He's a friend of mine now. He came on the radio show to talk about cyber security. He explained about banking scams and how to keep your information safe, what the cops can and can't do with your information, and what happens during a background check. The show was really well-received because we'd never done one like that before.

This same guy asked me to volunteer as a social media person for a cyber security tech challenge that he was doing with high school students. I sat in those meetings with technical people and had no idea what they were saying. They could've been talking complete nonsense to me, and I wouldn't have known. I kept on having more and more questions but I also wanted to learn more and more.

At the time, there were more tuition waivers becoming available pretty much everywhere. I qualified for the waiver because I had been in the foster care system. More bursaries and scholarships were becoming available too. The Advancing Futures Bursary came out a couple of years later, and Voices had their scholarships. Before, I felt I couldn't really go to school because I couldn't afford it. Also, I didn't want to go because I didn't want all the trouble of going to school and then not getting a job after (like what happened with broadcasting school). But I started thinking that with all these bursaries and scholarships available, I could afford to go to school.

I ended up at University of Winnipeg because it was the only place I could get in at the time. I hadn't finished high school so I didn't have any of my Grade 12 courses. I didn't qualify for most programs at most institutions and the ones I did qualify for were definitely not anything I wanted to take. I was twenty-eight, I didn't want to go back to high school, but U of W had a math class I could take to upgrade my math so that it would be a Grade 12 equivalent. And the language test showed that I was more than proficient enough to meet the English requirement, so I got admitted as a mature student,

At the U of W the first year I was actually rejected for tuition waivers because I had been out of school so long that they couldn't trust I could successfully go back. I didn't have my high school, and they didn't really give a crap how smart and dedicated I was and how much support I had. But, fortunately, I got a scholarship from Voices every year I was in school. The scholarships are $500 to $2,000 each. So I had one for maybe $1,000, and then I got student loans to help cover tuition for my first year.

When I had been in broadcasting college earlier and then didn't find work, I was an irresponsible twenty-five-year-old and didn't pay my student loans back. I thought, *screw that*. When I wanted to go to U of W I could apply for student loans again but I would have to pay off all the interest, which at the time was around $1,000. I'd had a really rough winter and ended up in the hospital because of my mental health. I had just been on a leave of absence from my job. I was supposed to have benefits, but they didn't pay out, and then the hospital lost my paperwork, which was my proof of that. When I did eventually go back to work, I was barely making $1,000 a month, so I spent my entire next three paychecks on paying off that balance and didn't pay rent. I was down to my last $80, which was supposed to be for my bus pass so I could get to work and start working again. Instead, I spent it on my university application fee and ended up walking from downtown to Polo Park in the dead of winter. That might have been when I got evicted—it was definitely all directly related. That was really hard, but it was worth it. It was a gamble. I wouldn't recommend that course of action to anyone, but I did what I had to do. So that was how I got into university.

I got accepted to U of W, which was awesome. I got my student loans and got my Voices money, but none of that stuff came through until after classes started. I'd completely forgotten about the fact that you need school supplies. I needed a laptop. Well shit, I had no money. So...what's a nice way of putting this? I ended up finding a sugar daddy to basically pay for my school supplies.

I started off in Business. I wanted to do both Business and Computer Science and planned to get both degrees. Until that math class was done, I couldn't do most of my computer science classes. As a mature student at U of W, I think you can take only three classes at a time for your first year until your GPA is high enough. If you pass your first year, then you can go up to a full course load. So I was full-time but not super full-time. I loved what I was learning and I loved being back in classes. It was also hard because I was now working at Tim Hortons. I'd have to open the Tim Hortons for 6:00 a.m. and then go to school for noon. On other days, I'd be in school all day and have to close the store at midnight because they were super bad about scheduling. That work routine sucked. I was tired.

I also felt out of my element at university because like half my classmates were essentially children, fresh out of high school, and

ANDREW MAHON

then the other half were older people who were changing careers and were married with families and children. This actually remained true for my entire academic career. I always felt in the middle because I wasn't eighteen and living at home with my parents, and I wasn't married with children. I had spent my twenties homeless, broke, and busy trying not to die. I had a very different experience from my classmates, so I felt really isolated and like I couldn't relate to anyone.

The first time I took the math equivalency course, I actually failed it. They condensed Grade 9 through Grade 12 math, like pre-calculus, into twelve weeks. For many students—a lot of international students or people who just hadn't scored well—it was a review of stuff they'd already taken. For me, this was all brand-new material. So it wasn't really surprising that I didn't do well the first time. Luckily, it was a zero-credit-hour course so it didn't affect my GPA. The bad news? That math class was only offered once a year, so I had to wait to take it again. I thought, *I guess I'm not doing computer science for another year. I'll just do another year of business school.*

Somewhere in my first year, I broke up with the guy who initially got me into tech, and it was not a good break up. It was devastating, and I needed to get away. I saw that U of W had an exchange program, so I decided that I wanted to do it. I felt I needed to have a different experience. It was weird to get to that point in my life and realize that despite the life I'd had, I felt incredibly sheltered. The U of W had really good partnerships with lots of different institutions all over the world. There were two schools that had tech programs. One was in India and the other was in Scotland. Based on my experiences dealing with the privacy issues, I decided I wanted to go into security, and Scotland had a really good program. There were no good security programs at that time here in Winnipeg. If I had stayed at U of W, I would've been lucky to get one security-related course. So I submitted my application and crossed my fingers.

It was around that time I started dating my current boyfriend, Colin. I had known him from the volunteering I'd done with the Cyber Defense Challenge. He messaged me one day saying, "Why don't I see you anymore?" I told him that because I had been so interested in what he and his friends were doing that I decided to go to school. I knew they'd get sick of answering all my questions!

He asked me out and I said, "Just so you know, I have applied to study abroad. It's really something I need to do." We started dating anyway. November 22nd, 2014. There was nothing set in stone yet, but six months into our relationship, I got accepted. I was going to Scotland for an entire year! So we decided to do the long-distance thing and I went to Scotland. It was really cool.

While I was there I went into a really technical program having zero technical knowledge. It was a second-year program. I had never taken level one. In Scotland, they were not interested in the fact that I had not taken anything previously. Their attitude was, *You'll catch up. You'll be fine.* At first, I didn't even know what the professors were talking about. So luckily this was something that my boyfriend did know well, so he was able to tutor me. We definitely spent a lot of time video chatting and texting. And for stuff he couldn't tutor me on, his friends knew that material, which was part of a standardized certification that's taught all over the world. As challenging as it was, I really liked all the technical stuff I was taking. It was super hands-on and I found that I was learning and retaining it better than if I was sitting in a classroom.

My relationship with Colin continued long-distance for the year that I was away. I thought if I stayed in university, I'd be looking at eight more years to finish both of my degrees. At this point, I had the math requirements, and the requirements I needed to get into Red River College (RRC). That had been my first choice anyways. So I decided to apply while I was still in Scotland. I returned to Canada in May 2016. I got back to Winnipeg and then I had one last co-op placement with U of W.

I technically stopped attending U of W in August of 2016, two days before I started at RRC. But in that period of time, I had to argue that I should still keep all of my scholarships and bursaries. Tuition waivers weren't transferrable. They were still relatively new and the schools were just rolling them out. So you'd have to apply to every school individually. Now they have a point person at Futures Forward who organizes all of that, so it's a lot easier because they can walk you through that process and advocate for you if you run into a situation like mine. But back then you had to apply for them at each school.

But in between me applying to RRC and actually getting formally accepted, most of the staff went on holidays and the last tuition waiver was given away. I'd already told U of W I was not coming back. Oh my god, what the heck was I going to do? I was freaking out. I arranged a meeting with an academic advisor. I had it in writing. She looked at my transcript. I was a really good student at U of W besides that one failed math class. So somehow she managed to find a way to get me a tuition waiver.

I feel foster kids who get these bursaries and tuition waivers are held to a higher standard. If they fail a course or decide to switch majors, they're under all kinds of scrutiny—"You're not dedicated or focused, you don't know what you want to do with your life."

When I switched schools I said, "I'm giving you solid arguments as to why I want to switch. It's literally changing into a more focused version of the program I'm already in at U of W. Many students change their major within the first two years and you're telling me I can't because I'm not focused? Are you kidding me? That's ridiculous." I was really just arguing for the same privileges they would afford another student living in her parents' basement.

I was thirty by the time I got to Red River. I had a hard time with that transition, partly because of switching from a smaller course load to a really big one. It was very different in a lot of other ways. But I finished classes there in April 2019 in Business Information Technology. I majored in networking and security so I learned lots about computers and programming and web development. I studied there two and a half years.

You'd expect that graduation would be the happiest time ever. I was so excited leading up to it, but about a month before graduation I was like, *Oh fuck. I didn't plan for this at all. I spent my entire life trying to end it. Actually finishing school was not part of the plan. What do I do?* I felt conflicted and stressed out because everyone was asking me if I was super excited to be graduating, but I didn't have a job lined up. I didn't picture living this long. I was so confused and felt lost and powerless again. So the depression came back for a brief period. I had a lot of really dark thoughts. Again, I didn't act on them, but it was the first time it had been that bad since I started university. I wasn't prepared for it because it was supposed to be such a joyous occasion. I wasn't expecting to be so overwhelmed.

What ended up snapping me out of it was my boyfriend losing his job two weeks before

I finished classes. He'd been working that job since he was seventeen and volunteering there since he was fifteen. They laid him off and he was devastated. It distracted me because he needed me more. So by the time he started feeling a bit better, the worst of it was over for me. Colin had supported me and helped me so much through school. A big reason that I wasn't under a lot of financial stress through RRC was because Colin was footing almost all the bills. That was huge and it meant a lot. There he was losing his job and I couldn't return that favour. I felt super guilty, but I wasn't unemployed for very long. It was a huge relief when we both found jobs quickly. My boyfriend and I both started brand-new jobs the same week.

At my RRC graduation it was cool and surreal to have all these people there supporting me. I had Colin, his mom, my parents (they were really excited for me going back to school); someone from Voices; Trevor, the current principal (and my Grade 9 teacher) from John G. Stewart; and Kevin, who was the principal when I went there. I was glad that the people who loved and supported me understood what a big deal this was. A lot of my RRC classmates just rolled their eyes and pretended like they were too cool for grad. But I didn't get a high school grad, this was my first graduation, and I had become really excited. It was great to have people around me who were also excited. My sister who lives in Vancouver and my best friend have also been really supportive, but neither of them were able to be at my graduation.

Colin is incredibly patient and thoughtful and kind. I'm a very tightly wound kind of person. He's not. He's very calm and chill. That always blows my mind. It's really nice that we balance each other out. I wouldn't be where I am today without him. I don't know how to explain it. He just loves me for who I am and cares about my dreams and my goals, even if he doesn't quite understand them. If it's important to me, it's important to him. It's still weird. I don't always think I deserve it. I'll say, "I don't understand what you're doing with me." He usually just laughs and shrugs it off. His mom told me recently that Colin told her before we were dating that he liked me because I always speak my mind and that's something he has a really hard time with.

After graduation, Colin and I got a hotel room at the Forks for a couple of days. It was really nice. Our original plan had been to go on a vacation. We had been saving up from my part-time job the entire time I'd been in school, but then Colin lost his job and we were in the process of moving, so that didn't happen. So we got a hotel room for a couple of days. We went for dinner and just kind of relaxed. I slept a lot because I was just so tired. I had started my new job a couple of weeks before the ceremony and then I'd taken that week off because we were moving right then.

I got a job at a small marketing company as an information security analyst, which is exactly what I wanted to do. I got really lucky. I didn't have a job lined up when I finished classes so I was freaking out. Not having a job is not an option. I'm an adult with grown up responsibilities, but I was unemployed for less than two weeks. My job was super exciting, but it would put most people to sleep. I wrote security policies and made sure that the company I worked for was being compliant with people's personal information. The company does a lot of online promotions and Twitter bots. If you're on Twitter and you see an ad, that's the kind of stuff they do.

I stayed there until 2020. My current job is in fraud and it is amazing. I work at a really supportive place where I've been able to grow and improve. I feel empowered to take control of my career.

Every year RRC has a conference for computer and business students. They get to meet different employers and learn about their industry. At one of the events there are round tables with different employers. In 2020 I was part of a table of women from the tech industry. Students asked us questions. It was exciting and so much fun.

I got told I was smart all the time growing up. But when I went back into foster care, I got beaten up a lot for being smart. It got worse at Knowles, so I just started acting stupid because it was a lot easier. And I did that for so long that I actually started to believe that I was really kind of dumb. Every now and then someone would try to tell me that I was smart, but I'd say I didn't know what they were talking about.

> I work at a really supportive place where I've been able to grow and improve. I feel empowered to take control of my career.

When I was fourteen or fifteen and I was at Manitoba Adolescent Treatment Center, they had me do a bunch of these tests, and I remember that I was doing math and reading at a second-year university level. I found out that most people who I worked with at my first job didn't even know I was a new graduate. My employer didn't usually hire people right out of school. So I guess I was probably just as smart, if not smarter, than most of the people working there; it's just that I didn't have as much experience. Since I started dating Colin, I finally learned to feel confident about being smart. He's the first person I've ever dated who's been as smart as I am. Actually he's probably smarter. So that's really nice.

After some discussion and a lot of treatment, the bipolar diagnosis was thrown out as soon as I was eighteen. And I no longer have the symptoms of borderline personality disorder. The good thing about that mental illness is it's one of few that can actually be treated successfully. So those two diagnoses don't exist for me.

I do remember that most of university and even my first year at Red River College I was still struggling with depressive and suicidal thoughts. I was at the point where I knew I didn't want to die, but I didn't know why. I was still struggling with feeling stuck and overwhelmed and I didn't know what to do. I felt like there was no way out. So those first three years of university, there were a lot of struggles for me.

Things got slightly better at Red River College. The workload was ten times more than university, but my supports were much different—I had my boyfriend and I had the support of the tuition waivers, so I didn't have to work all through school. I kept a part-time job at the school convenience store where I worked three hours a week. It wasn't a necessity, but I really liked the people I worked with. They were fun.

I'm a lot better about my anger and a lot more chill than I used to be. Over the years in my adult life, I did eventually do short bits of therapy to deal with my anger and sadness—some talk therapy and some cognitive behaviour therapy (CBT). That helped a lot with the anger, but I still had some symptoms of depression and anxiety. Shortly after I started at RRC I finally found a good doctor, a GP. I was really embarrassed, but I told her about my struggles with depressive thoughts. When the thoughts did come back, it was usually around times of stress, like exam times. But I had never really done a lot about it because, as you can imagine, my experiences with medication as a teenager had left me with a fairly extreme aversion to taking medication. My doctor was really understanding. This time, I actually conceded and decided to try an antidepressant. It was very helpful. Those stressful times got a lot better, so I'm coping with things well.

Another thing that has helped is trying to figure out where the anger comes from. Once I identify that, I can actually do something about it. Like sometimes I feel angry because I'm overwhelmed. When I do, I make lists, a lot of lists. Often, by the time I write it all out, it's not as bad as I was thinking in my head.

Over the last few years, I've started to learn that as much as people try to hide it or pretend like it's not there, everyone has kinda the same stuff. Everyone's anxious sometimes, everyone can feel awkward in front of people, nobody has enough time in their day. So if all of these people can get by, survive life, and be relatively normal, that means I can too.

A big thing that helped me get unstuck when I was in university was math. It changed my perceptions. Math was a simple way of explaining really complicated things. Everywhere else in my life there were rules that sometimes applied, sometimes didn't, and they were dependent on the day and the person I was dealing with. Math was not one of those things. It taught me how to reason a bit better, and gave me some sort of comfort.

Today I feel I was incredibly blessed to have graduated right before the pandemic. I look back at how scared and stressed I was in my early adult years and I don't think I could have survived the pandemic if I didn't make the changes I did.

I'm really excited to be part of the book because I have a different narrative when it comes to being in foster care. I'm really proud of the fact that I graduated with honours from a program that fifty percent of people drop out of in the first year. I got the job I wanted. I have an amazing relationship with my boyfriend. I'm lucky and I'm proud of those things.

I like to tell people that foster care gives you some unique job skills that no one thinks of. For example I am adaptable. It's a good skill to have. I feel like a lot of the chaotic and tumultuous experiences I had in care and my early adulthood make coping with competing priorities, additional processes, and changes in structure and leadership easier. Also, I am used to dealing with a lot of generally difficult people. On the one hand, being in foster care taught me not to question things, to just shut up and keep my head down. But on the other hand, it taught me how to stand up for myself too.

I always dreamed of having a professional life, working in a business. I always thought that was a stupid dream until one day when Marie from Voices picked me up from a practicum placement where I was working. She had a youth in the car who didn't realize that I was also from care until at some point I mentioned it. The girl said, "Wait, you came from care and you work in a real business? You can do that?" I think that's probably one of my favourite moments working for Voices and why I stay involved. I realize how powerful it can be for youth to meet someone who went on to do something completely different.

I like to tell people that foster care gives you some unique job skills that no one thinks of.

In general, I do have survivor's guilt. I have this super awesome life. And I feel weird and guilty enjoying it because I know that most other people from care don't end up with lives like this. I'm like, "Well why do I deserve to succeed, and the others don't? What makes me so special?" I don't have a good way of reconciling that, because I have no explanation. There are other smart people and people who went to school. Most people who've been in care want to have a better life. I do hear I am hard on myself a lot. I'm trying to get better, but when I look at all I've accomplished and where I've gotten to, I don't know if I could have gotten here if I'd been soft on myself. I hold myself to some pretty unreasonably high standards. I know they are, but I do meet them.

My life seems just normal to me. It's really hard for me to realize that all this—being called Psycho Sarah, going through foster care, poverty, homelessness—aren't normal for everyone else. Most people don't have these struggles. It also took a while for me to realize that most people don't have the mood swings I've had either, but they also didn't have these really tough things to deal with. I was dealing with some big things that were way too heavy for a child to deal with. It took a while for me to come to terms with the fact that screaming and anger are a very normal reaction to some very abnormal situations. It probably wasn't me being crazy; it was the situation that was crazy.

I have a hard time with the whole concept of resilience. I don't know where it comes from. When I was super depressed and would do nothing but sit in my room on welfare, people would say *You're so resilient because you've had such a hard life*. And now that I'm living a good life, they say *Oh, you're so resilient because you've had such a hard life*. Up until I was twenty-eight I spent a good chunk of my life trying to end it, so what part is resilient? I don't think I'm resilient by choice; I've just tried to do the best I could. I do know I am so incredibly grateful for my life now.

I do live in fear of everything being taken away, that this is all a dream and I am going to wake up back where I was. When those thoughts creep up, I just try to tell myself that even if this is a dream, or it's temporary, let's just enjoy the reprieve. Maybe one day I'll feel more confident and secure in my stability.

Most of my life I didn't feel like I had any choice. I was powerless against my foster parents and Knowles, and then I was powerless against an abusive boyfriend that I couldn't get away from. I was completely powerless against crippling poverty when I was trying to get a job and have an apartment so I didn't end up on the street. When I finally left that abusive relationship I never wanted to be in a position where I had to do that again. I didn't know how or even if I could have any different life. I really felt like there was no way out.

But I do not feel powerless today. When I started to go to school again, I started to have more of a choice. And now as I get better at my career, I will have more choices afforded to me and that makes it a lot easier to not feel completely hopeless. My biggest goal has been to have the power of choice. When you have a choice, there's a way out.

> I do live in fear of everything being taken away, that this is all a dream and I am going to wake up back where I was.

I met Trevor Holroyd when I visited John G. Stewart School to talk with the students there. When Trevor heard about the topic of this book, he enthusiastically told me about a student he stayed in touch with and was the most successful student he could remember. That former student was Sarah. He introduced us via email. I am grateful to them both.

Sarah and I talked about studies which show that people coming out of foster care can have the same kind of posttraumatic stress disorder (PTSD) as soldiers coming home from war. Sarah, as well as other participants in this book, have shown incredible courage and strength in working through their own version of PTSD and its symptoms.

It was hard to talk with Sarah about her suicide attempts. But as Sarah pointed out, her suicide attempts are an important part of her story. Sarah spoke of this because she wants to help us and give us hope, not burden us. I just can't imagine Sarah's voice being silenced.

Rachel

I think that the bravest thing we can ever do is walk in truth. For me, that's letting people know the truth about my life.

We all have our own story and our own hurt and pain. People want to protect the truth, but it needs to come out; that's how we heal. I love myself, and I'm going to make my life better. I am speaking from a survivor's perspective. A lot of people have trust issues but if we are brave enough to share our stories, they can become great teaching tools. It is good for us survivors to teach. But in telling my story I don't want pity. There's no pity in what I'm saying. I don't let my time in hell define me today. If I hadn't gone through what I have gone through, I don't think I'd be as strong as I am now. Many of us have not reached our full potential yet, but eventually

we can with enough nurturing, caring, and empathy. Empathy is really important. Empathy has taught me to put myself in another woman's shoes. It is an act of kindness and love.

I am a survivor of the Child and Family Services (CFS) system. I know it very well. I was once a little girl in foster care. Back then it was called Children's Aid. Later my kids were taken by CFS, but I've had them back for more than ten years. I do a lot of work in the child welfare system supporting high-risk youth, and I am a foster mom too. I attribute a lot of my pain to that system. In the beginning I had a healthy distaste for CFS, but not for all of it. CFS was put in place to protect our younger children because we're living in a world right now where kids aren't valued. Systems are put in place for reasons. But it hurts when they take us from our families. People, especially our own (Indigenous) people, like to say that we don't need CFS; that all they do is take our children. But that system needs to be there because what our kids are going through right now is absolute hell. Authorities are working with agencies, so hopefully things will get better.

There are only a few nice memories I have from when I was a little girl. My family lived in the Manitoba Housing Complex on Keenleyside Street. Our house had just the basics. I know my mom loved us. We'd come back from daycare, and my mom would always have lunch made. My biological dad wasn't home much.

But then my memories jump right into *the meat* (the horrible stuff), right? My biological dad, he'd be drunk. He was an extreme alcoholic. He was the most physically abusive guy ever. There was a lot of domestic violence. The beatings were never-ending for my mom. My biological dad was really big,

like 6'5", 6'7". He ripped out chunks of her hair and dragged her across the floor. And it wasn't just physical; it was sexual, verbal and emotional abuse too. My mom was so fragile. She sat like a shaking leaf with her head down all the time. She wasn't allowed to look at anybody. My biological dad was controlling. If my mom went to the store, she was accused of something. If she went to the daycare, she was accused of something.

My mom always tried her best for us, but she drank too. I think she drank so she didn't feel the beatings. Back when I was a child, I don't think there were many resources for domestic violence. Domestic violence supports have just opened up recently. It's one of the highest reasons for child apprehensions.

There were a lot of drinking parties at our place. I remember us kids all hiding under the bed while people were having sex on it. It was supposed to be our room. Or we'd be hiding in the closet while they were drinking.

My mom's childhood was marked by seeing so much domestic violence and poverty, growing up back home in our Métis community of Duck Bay. My grandpa beat my grandma so bad. I understand that he almost killed my grandma. He once threw her out of a moving car. She lost two babies in the womb from being hit. But back then domestic violence was dismissed and it was taboo to talk about it. My grandma had eleven children in total. She never had a drop of alcohol until she was thirty-nine or forty, after they moved to the city and she left my grandpa. (My grandma stopped drinking over twenty years ago now.)

My mom moved to Winnipeg with her family. That's where she met my biological dad, Raymond, when she was sixteen. Their relationship quickly became toxic. She got pregnant almost every year after that. She had six kids in the ten years they were together. She had my brother Raymond first, and then I came along eighteen months later. I was born in '74. Then after came my sisters: Mavis, Lee, and Crystal. My brother Quinton was born in 1980 and was taken away from our family the following year in the Eighties scoop. My mom thought she was signing papers for visitation rights, but instead they were papers for his adoption to the United States.

My biological dad was pretty privileged. He was French and white. He had a mom and dad who kept him until he was eighteen. He had a good job. He used to call us his dirty little Indians. We thought that was cute. It was attention for us. But that's horrible. Growing up he'd say that my mom's family was a bunch of welfare bums. He was always on the road truck driving. Him being away a lot saved my mom from even more beatings. Things could have been much worse.

My biological dad did eighteen months in Stony Mountain for trying to force an extended family member to have sex with him when she was fifteen. He didn't only abuse my mom, he abused my whole family: emotionally, sexually, physically, verbally. My grandma and my Auntie Joan were protective of my mom because they knew what she was going through. They were always trying to stop the abuse. My grandma left my grandpa because of domestic violence too. There was intergenerational trauma. My Auntie Joan tells me so much about the past that I didn't know. She gives me old photos too. A lot of what I know from the past comes from her.

My biological dad beat me too. My auntie Joan told me, "My girl, you had black eyes. My girl you were just small. We couldn't believe it. We were trying to get your mom to press charges against your dad. You were always beaten."

My memories go to the drinking and to my biological dad always wanting to keep me behind. My auntie Joan told me that every time my mom left to find safety, he would always say, "Well, you're not taking my Rachey." It was really volatile. My grandma, my auntie and my mom would get in there to fight him about taking us kids because my biological dad would challenge them. He would fight anybody, even women. They always managed to get my brother Raymond, but my biological dad would hang on to me.

My biological dad was my first perpetrator. He would abuse me, multiple times. That's why he always wanted me left behind. It made me so sick. I blocked the abuse out for a long time. I didn't want to remember it. I actually started to remember when I was in jail from 1996 to '99. I'm able to talk about it now because I've done a lot of healing.

In 1999, while I was doing that sentence in jail, I phoned my biological dad and confronted him. I said, "I know what you did to me." He was still of sound mind then (before he got Alzheimer's).

> I blocked the abuse out for a long time. I didn't want to remember it.

He said, "Oh, quit talking F'ing crazy."

I said, "I know what you did to me." He hung up on me.

I also wrote my mom a letter from jail and told her what had happened to me. When my mom read the letter my aunties were over at her place. My mom told them, "No, that didn't happen. I know I never left Rachel." But my mom was still in denial. My aunties had a talk with her. My auntie Joan said, "Think about all those times Ray (my biological dad) would want Rachel to stay behind. Why would a child say this? Kids don't lie about this kind of thing. Your daughter's trying to heal. She's trying to tell you something. You should listen."

So my mom lived with a lot of guilt towards the end of her time. She told me, "I always loved you." I believed her, but I don't regret telling my mom. I'm glad my mom knew why I was so messed up.

My mom was with my biological dad for ten years until she just completely had enough and left. By then all of us kids were in care. In 1981 when my youngest brother was taken, it broke her. She lived with her mom and was grieving, drinking, and probably trying to cope with her pain. Us kids would have a few visits there. In 1984 my mom met my stepfather, Joseph Flatfoot. I'm thankful my mom met him. He never once laid his hands on her. He broke the cycle of abuse for my mom. He accepted her as a broken woman and helped her heal. My stepdad saved my mom's life. I call him dad. He is very special in all our lives. He is always encouraging us. He is family-oriented, a very hard worker, and gentle. He was also a kid in care in the CFS system. He is a very Godly man. It's been ten years since my mom passed, and he lives with us now.

I'm thinking that the first time I was taken from my parents I was three, in 1977. I remember us being taken back home to our parents a few times (back then CFS gave parents a chance). I don't think that there were enough supports put in place. I remember going to daycare but being in and out of my mom's life. So obviously CFS was involved early. I remember us kids all going to CFS offices at 114 Garry St.

The last time we were taken, I know for sure it was 1978. We were made permanent wards, which meant we were wards of the government. We didn't belong to my mom or my family; we belonged to Children's Aid. We were taken because of excessive alcohol and domestic violence. My mom fled and left all of us kids at home. I had gone next door and knocked on the door and said, "Look, do you have any food? We're hungry." We'd been drinking beet juice and sauerkraut juice. We had nothing, nothing to eat. They called Children's Aid, who came and put us all in a car.

They took me, my brother Raymond, and my sisters Crystal, Lee, and Mavis. My sister Crystal was just a baby. I was maybe five. I remember the CFS workers telling us they were going to take us to McDonald's. Every time we passed a McDonald's on that drive, I shouted, "Well, there's McDonald's!" We never did go to McDonald's; instead we were taken to a house at 1824 Chancellor Drive. There was a lady there named Mrs. Aboabo. I think we went temporarily but we must've stayed a while because I know we had family visits there. Auntie Joan, Auntie Loretta, Uncle Bert, and my mom came.

My auntie Joan's the one that requested visits all the time. She kept in touch with CFS wherever we were. My mom would visit us while we were in care too. Auntie Joan and my mom were very, very close. My auntie was the one that always held my mom together. She was the mentor of our family. She phones me every day. She's just one of the best women.

I always held anger towards my mom. But I don't think it was my mom's fault. I think that there were no systems in place for domestic-violence victims back in the day. I know my mom would have taken us to a shelter if they were around. So I had to do a lot of forgiving with my mom because I always thought, *Why did you lose us? Why did we have to go through this?*

All five of us were placed with Mrs. Aboabo temporarily, but then they split us up. My understanding is that my sisters went to foster homes in my community of Duck Bay. My brother and I were older and had already had a lot of trauma, so they took us to the foster home of people named Jack and Savannah. Holy Mack! They were two horrible, horrible people. We were so abused. They had another brother and sister set of foster kids there too. Savannah wasn't around the house much. It was mostly Jack and Savannah's mother who beat us.

We were brutally beaten on our ears. I got a quarter-size hole in my left eardrum. A doctor found it years later. I was pulled off a bunk bed by the ear so hard. But starving was the most common problem. Jack and Savannah had food, but us kids didn't have any. Me and Raymond were always made to go outside and play in the yard and we would fill ourselves up with crabapples. Or we'd sit up until they'd gone to sleep and we'd sneak downstairs together to get food from the fridge. If Jack or Savannah found our hidden stash of food or crumbs in our beds, we got a good beating or we'd be dragged around by our hair. That's also the foster home where I got my nose broken. I was trying to steal pennies because I thought I'd take a handful and get candies to fill my belly up. Then Savannah's mom punched me square in the face with her fist.

Us kids dreaded nighttime. Savannah went out in the evenings and Jack would sit there drinking little stubby bottles of Extra Old Stock beer. Jack got more furious the longer Savannah was gone and we were the ones he picked on. We had to be so quiet in our beds. A couple of times a week for punishment, we were made to stand in a corner on one leg and put our arms up. This was from maybe two to four in the morning. My brother and I would always get a beating. If I cried, I was told not to cry. When Savannah finally came home very late at night, Jack would accuse her of "fucking around" and they'd fight about *the spa*. I don't know if she was a call girl or what. I just remember them fighting about the spa every night.

Raymond and I were always shoved downstairs. We'd spend like six hours a day down there. We weren't allowed to come upstairs. We'd hear them laughing and having a good old time. There was no TV, only two couches so we'd build a fort and just make do by talking to each other, saying, "Oh, we're going to get out of here. One day we're going to be older and we won't have to put up with this." But we were happy that at least we weren't getting hit or punished at that moment.

The best thing about that foster home was that they had a niece and when she came over she would let the other little girl and me be little girls. She always made French braids in our hair, and she'd put on music. I have a memory of helping put out cookies and milk for Santa. That was the first time I ever got Christmas presents that I can remember, other than the daycare giving me presents.

I would guess we stayed in that foster home about a year, maybe more. Nobody saw us regularly—no social workers, not my mom. One day my brother finally had enough. Savannah was carrying grocery bags into the house and my brother was standing inside by the stairs to the basement. He opened the door, looked at her and pushed her right down the basement stairs. She got a broken leg and CFS moved us out. I don't remember nobody asking us what happened. We looked like these monster children I'm assuming, because nobody knows the real reason why that happened. You don't just push somebody.

I don't even know where I went after that placement, but I went to a string of foster homes. All over. I did live in two nice foster homes. I lived with Rose Genaille on Ross Street. She was from our community of Duck Bay. She has died now. That's where I was treated the fairest. It was like a real home. Her sisters and daughters treated me well. When my sister and I lived with her, we'd go visit our grandma and aunties because they lived just down the street at 391 Ross. My grandma lived there for twenty years, so I always knew where to find her. I don't know why they took me out of Rose's place.

My sister and I also lived with a nice family of a lady named Maryanne Linski. I still talk to her today. Me and my sister Mavis went there. Maryanne was the best woman. She treated us fairly and gently, and always kept her word. She was a nurturing woman. She took pride in us and still has our pictures hanging up on her wall. She would buy us dresses and we'd have matching ribbons in our hair. I think I stayed there for eighteen months or two years. While I was there I went to Norquay School for two grades—probably Grades 2 and 3. It was the best home I ever stayed in. But Maryanne started getting really bad ulcers, where she was bleeding, and because it was a medical issue, we had to leave.

I was the type of little girl that was not sit-able. I needed constant movement, so I wasn't the type to sit and be in one home for long because if you brought me in the front, I was out the back. Every time I switched a foster house, I'd switch schools. I couldn't sit still, and I didn't understand a lot in school. I don't think I did well. I probably have a learning disability. I learn in a different way—more visual and verbal. Sometimes I work differently, even now as an adult. As a kid I'd had too much trauma to be able to sit and engage in the classroom. I'd be worrying about what might happen that night. The trauma was overwhelming. But trauma wasn't even a word that I heard back then. Now that I'm older, I see that the trauma was always right there.

I was in four foster homes in Dauphin that I remember. I'm guessing I was about eleven at the time. I remember being in this one foster home, sitting around the table and I didn't know how to use a knife. I wanted to pick up my meat with my hands, but I didn't want to do that in front of them. So I was trying to cut it and then the meat flew off my plate and I just let the dog eat it. They had their own kids, but they didn't judge me. They were always offering me more food. It was a good home. But the sense of security still wasn't there, even in this two-parent functioning home. I couldn't adapt to the kindness because I was so conditioned to being treated like shit. I went there with no extra clothes. I remember having to wash my panties each night. I'd be wearing my panties for a week. I'll never forget. I was scared to ask for panties or clothes. I was always so scared to make any mistakes in case I'd get a beating again. That's how I lived for so long. By my early teen years, I had a lot of anger and hatred. I know "hatred" is a strong word, but that's how I felt.

I would skip a lot of school in Dauphin. I would venture out around the town looking for my family. My grandma's sister lived there. That foster home lasted for about two months, maybe three. I just couldn't fit in. It wasn't the foster family's fault. It was probably me, because I was so used to movement that I couldn't actually settle down to think. It felt strange to stay in one spot, one home. So then, it'd happen like clockwork: "Okay, yeah, you're moving. Pack yourself up." *Boom.* I was out. Everything would be thrown into a garbage bag, and I'd move on to the next house. It was constantly different places. It was crazy.

They put me in homes in Dauphin, Duck Bay, Camperville. Even when family tried to take me, I was unmanageable. I was moved around a lot, but I also kept running away. I was a chronic runner. I think I was just accustomed to movement. Whatever foster home I was in, the police department would have to come look for me. I'd go to search for my mom, or I'd run back to my family. Eventually they brought me back to Winnipeg because it was not feasible to find placements for me anywhere else. At that time I was not deemed at risk yet, I was just another kid in care. I remember being ten or eleven years old and looking for my mom in the bars.

Before I turned eighteen, I had been through over fifty-six placements: lockups, institutions, foster homes, emergency placement facilities. Those are just the ones I can remember. They were always temporary. One place took me back seven times! When I asked ANCR (Child and Family All Nations Co-ordinated Response Network) for my records, they told me they didn't have them, and that even if they did, the details would be all blacked out. How does one ever get justice if we don't get to know about our lives? We would like to know what happened in our lives so we can move forward. Why did we become how we are? Nobody really knows the beginning of my life because it wasn't documented. I've hit so many dead ends trying to find out about my childhood that I've given up. It's really frustrating. I know that's not the case for kids in care today. Now everything is documented in emails and on the computers.

I remember being eight years old and struggling to cope. I was sitting on a haystack and trying to sniff gas. I didn't want to feel. I kind of knew sniffing would take me into a different world because I had seen people back in my community doing it and they would be laughing and acting funny. I thought *Oh, I'll try it too*. I didn't want to be sad anymore.

Then I started experimenting: drinking, smoking pot. At age eleven or twelve, I was already snorting lines of cocaine. At thirteen, I was fully into drugs and going into bars. I'd go down Main Street and do some visiting on the way to seeing my family (my mom, my aunties, my granny all lived in the core area). Sometimes I never even made it to my family's place. Nobody in the bars even knew my age or cared. Everyone thought I was eighteen because I always hung around with older people. I had the shape of a woman. I looked at it as part of the fun of partying, but it was a form of exploitation (but I didn't realize that). It was easy to get a drink, or get high. Everything was free for a young Indigenous girl. I thought it was exciting. I

was vulnerable and looking for security and belonging. I was trying to find my place in the world. Everything was already stolen from me at an early age; I had already been taken advantage of, so it was normalized for me. I was seeking this because it was all that I knew.

Some people might judge me for how I acted, saying, "Well, you had a choice." But I don't buy that. I have choices now, but not back in the day. I wasn't given a choice when I was young. If you're not given a choice, what the hell do you pick from? You just go about your life the way it is and you cope in whatever way you can.

Clearly a lot of systems failed me as a young woman. I was in Seven Oaks Youth Center when I was around fourteen or fifteen. It wasn't even a youth center; it was really a warehouse for youth in care because there were no foster placements for us. My boyfriend (who I consider my perpetrator) was twenty-six or twenty-seven and allowed to visit me there and bring me candies, munchies, and clothes. He'd just got out of Headingley Correctional. He was a convicted sexual offender (which I did not know). Nobody looked up his history. He had a good job working with Hydro. I think they looked at that credential more than at me as a young vulnerable, Indigenous girl. Nobody looked at me. If they would've looked up his history, they would've seen the danger. Why didn't anybody ask if this guy was allowed to visit me? He was on the pedophile list. That was not right. Systems need to be held accountable.

At fifteen I became pregnant with this guy's baby. I was already into drugs before my son was born, but I had a good pregnancy. I stayed at Villa Rosa. I liked it there. It was a beautiful place to be when I was pregnant. Lots of food. We had structure. We would do pottery and make our own baby blankets. Nobody was allowed to visit during those months. I really enjoyed being there.

My first son was born November 18, 1990. After that, I moved out of Villa Rosa and the programs stopped. The requirement there was that I have a healthy baby, and I did. At first CFS put me in this home with an eighty-year-old lady. She was to be my helper. But she would leave from Thursday until Sunday, or sometimes Monday morning. I ended up moving in with my baby's father because CFS told him that if he wanted to be in my child's life, we would have to move into his place, and he would have to support us. At that point all funds from CFS stopped for me and he provided for me and the baby. I received nothing more from the agency, not even a visit.

Only a month or two later, I phoned a CFS worker crying and told her to come and get the baby and make him safe. His dad was at work and going to school at night, so I didn't see him all day. My baby was crying over and over. I remembered being told at Villa Rosa, *Don't ever shake your baby*, so I just let him cry. I didn't know if his belly was sore, or what was the matter. I was holding him, but I put him back in his crib because I didn't know what to do. I thought, *I can't be mean to my baby*, so I closed the door and phoned a worker. They came and got my baby. That phone call was a cry for help as a young mom, but the worker didn't ask me how I was doing. And then my baby's dad came home and got really angry. He got the baby back in three days. I signed the guardianship of my son over to his father. I left because I didn't have a clue how to parent. I was a kid myself. He raised his son. (I love my son, but we didn't have much contact while he was growing up.

We have recently been reunited. He lives in Calgary and is doing really good. His first child will be born in 2022, and I will become a grandma.)

I had moved out, had no money and I was just trying to survive. Wherever I parked my ass was where I slept. I had no fixed address. CFS did not house me. Then I was introduced to banging (shooting up, needles). I started right after my first son was born. When I started the needles, addiction came fast. *Boom*. I was already going into the gang traphouses. Back in my day they were called shooting galleries. There are still lots around here that should be shut down.

People were everywhere. I wasn't doing the injecting. I was sitting there with my arm out and somebody else would hit me all the time. It was pure cocaine. I would be throwing up. I overdosed twice. I woke up on the floor grinding my teeth. I heard a voice say, "Holy shit. Well, we'll just have to give her smaller ones." There was so much dope. I was high for days. From then on, my life was fully entrenched. That's a word I use for being completely stuck in the drug life, the gang life, the street life, and the madness that comes with it (the scamming, the drugs, the

exploitation, the stealing). I was involved in so much more than any child should be, but to me it was just normal.

I would go down to the CFS office and they'd give me a sheet of bus tickets. I don't know if they were worth twenty bucks, or seventeen, but it was a lot back then because you could get drunk if you sold them. I don't know if I went every two weeks or every month. I was messed up—blood spots on my clothes from shooting up. You'd think that somebody at CFS would have actually noticed my mental health or how I looked. Nobody ever checked up on me. I can say that now, honestly, in a way that doesn't traumatize me anymore.

At that point, I was already hanging out with my older lady friends. We were going to bars like Bumpers. I had no business being in that bar. It was run by gangs back in the day. I was getting to know people: who's selling, who's doing what. The gangs exploited women too—*Oh, look at this one. She's new to the streets*. Mind you, I never was exploited by them sexually. But I was fifteen and doing lines in a traphouse. That's exploitation. First you're the new face and invited to a lot of parties, then the gangs get you to do little missions (errands, delivering packages) for them and you feel important, but eventually your destination is the street corner. That's grooming. Those are the stages of exploitation. They were gearing me up for that shitty life. If the guys tried to bother me, they would hear it. *Get out of here, fuck off.* I was fortunate because I stood my ground. They knew I was a mean one. I didn't want to be bothered, but it doesn't mean that they didn't exploit me. I could never, ever say they didn't because that's the ultimate goal of any gang—to exploit. There are many forms of exploitation: sexual, selling or running drugs, trading for favours.

My first charge was possession of two pounds of hash. The police knew it wasn't mine, but I took the charge. I had the keys to the apartment where they'd found the drugs. The police wanted the name of the person renting the apartment, but I wouldn't give it, so I took the charge.

I spent my eighteenth birthday on a street corner by the West Hotel. I was being exploited. My exploitation had begun with my biological father when I was very young. Then I was exploited by an older woman that I knew. I was shown what to do by her. She said, "Hey all you have to do is walk down there by the Salter Street Bridge and somebody will pick you up." I thought, *Well, I guess so.* I was floored. I wondered, *What do I do?* But sure enough, somebody stopped, and he gave me forty dollars. I took off running and kept the money. I thought, *That was easy.* But life did not get easier; it got worse. I was fully out there on the street corner at seventeen. The party was over.

Nobody from CFS came to look for me on my birthday. But I ran into my mom that day at the bar. I went there on my way home from the street corner. My mom asked me what I was doing there. It gave me comfort that she cared, but I was so embarrassed. My mom loved me and didn't want that life for me. It broke her heart.

My first time in an adult prison was when I was seventeen. I transferred from the Manitoba Youth Centre to the Remand Centre. I was one of the first females in there. I thought being in prison was like a holiday because I got to smoke and work in the kitchen. All the women on my range (unit) took care of me. I was kind of the child of the range. We ate good. I had three meals a day, and I always got to have extra food. I had a nice soft bed, and I knew that I wasn't going to be abused, or picked on, or sexually assaulted in my sleep. I didn't have to do a blowjob for somewhere to sleep. I was safe. For me it was like a second home. But my gosh, I wouldn't call it a second home now.

I met Neal in 1994. He was much older than me. I know now that I ended up with older guys because the cycle of abuse and being used wasn't broken, and I was vulnerable. He's passed away now, but I was with him for ten years. He exploited me for the duration of our time together, but I never really understood that I was constantly being trafficked or sold. I had been warned, but I thought that he cared about me and loved me. I didn't understand what love was. I was never taught what a healthy relationship was. I just went along with everything. I'd be on a street corner, with him standing ten feet away watching me. He'd always collect the money. I came home with nothing. I stayed with him because I needed somewhere safe to sleep and get high. I had nowhere else to go. And nothing is for free—I know that. My time with Neal was a living hell.

I became pregnant with Neal's baby. I actually went into labour while standing on the street corner of Pritchard and Aikens. I was huge. My second son was born in 1996. Right after, Neal told me that his family was going to keep the baby because the baby would have been taken away by CFS anyway. I was heartbroken. My son went to live with Neal's family. Twelve hours later, it was straight back to the corner of Flora and Aikens for me. Neal was always watching me. If I wasn't doing that, living that way, I was in prison.

Neal was the second exploiter of my life; my biological dad was my first. Finally, my eyes became opened. I thought, I can't live like this; this is wrong. I was being sent out ten, maybe twenty times a day, five days in a row. Over and over. I started to fight back. But every time I fought back and the police were called, I always looked like the one responsible. Neal didn't really have many charges—nothing outlandish—so when the police looked at my files, I was always the one blamed. Neal knew how to work it so he looked like the victim. I'd take the charge, eventually get out on bail, and go back to Neal because I didn't know what else to do. Over and over. No one ever took the time to ask me why I had attacked him, or why I had hit him with a bat. There needed to be a different kind of preventative approach.

The police were part of the problem. Several times I had to do a sexual act for a police officer, for example to get off an unendorsed warrant (you could be set free from this kind of warrant) I had for prostitution. They were even in their uniform! (That happened, but twenty years later, things have changed. I want to acknowledge that this happens much less today. There are good cops out there.)

I was in jail again and got bail in the spring of '98. I went to the St. Norbert Foundation, but I took off from there right away. I was out for only four or five days and I went back to see Neal because that's the only life I knew, right? I had nowhere else to go. Four days later, I was walking down Selkirk Avenue and got caught by the police. They took me back to jail. I found out in there that I was pregnant.

I was back in jail because I had racked up some charges in 1993, but I wasn't convicted right away because I was using a bunch of aliases. Those charges would eventually catch up with me and I would be convicted in 1998. Back in '93 there was this john. He was an actual pedophile registered with the Winnipeg Police Service. He had picked up me and my girlfriend and taken us to his apartment at the Fort Garry Place. My friend was sleeping with him at the time, and we lived with him about six months. There were times when he was using us, exploiting both of us. He would buy us underwear and bras and make us walk around in them. He would take us to the revolving restaurant up top and get us an unlimited supply of dope. He was white, wealthy, and owned a car lot. We'd go there and pick any car we wanted to drive. We were just kids. I was not thinking of the bigger picture because I was not of sound mind.

One day I was with some people, and told them I knew this guy who had money. I took them to his place and I knocked on the door. When he opened it they jumped him. I sat and had a drink while they tied him up and robbed him. Now, I know that if you are with somebody and they are doing something unlawful, you will be charged. So in 1998, I got charged for those 1993 offenses and went to the women's prison in Portage la Prairie for a while.

In the jail yard there were these big, tall fences. You couldn't even see through them, but I knew there was a Child and Family Services building next to the prison on Tupper Street in Portage. I phoned there and said, "Look, I'm having a baby. I'm in the Portage Correctional right next to you and I would like somebody to come in and see me." So they sent a worker over and we worked out a case plan. I met the woman who was going to take my baby from the hospital and care for him until I was out on parole. Her name was Rose. She was married to a Métis man. I've always identified as Métis, so I liked that.

When I went into labour at the prison, I was screaming at the cell door for two hours. We were in dorms with five beds so every one of my cellmates could hear me screaming. When my water broke, one of the other inmates shouted, "Listen here. I'm going to fucking call the ombudsman. You guys have got to take her to the hospital." I could barely walk. They took me by van to the hospital, but I still had handcuffs on during the ride. They did not handcuff me while I was at the hospital. A female guard stayed with me in the delivery room 'til I had my baby. Then they had two

A female guard stayed with me in the delivery room 'til I had my baby. Then they had two security guards outside my door.

security guards outside my door. I stayed there for twelve hours after I had my son. He was 9 pounds, 14 ounces. The nurse came and brought him to see me one last time. I left the hospital to go back to jail, but my baby stayed behind in the hospital. I felt I was leaving a part of myself behind there. That was the worst, most heartbreaking feeling.

My baby got to come and see me in jail. Rose brought him three times every week. She was one of the nicest ladies I've ever known. He was always dressed so cute. He had little ties, and at one point he even came wearing a little Métis sash. He was a butterball.

I was going up for parole and told them that if I got it, I wanted my baby to come with me to St. Norbert Foundation where I'd be staying. But when I got released, I wasn't allowed to see him. I had become so attached to my son, but they wanted me to focus on myself for thirty days. I said, "I just focused on myself for fucking ten months. Why can't I have my baby visit me during these thirty days?" Rose wrote me letters that had a daily journal of what he was doing. Those letters made me cry, but they also inspired me. My whole goal while I was at the Foundation was to get my baby back. I asked the staff for that so many times. After two weeks, Rose was able to bring my baby to see me twice a week. The staff promised me that I would see him and they kept their word. I think my baby was about three, maybe four months old. But he did eventually come to live with me in St Norbert after about forty days. I stayed there seven months.

Having my baby while I was in jail could have been worse. A least my son wasn't taken somewhere for good. And I got to meet Rose before my baby was born. She had a wonderful heart.

I was on parole out in the community, and I found a place to live. My ex, Neal, and both of our sons came to live with me there. But Neal sent me back out on the streets again. That lasted about three months, until I was arrested and went back to prison. I lost both my boys. They went to live with their aunt (Neal's sister). She was a very good woman. I have nothing bad to say about her. The boys are both gentle. They were taught about their culture from their family. I commend their auntie for keeping them so they did not go through a bunch of foster homes.

When I got released from jail in 2000, I left Neal. I just never went back. While I was in the institution, I was sound in mind (not on drugs). I had a lot of clarity and a lot of time to think. Even while sober, I knew that I had something sitting there inside me that always said, *If I go back to him I'm going to kill him.* There had been so much abuse, so much selling my body and doing sexual acts when I didn't want to. If I was sober and could think this way, obviously there was the potential of my acting on this. I knew I couldn't go back to him. I never saw him again.

My current husband Matt and I met in September of 2000. We got married in 2010. We had all of our four children first: two boys and two girls. Ironically, I met Matt in a drug house. His dad sent him out to sell drugs, and I was a buyer. It wasn't the best way to meet. It was his first week working at the traphouse. Matt was curious about us exploited women. He asked me, "Why do you use? Why are you out here on the streets?" I rambled on to him (I was really messed up) but I remember thinking, *This guy is really listening. He's trying to make sense of people's lives.* Matt always used to say, "You girls deserve so much more than this." Matt took me for what I was. I was so broken when we met. When I'd go to the drug house, I'd always ask when Matt was coming on shift (a shift was twenty-four hours long), because he treated me differently.

Matt had always been called down. During his school years, he was the one who people said wasn't going to be nothing. He was the one picking up charges. At twelve years old, *Boom*, he was in the youth center. He ran around the streets like crazy. But he was handed that life. I think he was in survival mode (I'm not making excuses). From day one Matt knew that what he was doing was not right. He felt he was destroying lives. We had lots of conversations. We'd talk about how women are looked down on as junkies, but he would tell me that he saw so much potential in me. I don't know why he picked me, but he said, "If I was going to be with anybody it was going to be the toughest one in the house." (I had already lived an entrenched life for fifteen years.) Matt was in CFS when he was a baby. I think that we were drawn together because we had the similar experience of no nurturing from our parents.

I grew up hearing that men will never change. But, if we can believe in our women, we need to believe in our men too. I've seen men change, like my husband did. Our relationship was really volatile in the beginning: lots of fighting, bad assaults. I fought back. But we didn't know any other way. I think he was trying to help me not inject, or use, or run away.

I had to stop a lot of behaviours to change my life. I had a hard time at first with Matt being five years younger than me. I thought he must want something. I didn't know how to be given something nice, because I always thought that I had to give something back, like a piece of my body. Matt'd say, "You don't need to do anything." He stuck with me through all that. It's really beautiful because Matt is very thoughtful. If he gets invited out now he'll say, "Well, I got to ask my wife." I want him to just go and have a good time.

Today Matt is doing a lot of work with young men aging out of CFS care and involved in the justice system. He feeds his spirit by working in a system that he feels chewed him up. He loves connecting with these young boys. He also does work with men in the community on domestic violence prevention and parenting skills.

When we first started to be together in 2001, I had short stretches of sobriety, one to two months. Then Matt did sixty days in jail for possession of drugs. I used a bit while he was gone, but when he returned, Matt helped me to stay sober, kept me out of situations that weren't good for me. During those stretches of sobriety, having Matt by my side was essential. I wouldn't have been able to survive without Matt. It was a whole new way of life for me.

I got pregnant right away. I had our oldest son in 2002, October 26th. CFS came to the hospital to visit me because I was on their Birth Alert watch. They wanted to take my baby because of my past involvement with CFS. Matt challenged them. He said, "Just because I met a woman who had prior CFS history, that shouldn't affect me." Why should Matt have to suffer because of my past? Matt told them they couldn't take our son. My baby was finally allowed to come home with us.

In 2020 the provincial government mandated CFS to stop the Birth Alerts. CFS is backing off. But the Birth Alert's been around for a long, long time. It's a system that was used where hospital social workers alerted the CFS system when a "high-risk" child was being born. I always knew about it. The birth alert was around when my brother was born in 1980 and adopted out. My mother made mention of it when I was fifteen and pregnant. She told me that the number one thing was to keep my prenatal appointments because that's what CFS would look at. It was common that when you went for a prenatal check-up, a hospital social worker would see you. They were constantly asking questions. There's a long list of red flags for their risk assessment: if the mom is young, if the parents are having a disagreement, if there are track marks on the mother, if she's disoriented, if she has missed prenatal appointments, if she's on social assistance or transient, if there are other children in care, or if the mom was once in the CFS system herself.

The Birth Alert gave CFS the authority to go poking its head in and monitoring the families. In the hospital, during labour or a few hours after the baby was born, the authorities would come and go through this whole list of questions with the family and the mom. The mom is already stressed out. Perhaps she's going through some domestic problems. There's a lot of apprehensions that wouldn't happen if there were preventative programs in place. If moms are given a chance and have exposure to programs in the first months, a lot of them change and do well. We now have some good programs that step in at the beginning of pregnancy. We need them, and we need to use kindness and nurturing—*I'm really sorry my girl that that has happened to you. How can I help you?*

Our CFS hub ANCR knows about every baby born in Manitoba. But is CFS notified with every baby? I don't think so. There have been a high, high, high rate of Indigenous woman who have been put on Birth Alert. Why was it only Indigenous women who were visited at the hospital? Racism played a huge role. I saw it every day working in child welfare. The average newcomer or Caucasian woman didn't have a clue what the Birth Alert was because she just went along and gave birth and then took her baby home.

The Birth Alert has scared Indigenous women for decades. Every baby I had was on the Birth Alert. Pretty much any woman I know who's a survivor woman has been part of a Birth Alert too. Once you got tagged by the Birth Alert system, you were more likely to have it for the remainder of your children. Every other province had done away with it before Manitoba did. I'm glad this practice is being stopped. I don't want my future grandchildren to be targeted. It's time to stop underestimating our youth. And now, most importantly, we survivor women don't have to be revictimized by telling CFS workers about our past.

I got pregnant again right after my son was born. I had our second son October 25th, 2003, and then our oldest daughter on October 27th 2004. I had a few benders where I went off and left, but I started to have longer stretches of sobriety, six to eight months. Every time I had a kid, I was scared CFS would come and take my child. But at the same time, I know I was responsible for putting CFS in my life. In 1996 I was living a very transient lifestyle and had no stability. Then in 1999 I was in prison. Those were obvious times when CFS was involved. I had a drug relapse back before 2007 and there was also the criminal element in my life. But no one ever asked me about the underlying issues, and why all this was happening in my life. This needs to happen.

Our three kids were taken by CFS on September 6, 2006. I was going up on twenty-four charges that were a combination of gun charges, robbery, forcible confinement, and uttering threats. One day during a fight, I had said to Matt, "I'm going to kill you," and I said it four or five times and got charged. And then there were all the breaches (not showing up in court). But I was in a state of crisis. I was yelling. This all happened in the middle of my kids being apprehended by CFS. I was high and being expelled from my home. I had a no-contact order so I could not return to my home. And they were taking Matt to jail. So, the police were going to penalize me more for being in a state of crisis? I was devastated. If only I could have had access to my culture, and people with experience to support me.

After our kids were taken, I did so much drugs because I wanted to die. I was devastated that our family was broken apart. I felt no hope. The judge handed down her custody orders for the kids on April 23th, 2007. The kids became permanent wards for one year. I was in jail at that time so I wasn't part of the weeklong trial for custody of the kids, but Matt was. Matt had realized that he had to put his kids and me first. He got straightened

around very quickly and was already on his healing journey. During his recovery, he had found full-time employment. One of the first comments that the judge put in her decision was *All hope is not lost for Mr. Willan. He will gain access to his children. He just needs to find a place to live, and do one program.* Matt was also devastated when our kids were taken. He visited our kids fifty-two weeks consecutively. He did not miss one visit. To this day, our kids have a very close bond with their father.

The judge ordered that all three children were to remain together. But the first thing CFS did was separate them, even though that was a violation of the judge's orders. Our oldest son lived with a really loving family. His foster dad, Brad, was a fireman. He and his wife, Rhonda, lived in Gimli. His foster mom loved my boy so much. I knew he was safe. But she succumbed to cancer in her forties and died. So my son went through lots of trauma too.

Having your child taken away is a traumatic experience. Why aren't the CFS workers following up with the traumatic experience they just made? That should be part of doing their job too. You don't come and rip somebody's life apart and then walk away. There's no support. That situation needs to change in child welfare. Child welfare is not a business; it's about human lives.

I went to jail for the last time on April 23rd, 2007. That's my recovery date too, because my turning point came while I was in prison. I heard that Matt had started a relationship with this girl. He was hanging out with her because he didn't have nowhere to go. He didn't have his own place and his mom was too toxic to live with. He was visiting the kids every week and working. This went on for about four months. He didn't know the direction my life was going to take, or if he was going to be with me. In the beginning Matt had told this girl that she wasn't going to get in between him and the mother of his children. But this girl was so head over heels with him, right? I thought, Okay, I love this guy. Matt is the most patient person. I'm going to lose Matt if I don't smarten up. I had to get rid of the drinking and drugs. (Matt's never done hard drugs.) I knew Matt loved me. This was my family. He's a good man, and I didn't want to lose him. We had lost custody of the kids and I thought, *This is*

going to be it. We won't get them back this time. Never again do I want to feel the agony of losing those kids, and maybe Matt too.

I was afraid sitting in that jail cell, but being there saved me. I didn't learn much, but I learned to live another day. I started to realize that my children were going to have a dead mother if I didn't change. I was really analyzing my life. Holy shit. I had every system "on" me that I could possibly have and I was so tired of fighting them. The very first thing I did when I wanted to change was to pray. I finally just surrendered. I found myself and I found God. There is no greater word than the word *Hope*. It correlates with God. In the darkest times I remember telling myself, *If anyone thinks they are better than me they are fucking wrong. How dare anyone judge me, I'm going to make it!*

Through prayer I was able to start healing. I got rid of the shame and the guilt. I just wanted to be a mom to my babies. I'd tell myself, *I'm going to make it. Nobody's going to stop me.* I thought about the Law of Attraction—believe in something and it'll happen—and then everything came into perspective.

When I stopped the drugs Matt told that other woman no.

I got out for treatment the first week in November 2007. I was so happy to get released. Matt and his grandpa picked me up from the jail. They took me driving and out to eat. I got to spend a full four hours with my mom. Her cancer had come back. I told her, "Mom, I promise you I'm going to make it."

I set up everything for my release while I was in jail. I did a lot of research, all on my own. I phoned around and at first no place wanted to take me because I was a violent offender—a V01. (I would scare you on paper, but I have a heart of gold.) The Native Women's Transition Centre was the only place that would take me. I went to Pritchard House first. Native Addictions Council of Manitoba offers a five-week treatment residential program there.

Pritchard House had a blackout period where you're not allowed to talk to nobody or use the phone for the first week. Us girls there would sit on the fence out front, at the corner of Salter and Pritchard because the weather was still nice. The very first day one of the girls walked up to me with six pieces of crack. She said, "Come on, come around the corner. They're not going to know."

I said, "Oh no. I'm fucking done. I want my babies. I'm not happy. I want to be sober. I don't want to fucking smoke that. Don't ask me."

Drugs are pretty evil. They steal every part of you, including your dignity. Everything you have, drugs take. So that's when I was ready to focus on my treatment, my spirit was ready. After five weeks, I went directly to Native Women's Transition Centre. I spent the next eighteen months there.

The following year on December 23rd, 2008, I went to court for the last time. This was for the sentencing of my last criminal charges in 2006. Judge Patti Umpherville was the judge. Initially the crown had asked for seven years because I had a prior history. I remember Judge Umpherville told me I had the most horrific Gladue Report she had ever seen in twenty years as a judge. (A Gladue Report is a presentencing report the courts can request when considering the sentencing of an Indigenous person. It allows the court to take into consideration the prior life experiences of that person before they are sentenced.)

The judge said to me, "The systems have failed, failed, failed. You were a victim of so much." She said that my case was the hardest of her career. She gave me my conditional sentence—two years house arrest. I was pregnant and going to get induced in a few days. She said, "I want you to go home and have your baby." Those were her words. Wow.

I said, "I will listen."

Judge Umpherville said, "You're going to walk out the doors today and you're going to have a healthy baby. Take care of your baby. This is what you're destined to do. But I want you to know that if you do breach any of these conditions (she read them all out to me) you will come back before me."

I didn't take the house arrest as a free ticket. I sincerely looked at it as my second chance to live. I never really called all of those other times *living*; that was not living my life, it was a nightmare. This time I was taking on a new way of living; I was living a serene life. My youngest daughter was born December 27th, 2008.

I returned to the Native Women's Transition (NWT) Centre with my youngest for a good part of my house arrest until May 2009. My mom was sick with cancer while I lived there, and I had permission to go and spend every second night with her. I was given a lot of flexibility. I loved it there. Being sober and a mom again, I spent so much time in awe while I was there. I was so grateful. Afterwards they hired me and I worked for them for five years. That was my first real job, and it opened a lot of doors for me.

While I was at the NWT Centre, I was allowed to visit my three other children for only one hour a month. I fought that. I phoned my CFS supervisor every single day and said, "You're not keeping my kids. I'm going to get them back." When I was in the midst of a fit, I always told CFS, "You're going to see, someday I'm going to be somebody and I'm going to fight you guys." I was hurt, right? I would yell at them, "You're never fucking keeping my kids. Those are my babies." They thought I had an anger problem. So I'd go do an anger management program, but I was still the same way. "Don't you fucking get it? I just want my kids." They thought I had a mental illness, but that's where I found my voice.

I had such a good probation officer for twenty-five years: Sandy Lafontaine. Sometimes I was mean to her. I'd tell her "Fuck you. I'm not listening to you." But she never gave up on me. Sandy was like a mom to me. She'd always follow up with me, give me little gift cards and meet me. Sandy probably understood my struggles, having been an older lady who had been a PO all her life. I still see her today.

When I wrote my Gladue Report in 2007 Sandy helped me. That was during a dozen long visits, writing out my life, starting from when I was a little girl. It was brutal, and intense and really raw to tell Sandy everything, but I couldn't bury my pain anymore. I knew this report could be my freedom. I wasn't the greatest person, but I didn't do all those things just because I wanted to; it was about my survival. Something I learned when writing my Gladue Report, was that every one of my convictions was against a male. None of them were female involved. When I wrote that Gladue Report, it was not a "get out of jail free" card. I had to do the work. I had to plead guilty to my charges. They were serious and warranted a long prison sentence. I wanted to know where my life was going. I wanted my kids back.

While I was at the transition centre, my husband visited our kids the whole time they were taken from us. Our oldest son came back to us June 25th, 2009. The other kids came

two weeks later. The day our oldest came home was the same day we laid my mom in the ground. So we had to make a decision. Matt got our son and I went to my mom's funeral.

My youngest daughter and I moved back in with Matt and our kids around October 2009. We were married but had been living separately because CFS said that we had to. Finally I thought, *This is ridiculous*. I threw all my furniture in the garbage, and I moved in with Matt. I told CFS, "I am living here now and there's nothing you can do about it." I was a good enough mother to raise my baby daughter, but not my other three kids? That was bullshit. CFS didn't say anything. I had grown enough at that point to say that the systems were not going to control me anymore. I took control of my life. It wasn't too late when we got our kids back from CFS. They were still young: four, five, and six.

My role model for mothering is my husband, Matt. When I met Matt, he told me that I would be a great mom. He always saw that in me. He is very encouraging and perceptive. Sometimes when I feel a bit disconnected from my kids because I am in survival mode, Matt will remind me that the kids need my attention.

It's really easy to sober up when you're in jail, but when you get out it's a whole different story. I kept myself on high alert from places, things, and people who could discourage me from being on this path I wanted. You got to keep your company kind of clean. If you're going back to your family or community and they're known to be snorting and doing drugs, you got to be careful.

Other people, especially women, cannot be happy for someone when they're doing good. There's a lot of hate out there. It's so tiring to see lateral violence like that. Lateral violence is when the Indigenous don't direct their anger or frustration at their oppressors, but instead at their own people. It's wild! For the first two or three years that I was sober, I went to bingo every night. Bingo was a safe addiction. It helped me. Now, after fourteen years of being sober and on the right path, I have no desire to go to bingo! Heck no!

I graduated from Yellowquill College
with the First Nations Child Family Service Worker Diploma in 2016. I've worked for a number of different organizations, always in outreach positions. I've worked with adult women and LGBTQ2S+ exploited adult persons, and then that's taken me to my work with exploited youth. I've worked in the core area with level-five females under the age of eighteen. That's the highest risk level. They are highly vulnerable: having Fetal Alcohol Syndrome, or anger issues, being exploited or involved with a gang. I used to be the same way. That's why I love them. I need to do this work. I choose to do it for the community that helped me.

I've also been working for Mitch Bourbonniere at Action Therapy since 2016. We do case planning, and Mitch decides which girls I will work with. He is very good at matching us up. I usually work with high-risk girls. They are youth who are on lockdown and really struggling mentally.

The youth are exploited, but there are many forms of exploitation: be it for their bodies, for a place to stay, for selling or running drugs. But I want to be careful; I don't want to stigmatize them or categorize them. Ninety-eight percent of the girls I work with are Indigenous.

Doing this frontline work, us outreach workers could die any day. We're just as susceptible as police officers. Sometimes even more so. I go in the crack shacks, shooting galleries—whatever you want to call them—dealing with the riffraff. One thing helping me to do the work is that I know many of these parents from the lifestyle I lived prior. I have an ability to connect with parents when all else fails with the agencies. I connect with their kids too. I'll say, "Hey, I used to babysit you." (I don't tell them I was getting high with their moms.) I've survived these streets long enough that I'm kind of considered old-school because I've been around for so long. Had I not had that experience I'd probably be chewed up out there. That's the reality.

If some people see a child that's ten or eleven, drunk, or holding a bottle of beer, they might think, *It's not my child, not my problem*. But I'll go and ask, "My girl, how are you doing? Where's your family?" (It's our duty to report any child abuse we see.) This work brings me validation, because when I was exploited, I wasn't being looked after. I know how it feels to have nobody look out for you. I think that's why I push so hard for these young girls I work with today. The work I do is always meaningful heart work. It is medicine work. I feel that's where I am needed. It's tough work but I'm tough too. The work feeds my spirit. I go home and am grateful for another day that I'm alive and breathing. I got a home and I have my kids.

These kids I work with have got to have that one person to go to. I know mine was my probation officer. I always tell the youth, "Reach out to the one person you trust. Look for someone healthy." Sometimes when you need help, the best people are not even your family. It's getting worse in society. The meth crisis is at an all-time high. That drug is just so cheap. So many girls are shooting up. But I commend our Winnipeg Police Service and drug enforcement for doing their jobs.

I'm no fool. I know when somebody's using. "Don't even lie to me," I say. (When I was young, I was the best at lying and being a manipulator. Those are survival traits.) I say, "I've been there, done that, so don't even go there with me."

"Oh Rachel, I've been clean for six weeks."

And I'm like, "Oh, really? Don't lie to me." I say. "My girl, if you want help…" and she'll break down. I give her a good strong hug. "My girl, I love you." I say, "You know you can do this. Your babies need you. You're a mom." I treat them in the way I would want to be treated.

I'm always mentoring. Our hearts carry love, kindness, nurturing. If someone's been damaged, we need to help them repair. I try and pass on what I know. I say, "This is a challenge for you, to fix up your life. But don't ever let your heart get mean, no. You got to have a strong interior to be able to move forward. No hanky-panky on your Facebook, Snapchat, nothing. You need to start acting like a mom."

I always look at my lived experience. I try and keep my mind on what helped me get sober. I was a horrible drinker. Just horrible. I would go to AA meetings and sit there, but I'd think, *One day that's going to be me up there.* I always thought that way and I looked at the brighter side. It wasn't easy, but I knew that I wasn't going to sit in my piss pot and blame everybody.

I still have all my mug shots. I carry them around because when I'm teaching our youth, I think it's important to show them that this was me then. I say, "This is where I used to be." But I also show them little things that I've done and how I've shared my story. It inspires them because I know that even the darkest, deepest, entrenched ones can bounce up. No matter what. I do believe that there's

ANDREW MAHON

room for change. "My girl," I say, "You're beautiful too."

I remember when I was a kid, my CFS worker telling me, "Oh, I understand."

I said, "No, you don't. You don't understand." I would throw chairs at my worker in the CFS office. "You'll never understand. You don't know." I said. I was just an angry little girl, right? But, the workers never once asked, "How was your day? What happened?" Nobody ever asked me about sexual abuse. Now today we would know the signs.

When I work with my girls, I really listen. I know when to cry with them and when to laugh with them. But the most important thing is to listen. I have a gift. I teach the girls their culture and we talk about identity. Not all hope was lost with me having had the life I had.

I have so much faith in the families I work with. I don't know if that's wrong, because then the next thing you know, a girl has overdosed or she's dead. It can be devastating. And I'm thinking, *Oh, I know she could've done it!* I get really conflicted as a frontline worker, but we can't judge. It's for Creator God to judge.

I harboured really ill feelings towards CFS for a long time. But I overcame that obviously, since I work with the system. It's a good feeling to know that everything I lived wasn't for nothing. My life experience will enhance those young girls' lives because I know they're going down the same path I went down. Sharing my story helps build connections. It takes away the rift between the worker (me) and the youth. This work cannot be done without survivors. Our people are seeking out people with lived experience to inspire them. There's nothing more important than our survivor children (our youth battling it out) learning from somebody with lived experience.

Child welfare needs to change. The approaches are so old. Government ministers need to listen to people who have already been through the CFS system. I'll never be embarrassed because I am a woman with lived experience. Book data is not enough; we need to learn from other people's stories.

We are in a time right now where CFS is seeking people who have lived these lives and have made tremendous changes, because they know they cannot do it alone. Us survivors are teaching the social workers. That didn't happen in my time. Our voices matter. We have a lot of gifts we bring to the table, and we are seeking redemption. There's been a lot of connecting and that's a beautiful thing. When dealing with CFS social workers, we always have to use kindness. (Things are changing quickly for them, and they often don't know where they stand.) We all need to be at the table together. Twenty years ago I would have never been hired with my criminal record, but today that is different. I think that is a sign of reconciliation. Change is a slow process, but still, it's happening.

Sometimes we need to challenge CFS staff, but I don't hold no animosity toward them. I have learned that there are other ways to cope than to be angry with the staff when I am fighting for my youth. I do know my value, though, and I'll never tolerate mean-spirited people or aggressive case managers. Sometimes a social worker will not treat me as I deserve. I will ask them not to use a certain tone of voice with me or not to treat me any less than other people they deal with. Holding people accountable on their nonsense is a gift. Not many people can do that.

The work I do is brutally hard, frontline work. The grief is heavy. It's emotionally and mentally draining. It'll burn you out so fast if you let it. Us older outreach workers are reliving our traumas from when we were children. (We're trying to repair that in a kind way.) People ask me what I do for self-care. It's weird, but working in level-five homes, that's what inspires me. Sometimes going to work is self-care to me. But I notice I can be stressing a lot too. You can burn yourself out from giving. I need to know boundaries when it comes to that.

So I've been trying to manage my stress. I'm digging in my toolbox. When I need time for myself, I have a special sacred space in our living room. I have things that are meaningful: my drum, my Métis sash, crosses, and pictures of people who've all passed away—my mom, my best friend, my uncle, my husband's dad. It's my special spot that nobody can touch. I put my traditional medicines there (sage, cedar, sweetgrass and tobacco) and I light the candles. It's healing.

I mix together my culture and Christianity. I am very proud of my culture, but I also believe in the Lord. I will never be ashamed of that. Ever. I don't care what others think of me. I'm not shy. My faith is my gift. The Lord is the one who held me up in a jail cell and gave me the strength to move forward in a good way.

As a little girl, I knew about God and I was made to go to Sunday school. As far as I can remember back, I've always prayed to God, when there was a shitty situation. I'd pray to God as a little girl, "God, please don't let him hurt me. Please God, let me eat today. Let me be safe. Let me be able to run away today." I prayed because I wanted a better life. It was instilled in me that there was a higher power. I told myself that it would help me.

I did go through a wicked phase of being mad at God. I still feel mad sometimes. How could I not question God with the things that have happened to me? I also went through a stage where I questioned why the Catholic

Church mortified my cultural history through residential schools. I had a hard time digesting that, and yet I still believe. It will be for forever that I will be trying to figure things out. But that's okay. I still believe there's a higher power.

I can remember early on when I first met Matt, sitting with him and talking about God. Matt is a man of God. You can open a bible and he can tell you something about that scripture (he loves to learn). Early on, Matt shared with me about why we're alive, and how God does good for us. There is never a day that I don't hear Matt say Jesus is Lord. It's one thing to say you believe in God, but another to practise your spirituality. I never had no component to my spirituality before I met Matt. I was living a sinful life. I used to say, "Oh God, just let me get out of jail" but nothing meaningful. When I met Matt, I started to have a spiritual part to me.

The first time I prayed in my jail cell, it felt weird. I felt ashamed. I felt like I was talking to a wall. Once I started praying—whether to The Creator or to God it's the same—I was better able to move forward and to be thankful. I surrendered. In the early days of my recovery, I used to pray for simple little things like my food, or getting picked for a program because then I could learn more. Everything that I would pray for was coming to me. I'd get a phone call from my PO asking if I wanted these couches a woman was getting rid of. They turned out to be almost brand new. Then my PO would bring me brand-new blankets. A lot of good things were coming my way. What changed is that I was missing what the Lord does. He provides. I thought, *If I do good things, good things happen.* I started to trust God more. It's what we believe in that helps us to be who we are and helps us to be alive for another day. I wouldn't be here today without the Lord.

I define my spirituality as my faith in God (or Creator) and I define my Indigenous culture as who I am. I separate them. I'm proud to be Indigenous. Ceremony has helped me too. There was no access to ceremony while I was in jail, but I reached out to the Indigenous community after I got out. Many organizations stepped up and helped me on my healing journey. They were a big support. I love all the teachings and ceremony: sharing circles and sweats. But when I go to a sweat lodge I stay outside. I have attempted to go inside but that didn't sit well because being confined affects my trauma. But I love the drum, the space and the Pow Wows. Ceremony makes my heart dance and makes me proud to be Indigenous.

When I became sober I thought it was important to give thanks. I went and talked to Greg Besant, the executive director of Métis Child and Family Services. He looked at me with tears in his eyes and said, "I'll never forget you because when you didn't have your kids, you phoned every day." I thanked him because I know he knows I bring a lot of my life to my work. He recognizes that. I feel I have been vindicated. I am not a bad person, I am not what you see "on paper." Him recognizing that I am changed and healed meant a lot.

The only person I had not got to thank was Judge Patti Umpherville. She's not on the bench anymore. But in 2020, someone located her email address for me, so I wrote to her. It was important to me to thank Patti and let her know about the changes I had made and what has happened with my life. I have broken many barriers. My life feels super and I am grateful. It was so important for me to have her know that. Writing that email,

and receiving her answer back, I felt a sense of redemption. That was a full-circle moment.

May 2016 I got a call and it was the coroner. They said, "Do you know a Raymond Joe Parent?"

I said, "Yeah, that's my biological dad. Why?"

They said, "We've had his body for twenty-eight days and nobody's claimed him. If nobody claims him, he's going to go into a mass grave." My biological dad was always the type that was running, running. He had beaten my uncle (my mom's brother) really bad, so my biological dad moved to Edmonton in about 1982 or '83. He ran from being confronted by me, and my mom, about the sexual abuse and the domestic violence. My biological dad eventually came back to Winnipeg but he refused to get any help from us kids. He went to Siloam Mission. In 2008 I went there and had a meal with him. Then all of a sudden, we didn't see him anywhere. I didn't know that Siloam Mission had fixed up all his taxes. He hadn't claimed his pension for over ten years. Siloam Mission helped him get into an old folks home.

I gave my biological dad a proper burial. His funeral cost almost $10,000. When I first went to go see his body at the funeral home, I told my auntie Joan, "Oh he's so evil." But I gave him a proper service regardless of how I felt, because I wanted to show my other siblings that we needed to do the proper thing. I have seven siblings in total. My mom had six with my biological dad and then two more with the man I called dad, my stepfather Joseph: Clifford and then Bridget, who is the baby. At the service, I was more worried about my siblings. I wanted to see them. We are scattered all over. I see one of my sisters more than any of the other ones. My biological dad wasn't a very liked man, but some of my family members came to his funeral just for us kids. Most importantly, I want a place in heaven. So I did the right thing regardless of how I felt. For me that was growth. I let my resentment go. I did what I'd had to do, and because I had done a lot of healing, I did it with grace.

Both prayer and sitting in prison helped me to forgive my mom, but one of the biggest things that helped was a teaching Mitch Bourbonniere gave at Aboriginal Visioning. It was a mentorship program I was doing during my first year of recovery in 2008. The teaching was on the medicine wheel, residential schools and family dynamics, and on why we Indigenous people are the way we are, and how we think, learn, and view the world. I was really intrigued. The first thing I thought was that my mom got the shitty end of the stick. I had never really put into context what my mom's and grandma's abuse was like—*That's why my mom was always mean. That's why my grandma was like that.* It all connected for me when I heard Mitch speak.

I'll never forget those teachings; that was such a gift. I realized my mom was victimized herself. She could have done better if people had understood her and if she wasn't ashamed to talk about her abuse and experiences with CFS. My mom loved me, but she was so beaten up. What was she going to do when she had been physically beaten and punched out by my biological dad? My mom did try, but she must have felt like a failure. At that moment during the teaching, I realized my mom did love me and I was just stunned. I had had such hatred for my mom. This opened up a whole new door: Holy man, my mom loved me.

When I was sober, I spent time with my mom before she died. She got to see the beginning of my recovery. One night I told her, "I know your life was hard." And so she knew that I knew.

I had never heard the words colonization and reconciliation before that teaching from Mitch. I was just floored. I wanted to go running around and tell everybody what I learned. My eyes were opened. I had never thought about these things, or learned about them before because I was too high, or just trying to survive. When my grandma was older, she told my auntie, who looked after her for many years, that she was in a residential school and was abused while she lived there. She never did chores there; instead, the priest always wanted her to sit on his lap. My grandma did not talk about that until later in her life.

My mom was a status Indian and also in a residential school. She never spoke about it either. I found out about the residential school from Auntie Joan after my mom died. My mom was in the school around 1964, before my grandma fled and brought all of her kids to Winnipeg. My grandma was already feeling the impact of her kids being taken. My grandmother didn't talk about that, neither did my mom. Now I can be the voice for my family.

Society (the bigger colonial systems out there) has just moved on from residential schools to something else, such as the Birth Alert, prison, and child welfare apprehension. So colonization is still here. Many of us are not treated properly. The Indigenous people in Manitoba are overrepresented in children in care, prison populations, Missing and Murdered Indigenous Women and Girls, drug addiction, and social assistance.

One of my most important focuses is the Murdered and Missing Indigenous Women and Girls (MMIWG) because I think of all the vulnerable girls out there. Women of all race and colour matter. I spoke in front of the MMIWG inquiry three times. The first time Matt and I gave a talk in Winnipeg about our relationship and how we have both changed. The second one I shared my life story along with another woman. Then I was asked to go to the National MMIWG Inquiry in Newfoundland in 2018 as the Manitoba survivor speaking about exploitation. Matt, Diane Red Sky, Danny Smyth (Winnipeg

Police Chief), and Darryl Ramkissoon (Counter Exploitation Unit Sergeant), came too. Matt didn't want to hear me talk about being exploited, and I don't blame him. After I finished speaking, some people there said I should write a book. I'm like, "I know. Trust me."

When the MMIWG commissioners visited Winnipeg, they asked Matt and me to take them on a tour of Winnipeg. We took them to Rossbrook House to show them what a twenty-four-hour safe space looks like. Oh my God, I spent so much time at Rossbrook House when I was a little girl. When I was young and I'd be visiting my mom or my granny and they were drinking, I wouldn't tell the CFS worker, because I knew they would take away my visits. I would go to Rossbrook House instead. My family lived in that central area close by. I went there to eat. They would give us bags of bread or donuts to take home. And when I was in my teen years, I would go there to sleep sometimes. Rossbrook House having their doors open twenty-four hours a day played a huge role in saving me from extra abuse and trauma.

Now Matt and I work together in the community service field. Walking alongside each other, healing and doing the work we do, is beautiful. We will take each of the kids we are working with out together for a day trip. We take them swimming or fishing, and we have one-on-one time with them during the day. It's good for those kids to see a couple where the two people are healthy together. So Matt and I get to know the kids we are each working with. Sometimes we'll tell the youth about the early days when things weren't so good for us. They get to hear about that and learn. There are no other couples with lived experience that do the work.

We've also fostered a lot of children, Matt and I. I would say about ten kids over the years since my recovery. They range in age from six months to seventeen years. I've also had two adult foster kids (eighteen and twenty) in extended care with us.

In life, a lot depends on who we chose as our life partner, so it's important to acknowledge my husband Matt. He is a very encouraging person. We have broken the cycle with our kids. Our oldest son graduated from high school in 2020. He is a hard worker, not selfish, and his intentions are good. He will make a good husband and dad someday. Our younger son is just finishing high school. He is intelligent and curious. He likes politics, Indigenous issues, and wants to learn about other countries. Our older daughter has a strong voice but is also a good listener. Our youngest daughter has brought us all a lot of joy. She has a very close bond with her older sister.

The number one thing in my life is my sobriety, because if I don't have that, I won't have my kids and I won't have my life. I was in twenty-three treatment centres before I finally got sober and 2021 is my fourteenth year of sobriety. Through my recovery, I've learned that no matter what kind of life I've had, I can still do whatever I want and be whoever I want to be. My message to the vulnerable girls I work with is to believe in themselves.

I believe that anybody can change, but they have to have support. You can't walk that walk alone. You can walk your walk with God and Creator, but at the end of the day, it's a heavy road because you need to physically get out what's hurting you inside. And it might take you twenty times talking about it, but you need to get it out and gone. Some people say writing your feelings on paper can help, but that's not my way of healing. Everybody's different. My husband and my auntie Joan have always supported me. They inspire me to keep moving forward regardless of the shitty past. The more I find out about my childhood, the more I'm able to let go.

I admire resiliency from people who've walked out of the fire of being homeless and entrenched in the drug culture, of drinking hairspray, shooting up, sleeping in parks. I've seen women turn their lives around. But, we can't forget our men. Nobody talks about our men. I see a gap in our attention to what needs to be done in our society—our men need to be sheltered and nurtured and loved too. Men don't talk about their trauma. They don't want to look weak, right? Men need to be brave and share their stories. We need more opportunities for men. We need more parenting programs for them too. The reality is that child welfare always makes the mom more responsible than the dad. What if we changed that around and they're both equally responsible? If the mom doesn't want to get help, let's give the dad that chance. There's no building relationships with dads in the child welfare system. That needs to change.

My journey has made me who I am today. It's pretty common when people say that, but I believe it. I'm thankful. If it wasn't for the people in my life, I wouldn't be where I am. I didn't do this alone. Whenever I have a crappy day, I have to reflect back and give gratitude. I got no business swearing and complaining when there's people that are worse off than me. So sometimes I have to stop and say, *Rachel, smarten up, you got no business being like that.* You can have bad days when you feel soured by people and I think *Oh God, I don't want to deal with this today.* But I have a home, I have my kids, I have my husband, I have food to eat. I have more than I need. For me, that's gratitude. I don't want to ever falter and be back to where I was. Today I'm so thankful for my life. It's unbelievable. I have lost many friends to murder, suicide, and overdoses. I am proud to be alive.

I met Rachel's husband, Matt, before I met Rachel. Our mutual friend Mitch Bourbonniere introduced me to him. Matt and I spoke to criminal law students together at the University of Manitoba about why people end up in crime and how they can change their lives. Matt was an amazing speaker, sharing his story with the students. Afterwards we got talking and Matt suggested that Rachel would be a great participant for this book. I am so glad he did. Rachel is very friendly, tender-hearted, and quick to offer her big deep laugh. I really enjoyed our time together. Rachel and Matt are a strong and inspiring couple. They dream of one day telling their shared story of transformation as a couple in order to encourage others.

Rachel wants to give thanks for everyone who believed in her along the way, including Margo Lee who was her counsellor at the Women's Correctional Centre, and Métis CFS for giving her back her children.

A small part of Rachel's story is taken from the public presence of her testimony for the MMIWG Inquiry found on CPAC.

Amy

I've started over a few times since coming out of care. After I aged out at nineteen, I eventually started going to university. I left Winnipeg when I was twenty-nine and hitch-hiked back, pregnant and homeless, at thirty-one. I made decisions and sometimes they led to life-learning lessons. It took me to those points where, fuck, I needed help. And that's okay; that's a part of life. I'm just grateful there are places that help people and have resources.

Thrive Resource Centre on Spence Street has really been there for me. Even if the help is just temporary—an organization or someone who's in your life for only a few months—you need to take advantage of that. Community organizations like Thrive offer programs that have such gold resources. That's what they're there for. You must take whatever supports you can find, and use anything available, even if it's only a $5 voucher. You can't feel bad about the decisions that you make, but eventually you've got to get up and help yourself if you want to get out of a terrible situation.

I have family from both Saskatchewan and Manitoba. There's eight of us kids and three dads. My mom was living with her kids on the reserve in Pelican Narrows Saskatchewan. She was having a tough time and left the reserve because of a bad relationship, so my five older siblings stayed with her mom (who we call Chapan, Cree for grandmother.) When my mom came to Manitoba to live in Thompson, that's where she met my dad.

I was born at the St. Boniface Hospital in Winnipeg, but we lived in Thompson, so we went back there after my birth. (I'm not sure why my mom came to Winnipeg for me to be born.) I have a younger brother and a younger sister. My older Saskatchewan siblings never came to Manitoba to live with us, so I have always been considered the oldest at home. Right now I have no siblings in the city. It's just me here. My younger brother lives in the North and sister lives in the Far North. My older siblings still live in Saskatchewan. My younger brother and I had the same dad. Our dad shot himself in the head three weeks before my third birthday.

When I was small I spent a lot of time going back and forth from Thompson to Pelican Narrows visiting my older siblings (holidays, Christmastime, and summertime) because that's where my mom's side of the family was. We also went to Nelson House and York Landing to see my dad's family. My dad committed suicide in Nelson House, so visiting there must have been hard for my mom. I travelled with my mom, my stepdad, and my younger brother and sister. But that was only part of the time because there were months at a time when I wasn't with them because I was already involved with CFS. I was in and out of care from the time I was a baby, probably by six months, maybe even before that. There was neglect because of alcoholism, and I was physically and sexually abused as a child.

My first foster parents were Annie and Warren. I have pictures of me as a baby—six or eight months old—on my foster dad Warren's belly, and birthday pictures with them when I was four or five years old. One of my fondest memories is being with my foster dad, planting sunflowers in the garden. I remember eating rhubarb, fresh from the garden, with sugar. I went back and forth for periods of time between Warren and Annie's and my mom and stepdad's. I left my mom and stepdad's home permanently when I was nine.

> I was in and out of care from the time I was a baby, probably by six months, maybe even before that.

There was lots of drinking, violence, and police involvement with my own family. I do have good memories from being with my mom. I don't think I'd be doing as well as I am today if my mom hadn't given me good memories. She tried her best. She was always a very hard worker and not one to live off welfare. My mom made sure that we had good Christmases. Our rooms were always kept up with nice bedding and furniture. I remember my walls being full of posters. We always had food in our fridge when times were good. But there were also times when I had to rob the drunks that were in my living room to feed my brother and sister. There are always extremes when you're dealing with alcoholism. My earliest childhood memories from the times living with my family would be trauma. My mom was coping with her own trauma too.

My mom is a residential school survivor. My mom went for ten years. My Chapan would send her clothes and parcels and she never received them. When my mom first went there, they poured the pesticide DDT on her hair. One of the stories I heard was that a young person had hung themselves in the mess hall, and the nuns told the kids, "This is what happened when you don't believe in God." This is the kind of stuff that's ingrained in residential school survivors' memories. You can't just get over that. People carry trauma for the rest of their lives, but sometimes they just learn to become better at functioning with it. My mom said residential school was a horrible, horrible place. Can you imagine a community where all the children are gone? And all you hear is silence?

My mom went to residential school from age six to sixteen. When she got out, she basically got married and started having babies. If you don't repair your trauma, then that really affects your mindset. Some people are beaten down so much that they don't even see that it *can* be repaired. There've been so many studies on the relationship between trauma and the brain. My mom didn't come to a place of healing and helping herself until she was in her forties.

When I was nine years old, I had enough of what was going on at home. One day I went to my best friend Jamie's house at lunchtime and I told her mom about the abuse that was going on at my home. Her name was Hope, and she was a social worker. I said, "I didn't want to live through that anymore."

I went back to school that afternoon and the counsellor came to talk to me because Hope had told someone at the school. I went back to Jamie's house after school because I didn't want to go home, but my mom showed up there banging on the door. She probably had a whole mixture of emotions, I can't say what she was really feeling, but she was mad and I was afraid, so I ran. I left through the back door with my mom chasing me. I ran and ran, halfway across Thompson to Warren and Annie's. But I couldn't stay there without the proper paperwork and process.

I went home one last time, and *it* happened one last time. The next day I was removed from my home by CFS. I was taken to the hospital for a medical exam. (The documentation from that medical exam confirmed what I had stated.) I was taken permanently (as far as I know—I haven't seen my records) to Warren and Annie's.

Not long after that my younger brother and sister were removed from the home as well. I felt I had a duty to take care of them, and I did that by telling what was going on in our home. My brother and sister have blamed me for being removed and for some of the emotional issues that they have from

not living with mom and dad. I've apologized over and over again. I always say to them, "Do you know what I protected you from?" If they don't know what I saved them from, then they never experienced the harshness of what I went through. I know my mom still holds me accountable for having the kids taken away. I just wanted to keep them safe. CFS placed my brother and sister together, but I stayed with Warren and Annie. I felt relief that I didn't have to worry about abuse anymore. I felt safe.

I did go to court to face my abuser. I was nine years old in court being interrogated by his defense lawyer. That lawyer was tearing me apart, saying that I was lying. How could they say I was making up a story like that, at that young age, having gone through the investigation, the trauma and the hospital, and being interviewed, and ending up in court? That messes with a child. My case was thrown out of court because while I was testifying I grabbed a water glass and smashed it. They used that against me. So my abuser got off.

There were different people within my life who abused me. That's not something that's comfortable to talk about. But it does happen and that's a part of our fucking experience. Indigenous children were introduced to abuse at such a young age in the residential schools and had no way of learning that this was wrong. The abuse there by individuals who were in charge was widespread and commonplace. This systemic dysfunction affected our family systems. Children left the residential schools and went into family situations and it all unfolded again. There's a reason that so many people are traumatized still. It was a part of my growing up.

I stayed with Warren and Annie a couple of years until they ended up getting divorced. I guess there were no other foster home placements available for me in Thompson at that time because when I left Warren and Annie's, I ended up in a receiving home. I stayed there for about six months. I was ten or eleven, but it's hard to remember. Moving around so much has caused me to lose timelines. I was always in a state of limbo, waiting for the social worker to tell me what decisions had been made. What does living under constant disruption do to a person? Maybe I blocked things out (that's a common part of brain patterns and brain functioning when trauma has been experienced). Constant unknowing

messes with a young developing brain, especially when a child is always expected to adjust and then function.

While I was in the receiving home, McDonald Youth Services (MYS) got involved. MYS is a placement agency. They were involved in finding my next foster family. My clinical case manager, Allan, worked with me closely to make sure I was placed appropriately. Allan was outstanding. He went above and beyond for kids in care. He was such a gem. I was told that I was going to be moving out of Thompson to Portage la Prairie. I was moving from the treed forest to the prairies. I didn't know what that would mean for me.

I don't know why the CFS system never explored placement within my own family. I do know my mom never put my dad's name on my birth certificate and she never gave my dad's information to CFS. I have quite a large family on my dad's side in Nelson House. My aunties and family told me they were never contacted by CFS about taking me. I also have my mom's family in Saskatchewan. I don't know what the process or procedures were between Manitoba and Saskatchewan at that time. I don't know if that was my mom's decision or a CFS system decision not to contact my dad's family in Nelson House or my mom's family in Saskatchewan.

When I was moved to Portage la Prairie, my mom and my aunties said it was like I had just disappeared one day. They didn't know what had happened to me; I was just gone. When I had been in care in Thompson, my mom had some kind of communication with CFS. When she was feeling good, she would come for our visits. She came a handful of times. We have pictures. My mom said that half the time she didn't want to go to the agency because she was looked at in such a bad way when she went there. She felt that she was really looked down upon and that no one ever wanted to help her. But it's important to understand that my mom was coming from a state of trauma. All these systems that were supposed to help her, had victimized her. So, she didn't want to come there and have those family visits. I get that now, but I also remember the desperate feeling while I sat there waiting and my mom not showing up. It was painful. Being a child, I didn't understand. I thought *oh my mom hates me.*

I lived with my foster parents, Peter and Allison, in Portage la Prairie for two years.

They were good to me. They loved me and I knew that. I loved them too. They had their own children and it was great to have siblings who loved me and treated me as one of their own. I never felt different in that home. They were such a beautiful family.

While I lived in Portage la Prairie, I went for regular play therapy sessions in Winnipeg. As a child, I was already outspoken and stood up for myself, so when I was offered play therapy, I said sure. About ten years ago, I messaged my play therapist on Facebook to say thank you because if I hadn't been in play therapy (with what I now understand about trauma, the brain, and reconnections) I wouldn't be the person I am today.

When I lived in Portage la Prairie I tried to go for a visit to the Rez in Saskatchewan to see my Chapan and my family. My worker gave me grief because there was so much paperwork for her to fill out when I would be going to another province, where the process was different. I understand that now because I worked for the system and I know about some of the provincial differences. But back then I remember feeling like shit because my social worker told me it was my fault she had to do so much work to arrange for me to go. My one-week visit turned out to be just six hours long. The social worker never explained why to me. She just told me that a short visit was all she could work out. It was so traumatizing for me because I just wanted to see my family.

Two respite workers drove me to Saskatchewan. I don't remember their names, but they were a really nice lesbian couple. I had a great time. When we drove back, their truck broke down, which was a real problem, but when we got back to Winnipeg they said, "You are such a beautiful young lady. Thank you." I never saw them again. They were such beautiful women.

My foster dad in Portage got this amazing job opportunity in the States. My foster parents wanted to adopt me and take me with them. I had heard them talking about that and I was really touched that the family wanted to adopt me, because they knew what that meant, right? That I would be theirs and they would take me as their own for good. But we had a meeting, and I learned that I wasn't able to be adopted. Provincial legislation about adopting out Indigenous children had changed. If the legislation hadn't changed, I would have ended up going to the States. I think if I would have gone with them, I probably would have been more successful because they had the money to provide me with an education. My life probably wouldn't have been such a struggle. But I don't really know that for sure because I would have been a native child with a white family in the States.

It was very hard to say goodbye to Peter and Allison because they were genuine. You get to be a pretty good judge of character when you're in care. You are constantly trying to figure out who you can trust. Whether you go to a new school, or to a new family, you get to know people's characters and their mannerisms. You know when someone's not *for you.*

I went from Peter and Allison's home in Portage la Prairie to Antoinette and Simon's in Winnipeg. They were a white Jewish foster family. Simon was such a character. He was going bald and had glasses and he had this giant grey station wagon that I was embarrassed to ride around in as he blasted Phil Collins music. But oh, I just loved him.

They had not celebrated Christmas or Halloween and they didn't have any pets. They changed some of their ways to accommodate me. I came to them with a fishbowl and two little fish. (I had named the orange one Marmalade and the white one Vanilla Ice.) They let me keep my fish and they started celebrating Christmas and Halloween. They did that because of me. I knew that that was love. Later on I would think that was pretty significant.

I got a lot of good lessons from my foster mom. She was a hard ass but I remember those hard ass lessons to this day. She was big on manners and doing the dishes. She also believed in consequences. I remember one time having to paint the fence. I don't remember what I did, but at the time I thought *I'm never doing that again!*

Simon and Antoinette made it known that they loved me too. They had four kids and there was also one other foster kid. But seeing the parents' dynamics with their children was difficult for me. It was hard to watch them doing what parents are supposed to do for their children—giving love all the time and keeping the home free of violence and abuse. I saw it was normal for a dad to hug and for kids to have the comfort of parents. That's how a dad is actually supposed to be. I did get that with Warren and Annie, and Peter and Allison, but it was different dynamics with Simon and Antoinette. I didn't feel as welcomed by their children. Simon and Antoinette loved me and made adjustments to their family life for me, which may have caused some kind of upset for their own children. I see that now, later in life. I got teased by my foster brothers. It probably seemed harmless to them but I still think about. I was a teenager going through teenage emotions. I felt like I didn't fit in anywhere.

I went to Grant Park High School. I met great people there and made a lot of friends, but I was an oddball being in foster care and going through the high school system. That was not easy because I was always labeled. Labels are so harsh and they come with a lot of misconceptions. It didn't matter where I went, I was still a foster child. I carried that label. Sometimes that provided me a way to identify with some people. An example is my neighbour below me. She was noisy so I finally went and knocked on her door. When we met, she told me she was nineteen and had just gotten out of care. I told her I had done independent living until I was nineteen. We started talking about the hardships and the obstacles. We had a bonding moment.

When I was fifteen turning sixteen, I didn't want to stay with Simon and Antoinette anymore. All my foster families were not Indigenous, and I wanted to live with my own kind, my own people. I had to fight for that. Every few months we had these meetings and I argued with the social worker and clinical case manager. That's how I came to live with Diane.

CFS approached Diane because she was an ex-respite worker, and she is Indigenous. She became my last foster-parent placement. She's known me since I was ten when she was my respite worker and drove out to Portage la Prairie to pick me up for my play therapy sessions in Winnipeg. She would have her daughter in her car seat in the back too. Diane is a mom to me. I still call her my mom. Most people here who know me know that when I say *my mom*, I mean Diane. But I will call her Diane for the purposes of this story.

The day I moved into Diane's I felt relief, acceptance. I didn't have to defend myself anymore. I was with other brown people and a family that accepted me because they already knew who I was. Diane has two children. I call them my brother and sister. I met Diane's daughter when she was just a

baby. Her son is younger. I had moved out before he was born.

Diane showed me how to love life and be grateful for it, how to be kind and be a nice mom. I came to live with Diane when she was just learning how to become a mom because her daughter was just a baby. Diane said, "You paved the way for me being a mother. You taught me a lot."

When I moved in with Diane, she didn't know how to cook, but she learned. Now she's the best cook. She'll say to me now, "Amy, my girl, do you remember when I used to feed you that awful goulash!?"

But surviving and living with trauma and abuse, I had to learn how to function. Diane taught *me*. When CFS takes kids from their families, the kids become broken down. (That's what happened in residential schools too.) My biological brain development was fucked up from the get-go since I was surrounded by abuse. My brain is wired for instant anger. I still work on correcting that. It's an everyday thing.

Diane has been a really big part of my success at being able to navigate and get through life. She is still my biggest support. It's so important to have a support system being in care because you're constantly going through attachment and then you're moved. I was very fortunate to have good respite workers, foster parents, and group home workers. Not a lot of children get that. I thank Creator all the time that I was blessed with such an awesome support system.

I see Diane regularly, but unfortunately, I don't have relationships with my other foster families. I've tried to reach out through email and Facebook. But you can only watch them on Facebook for so long until you realize that really, I'm not a part of their lives anymore. There's more awareness now about kids in care and the effects of the Sixties Scoop, and then there's politics and red tape. Foster parents are part of a government entity. That might be hard on them. I can see why they would pull away and not want to be associated with their foster children. Not reconnecting hurts though. That is another part of the trauma of being in foster care that no one really talks about. My foster families were such a big part of my life. I'd like to thank them for their positive impact. I really appreciate what they did for me. I wish I could give them all a hug.

As adults who were once foster children, there are a lot of missing pieces for us, and a lot we can't explore because of the other side of the red tape. I have questions and I can't even ask them. I could apply for all the documents, but then, maybe I don't really want to know everything. But I would like to know the dates though, so I can piece together some of my own life.

Kids in care go through so many relationships, which is very detrimental to a person. We can have such a disorganized way of dealing with people. How are we to know about managing those feelings and those relationship dynamics? We are expected to adapt and adjust. Most people wouldn't expect their own kids to function if they were taken from a familiar situation as often as we were. For kids in care, the situation never becomes familiar; what becomes familiar is the removal. How the fuck can we be expected to function and be a working part of society? Those are the dynamics no one wants to talk about. As I grew up in that complex environment, I became an overthinker. I look at every situation from every angle.

I am functioning as an adult, but I know I can always run home, where there is an open door. Diane says, "I love you, my girl.

I don't have to worry about you, but I know that when you come home, there's a reason why." But I also don't want to be a burden; Diane's got her own kids. Later on when I had my own kids, Diane helped me to become a better mom because she was so kind, and she taught me that's how moms should be. She also taught me to continue to seek help if I really need it.

I left Diane's house when I was seventeen and a half. I was about three or four months away from high school graduation. I thought I was grown up and I wanted to take care of myself because I was used to that from a very young age. I did cooking and cleaning and took care of my younger brother and sister well before that. I cleaned up after the adults' parties. I had a strong sense of independence after so many years of people telling me what to do. I was ready to be on my own. Also, I didn't want to hurt Diane by being rebellious. I went in the CFS program for independent living and aging out of care. Then I could do whatever I wanted to without being mean to my mom Diane.

I had a strong sense of independence after so many years of people telling me what to do. I was ready to be on my own.

MYS helped me move out. They set me up with an independent living worker and provided me with money to cover the startup costs. But the amount was very minimal. At that time, you could stay on independent living until you were twenty-one if you fit the criteria and were doing what they wanted you to do, like going to school.

I was still going to Maples Collegiate after I moved out. I ended up graduating and I did everything for that rite of passage. Even though I was on my own when I graduated, I went to Diane's to get dressed up. She gave me my corsage and I got picked up there in the limo with my girlfriends. At the ceremony I did not get my diploma because I still had to get my last math credit. The school was good enough to let me walk across the stage and get my diploma (even though it was empty). I still had the party and everything. The next year I went to Grant Park to finish my math credit, because that's where they had adult education classes.

Finally I got tired of people still telling me what to do and I left the Independent Living

Program and went on assistance. Being a young kid on assistance is really tough. In care, you're not really taught about life skills: credit cards, credit, budgeting, taxes, stuff like that. Those are things that really matter when you move out. I stayed on assistance only for a few months. When I was nineteen, I ended up living with an old respite worker of mine, Kim, from when I lived with Diane. But then I just didn't want to live on assistance anymore because I wanted to be a productive member of society, so I went to work at Robin's Donuts on Logan and McPhillips. I didn't like the uniform. I wore the shirt and the hat, but I refused to wear the brown pants. I got away with it for about three months. It was so funny. The boss was a real nice guy but he finally told me I had to wear the pants, so I quit. I ended up working at a daycare on Selkirk Ave. And then, not long after that I applied to MYS to become a respite worker.

I started doing respite for Diane and the foster families that I knew. I also worked at MYS's mental health units, their boys and girls transition houses, and assisting with independent living with some of the kids. I worked for them until I was about twenty-eight. I also worked for the provincial government with kids in CFS, doing respite care and with youth in care at the Golden Eagle Co-ed Emergency Placement Unit (Zawe Ginew). That was Project Neechewam Inc. I worked there from 2007-2010. I started at the bottom as a youth care worker, moved to team leader and then intake and discharge facilitator.

When I was working in emergency placement, I read some of the kids' files. I read about kids being given a lot of medications. How can it be OK to give these medications to kids when they were still growing? I'm glad that I wasn't medicated and that no one pushed pills on me.

I got along really well with most of the kids I worked with; only a few gave me a hard time. I was always upfront and truthful, and that's what they appreciated. I told them, "You know what? I'm here for the moment, the moment right now. Let's make the best of it, because I don't know what's going to happen tomorrow." I came from a different perspective than other workers because of having been in care. It wasn't hard for me to put my foot down because I was very honest and truthful with them.

I started at the University of Winnipeg in 2000 at the age of twenty-one. I remember someone telling me that going to university was *an opportunity*. I knew that there was money earmarked for post-secondary education through my Indian band. So that was my motivation. Those eight years (off and on) at university were really hard. I went full time for two years in the beginning, but they were really tough. That's why I didn't go back for a while. I hadn't understood what I was getting myself into. My first year I took all intro courses: psych, sociology, criminology. I took Intro to Moral Philosophy too! I worked really hard. My marks were okay, but they weren't the greatest. It was tough to do all the work to be prepared.

It was hard for someone like me to go to university. There were very low numbers of us Indigenous people there. I didn't know if I belonged. I faced racism, judgment, and prejudice from my peers—other university students. I assumed these people would have some decency and respect about them since they were there at the university and studying, but I didn't find that.

The Aboriginal Student Services Centre (ASSC) was the one piece of connection that kept me in university. If it hadn't been there, I wouldn't have stayed. I didn't know what the fuck I was doing. I had to pretend that I knew. When I connected with the Aboriginal Students Centre, it was off in the basement. I thought *This is where they put us*? We had to go through tunnels and around pipes to get to our little room. (Now it's in a beautiful second floor space, but it took some time to get there.)

In 2001 I took Intro to Conflict Resolution. It appealed to me because my whole life has been one big conflict. Not that it's been my own conflict. It's been the overlapping systems that have contributed to the conflict in my life. The class just blew me away. I was shown how conflict could be turned into a really beautiful thing of working through problems and working through life. I thought *There's a whole course on this! Wow, okay, I guess I've been doing something right*. In my class I was able to talk about some of the most horrible things that went on in my life and it was okay. It made people uncomfortable, but conflict has a way of doing that. Conflict is not always resolved, but it can be addressed. The course started to open up my worldview. It made me feel peaceful.

My early university years were very important and had a lot to do with me figuring myself out as an Indigenous person. I started to learn who I was and what had been done to us. I didn't know the history of my people and residential schools and child welfare until I started going to university. When I started learning about our history I could then understand why my mom and my family were the way they were. It was mind blowing. I realized that *we are not responsible for being fucked up*. I learned that my people couldn't fucking function because of government interference. We still have the Indian Act right? That's the most racist document and it's still dictating the lives of Indigenous people today! Government interference shaped my parents, and a whole generation of people, to the point where they couldn't fucking function.

I went through the alternative dispute resolution (ADR) process with my mom and I listened as she told her story to the adjudicators, the government and church officials. It wasn't her fault what she went through. Our people had no choice. With her being taken from her family, there was a total disruption of family values. My mom was supposed to take care of me, but she was never shown how to be a mom. That was taken away from her. My mom and I still struggle, but she's my mom and I love her.

I've always had a voice but learning at university about the history of my people was the beginning of me getting my Indigenous voice and defending myself for being Indigenous. In class I talked about the residential schools abuse and some of the stuff that I'd been through within my own family. It made some people really uncomfortable. They didn't want me to talk about it, but I felt I had to. That is the conversation I needed to be having because that's the reality I had lived through.

In my Intro to Conflict Resolution class, we had to do this group project. It was something to do with restorative justice. We ended up talking about residential schools and the realities of some of the stuff that Indigenous people have dealt with and are still dealing with it. In my group we had this arrogant man. He told us he used to drive down Main Street and flick his cigarette butts and his change at Indigenous people. He did not give two shits. He was very honest about this. I shared my experiences with my group. That guy was so uncomfortable with the topic, but by the end of this project his point of view had changed. He had an understanding of what happened in residential schools.

Afterwards I remember thinking, *This is conflict resolution. This is restorative justice. If I can do this with one person, I can do this with others too*. I call it planting seeds. I remember learning that from going to therapy as a kid, *planting a seed*. You just put it out there and then it grows. That also goes with my spirit name—Purple Lilac Tree.

A woman named Marilyn gave me my name. My cousin April took me to this specific ceremony for anybody who wanted to have healing or get their spirit name. We were seventeen or eighteen years old. I offered Marilyn tobacco and a gift. That was my first real introduction to ceremony. She told me my name in Cree. I don't have the language capabilities to pronounce it. Kind of sad, but that's part of genocide—loss of language, right? She said, "In short, it means purple lilac tree."

I'm still learning the meaning of my name. When you learn your name, it's a continual journey, a lifelong process. There can be many different elements to the name. For mine there's the tree, the seasons, and what happens in each one, and how that affects the tree. Then there are my roots, which can go very, very deep so you end up having a very strong tree.

It was good to go to that ceremony. It felt real wholesome, but I also felt removed. I knew that was my culture, but I didn't know how to relate to it because I hadn't grown up in it. I had been made to believe that my cultural practices—singing, chanting and drumming—were evil.

As a young girl living with my mom, every Sunday she would dress me up and I would be forced to go to church. I had to walk by myself in my Sunday best and sit there and listen to the sermon, take communion and go home. Sometimes my mom and my siblings would come along with me, but not consistently. I got baptized and went through the whole white dress first communion thing, but I never understood why. It was just so foreign to me. I felt I was the little brown girl in a room full of white people.

My Chapan was a big part of my life. She was such a devout Catholic. I lost her to COVID in 2021. She lived to age ninety-seven. When she was a girl, the nuns took her from school and made her work in the sanatorium, which was for sick people. My Chapan used to say, "Nosim (granddaughter), many bodies came in and not many left." The patients would be rolled down the hallway in the basement, to the crematorium, where they would be put in and burned. When family members came to look for them, the staff never had an answer. The nuns didn't even tell them where their loved one had gone. My Chapan would put her head down and shake it, and you could just see the weight of that experience. At the same time, I could also see the confusion that my Chapan went through because she was so devout in her religious ways.

My mom is Catholic too. When my mom was in the hospital with COVID in 2020, she had stopped breathing (code blue) and the doctors brought her back. My mom told me, "My girl, I was at a big fire." When my mom had that near-death experience, she was exposed to the other side. She asked me, "What is this, my girl?"

I said, "Mom, you were at the sacred fire." We light fires when people pass, to light the way for them to go home (to the spiritual side).

A part of my Indigenous identity has been healing the sacred relationship between my mother and me. I believe that once that is broken, it has to be repaired. I am trying to help my mom be comfortable with our culture, because that is who we are. But I also understand that is counter to what my mom was taught. At residential school, they made my mom believe that everything about her was wrong. But I feel like she is blessed now after seeing that sacred fire and coming back from her death.

I believe in the unseen, and I believe in a lot more than what is *now*, in this reality. I know that there's more. I've been through too much in my life to believe that this is *just it*. Ceremony is a part of my life. My daughter and I go to ceremonies. She loves them. I struggle with walking the Red Road because to walk it, you have to be free of alcohol. (There's a reason why it's called fire water and spirits; your spirit takes off when drinking.) I still like to have a drink every once in a while—a nice cold rye and Coke on a summer day. When I do indulge, I choose to abstain from touching my smudging bundle for a few days.

I have learned to forgive my dad for his suicide. Ceremony is a part of my life and I went through ceremony so my dad could be taken away to the spirit world. I have learned many teachings throughout my journey and one of those is about suicide amongst our people. Before colonization, it was never part of our culture, or our way of being, for an Indigenous person to take their own life. I don't know what my dad went through, but from what I've heard, it wasn't the best. He suffered and was not able to hold on. I think about him often, wishing, and wanting, that he would still be with us. I have learned in his death that life is precious and so very complicated. And that sometimes family would rather forget the ones who are tied to the person who has taken their own life. I also see the complications of suicide and addictions and how it affects all community members. My dad was handsome, with this full-bodied dark brown hair and a dark brown sun-soaked look. I love my dad, Gabriel. I wish I would have known him growing up. My aunties have said, "He loved you so much, you were his world." I know he is with me spiritually.

In 2004 I had my son, so I stopped going to university. (I started back up again in 2005, taking courses while I was also working. I joined the student council and helped run things as I got more comfortable.) My son's dad and I are friends, but we never had a relationship where we wanted to commit to each other or move in together, so I had my son on my own. My mom was involved with my son. She was with me when he was born.

My son is such a beautiful child. We lived in Winnipeg up until he was six and I was twenty-nine. In 2009 my son and I were supposed to move in with my boyfriend at the time. We had planned to start a life together, but I found out on Facebook that he was cheating. I had already given notice on my apartment, gotten rid of most of my furniture, and everything was packed up. I had nowhere to go. I was left without a lease and I had used most of my money to rent the new apartment. I didn't know what the fuck to do. I had just found out that everything had been a lie, and I was very upset so I called my mom, and she and my stepdad came to pick up my son.

I found another place to live for about nine months. I was really lucky that I had the money for it or I would have had to couch surf, but people always provide. My ex and I went back and forth for a little bit before the relationship ended for good. It was an awful breakup. I ran away from the city because he tried to kill me. One night he had me up against the wall and head butted me (he is a big guy). When I woke up, he was holding a computer over my head and was threatening me. Things got settled down but the next morning when he went to work, I called one of my best friends. I was lucky that she was in the city. I packed up what I could in my bag and she picked me up and took me to her home on the Rez, Fisher River. Eventually I ended up in Peguis First Nation. They are right beside each other. I don't recommend that people run away, but that's what I did.

I was very afraid, but I didn't call the cops. I know how the justice system treats our people and how it deals with women who have experienced domestic abuse. The justice system has failed us so many times. I have seen examples of how long domestic abuse cases are drawn out within the system. I know I should have called the police, but I didn't.

I was grateful my son was safe. In talking with my mom and my stepdad, I thought about how raising a child is a privilege. My mom never raised any of her kids. I love my mom and I forgave her because of what she went through, I understood. So I gave her a second chance to be a parent. My mom and my stepdad have worked on themselves through the years. Going through the Alternative Dispute Resolution process, my mom had access to therapy. I told my mom, "I want you to experience the gift of raising a child with a sober state of mind."

My son has lived with them in Thompson since then. He's been with them eleven years now. I told him, "I love your granny. She needs to raise you because she went through so much." He is happy and doesn't want to come back to the city.

After I got to the Rez, I lived with my best friend Karen. I was a waitress and a bartender at a bar in the Interlake. That's where I met a lot of great people and made another best friend, Cheryl-Lee. I partied and had fun for a year and a half. But when I got pregnant, I couldn't stay out there and have a baby and be dependent upon someone else. One day I

I know how the justice system treats our people and how it deals with women who have experienced domestic abuse. The justice system has failed us so many times.

had just had enough of my baby's dad, and I packed up my duffel bag and hitchhiked back to Winnipeg. I needed my own space. That was 2012. I was thirty-two and four months pregnant. I left at the end of the month, on a payday when I knew there was going to be lots of traffic from Peguis to Winnipeg. Sure enough, someone I knew picked me up. I got dropped off right at Polo Park.

When I first came back to the city, I contacted Diane and told her I was back. I asked her if I could use her address in case someone needed to reach me. But I didn't want to burden her, so I couch surfed with friends. I tried to apply for work, but upon disclosing that I was pregnant, nobody wanted to hire me. It didn't matter what experience I had. I get that.

I became homeless. When you're homeless you spend a lot of time walking around and I ran into some of the kids I used to work with. "What are you doing here, Amy? You don't belong here." *Life. It's life my dears.* They knew I was having a hard time. It used to be me who helped them, but they helped me (told me where to go to get food and help). It's funny how things can come full circle.

I ended up at Sunrise Village at the Salvation Army on Main Street. What a horrible, horrible place. My first night there was just awful. I heard people drinking and yelling and throwing beer bottles. The bar was close by and the drunk tank was right next to the shelter. It was hard to sleep. I didn't feel very relaxed. It sounded like someone was being attacked in the back lane. That was the reality of that little area there by the Salvation Army and Thunderbird House. I ended up sharing a room with this woman, and she was pregnant as well. Her family had kicked her out. It's hard living with someone you don't know. You've got to watch your belongings. I also had to tell her to wash. It would be three, four days and she wouldn't have showered. You gotta worry about bedbugs too. I never even knew what bedbugs were before then.

But, like I said, I ran into kids I used to work with. The homeless community is made up of the nicest people you will ever meet. They'll help you out. They sat with me. I saw this girl I used to work with. We had kept in touch throughout the years, and we're still connected. She said, "Go to Pregnancy and Family Support Services. PFSS." That's how I got to know Thrive. (The Thrive Resource Centre used to be called Pregnancy and

Family Support Services.) She showed me where it was on Spence Street.

At Thrive I started off by using their phone to call the welfare office, and then I used their computer. Thrive had a free therapist, so after a while, I accessed their counselling. I needed to start talking to someone because that's the first point of helping yourself, right? At one point when I worked at MYS, I used to direct people to go to these resources. Now I was accessing them myself. Then, I started with the prenatal classes at Thrive and their nutrition bingos. They were welcoming, so whatever they offered, I started attending. I did it all.

I applied for welfare about a month after I returned to Winnipeg. It was an awful experience. I was made to feel like I was worthless. I'd already been a taxpayer for thirteen years. I had only accessed Maternity Employment Insurance once when I had my son, but I had worked for that. People access social assistance for many different reasons. When I tried to access it, I experienced such ugliness from workers. They made me feel I was just doing it to *use* the system. Even my worker who was Native gave me a hard time. I was trying to ask questions so I could understand. I said, "Why are you treating me like this?"

The worker said, "We can end this meeting right now and reschedule."

I learned right then and there that you don't ask questions and you don't challenge workers who are in these power positions.

When I started accessing services, then I started sharing my story. All of a sudden there were authorities involved, right? And that's the scary thing about when you're involving yourself in community resources; these people sitting on the other side of the desk, they hold the power. It's really hard to navigate the system and to know, *Okay, who's really going to help me?* We see it time and time again, especially in the EIA system.

And then I found out that All Nations Coordinated Response Network (ANCR) placed a Birth Alert on my unborn baby. ANCR is the first point of contact for anyone relaying a concern about a child. Then CFS is made up of a number of agencies that manage the files of all children in care. ANCR had sent a letter to Diane's place, so I called. Someone had anonymously called ANCR and asserted that I was homeless and wasn't going to have housing for my baby by the time it was born.

I don't know who called on me. Who would do that? Why didn't they just come talk to me? EIA knew I had used my mom Diane's address and ANCR and EIA work hand in hand. I suspected it was someone at EIA who told ANCR (but this is just speculation). I had revealed to one of the workers my concerns about being pregnant and homeless. I started thinking about who I could trust. I didn't want to work with someone I couldn't trust.

But anyone can anonymously phone the child welfare system and report on anyone else. A person can say anything and they don't have to prove whatever the allegations are. Automatically ANCR will contact you and open a file for three months. They don't tell you who calls. ANCR and CFS can become a system for vindictive people. I've known many people who've called just to fuck up someone's life, and *Boom*, right off the hop, their parenting rights are under scrutiny.

Trying to piece together who made the initial phone call is another part of the trauma. Everybody was a suspect. I was questioning professionals and friends and family, and then questioning myself. If the person calling was truly concerned, I get the concern, it's about a child. But at the same time, holy moly!

ANCR is a very cold place to walk into. Right away I was seen as a bad guy. They pulled up my past history of being a child in care and asked me all about it. *Why had I been in care?* I asked them what this had to do with me now or with helping me find housing? If you are or were a kid in care, CFS can and does use it against you. I know this as fact because of having worked in the system with social workers, emergency placement workers, advocates, and lawyers. I said, "No, you're not going to do that to me. This is about me and my child right now. You guys need to help me." They did not offer any assistance. I was able to have that conversation with these professional people, proving that they shouldn't have automatically assumed that I was fucking stupid because I was an Indian. They already had me stereotyped, when they knew jack shit about me.

The system is hard to navigate. Like, I needed housing to be able to bring my baby home, so I was trying to look for an apartment, but I didn't have enough money for the damage deposit. The only money I had was from EIA—enough for a single room, because EIA doesn't switch you over from a single income to a family income until you are seven months pregnant. So for a couple of months, I was on a single allowance, walking the fucking streets trying to find a place to live. Nobody wanted to even give me bus tickets. I walked so much that I bled and ended up in the hospital. Then welfare finally gave me bus tickets.

When I went to ANCR, they gave me an appointment at Addiction Foundation of Manitoba (AFM) because people who are involved in ANCR have to take a drug test, especially new clients. They wanted me to go that day; I think it was 4:30. But I already had an apartment viewing at the same time. With the lack of affordable housing, either you're the first person there for the apartment or forget it. ANCR wouldn't give me another appointment time for the drug test, so I was left with this fucking impossible decision. I went to see the apartment because that's what I needed the most. The next morning, I went to AFM at 9:00 a.m. and tried to explain why I had not come to the appointment the day before. The guy there told me I had to go back to ANCR to make another appointment. I went back right after that, but they denied me the appointment. They said I had to wait for my appointment with my new social worker.

When I was in the initial ANCR meeting, they had opened a file on my unborn baby and asked what CFS agency I would like to go with. They assumed that I would pick a First Nations agency, but I picked Métis CFS because I used to work in their emergency placement unit. ANCR questioned why I was choosing Métis CFS. I knew it was my right to pick whichever agency I wanted. ANCR was not supportive.

When I met my social worker at Métis CFS, there was an assumption that I would not have a home for my baby. There was no other discussion about what I might need; instead it was about what I had set up and what supports I had. They didn't offer to help me because sometimes CFS sees that help as being a crutch for the client.

I really needed to secure housing so I could tell CFS I had somewhere for my baby to live. When I was seven and a half months pregnant, I found something with the help of Diane and my foster aunt and uncle (her brother and his wife). EIA gives you only a certain amount of money for a security deposit, and I didn't have enough for this one-bedroom apartment that I had found. I told the woman on the phone, "I don't need to look at it, I'll just take it." At that point, Diane kicked in the rest of the money. Wow. And then Diane's brother and wife kicked in the furniture. I had everything that I needed when I moved into this place. I could not have been blessed with better or more caring people. I would not have had custody of my daughter if they hadn't stepped up and helped me.

When I told my EIA worker I had housing, she gave me a hard time about the amount of money that I would have to pay for rent. She knew that I was trying to secure housing so I could keep my baby. I also met with the social worker so she knew I had a place to live.

The welfare system was bullshit. The ANCR system was bullshit. It is as if they want to keep you down. EIA won't tell you that you're entitled to something (like a disability credit or diabetic allowance) unless you ask. What if there's a language barrier? Thankfully, I already understood the system from working in it, and I was able to stand up for myself. If I had no prior knowledge, they would have eaten me up. They would've taken my child right from birth. I also had the support system of my foster family who already worked for the CFS system, so they understood everything that was going on.

And I still had other connections like my clinical case manager, who was still involved in my life. And thank goodness for community resources at Thrive.

When I went into labour with my daughter, Diane took me to the hospital. The nurses in triage started speaking in a professional language that they didn't think I would understand, but I was listening. They used the word BA (for Birth Alert). They were planning to take my baby from me once she was born. They spoke about me in such a way that if I had no confidence, I would have believed that I wasn't worth anything and didn't deserve to have my baby come home with me. All their talk made me wonder, who has access to my history?

I piped up and said, "Just so you know, I can understand everything you are saying. And you know what? I think you need to check with my social worker, because this birth alert and all these restrictions have been lifted." They changed their tune quick. They were quiet after that. Thankfully, I was able to speak up for myself.

With my baby I had a very traumatic birth. She got stuck and she was born bruised. She was a ten-pound turkey! I had this tiny little nurse, of Asian descent, and after I pushed her out the first question the nurse asked was, "Your baby's ten pounds, did you eat a lot of McDonald's?"

I looked at her and said, "What? No."

"Well then you must be diabetic," she said. "What?" I said "No."

"Well then you must've had gestational diabetes?" she said. My legs were still in the stirrups. I was just floored.

And I looked at her and said, "I'm on welfare and I didn't have enough money to eat McDonald's every day. I just ate well."

I couldn't believe it. This is the kind of shit that my people are faced with all the time. None of this gets documented because people are reluctant to speak up.

After I got home from the hospital, my social worker came to my place to meet my baby. When she visited, she said, "Oh my god, I am shocked. I thought you were just in a rooming apartment." I had a fully finished apartment, with everything I needed. CFS closed the file for my baby by the time she was six months.

> I still have this pamphlet with the post-it note because that is my official documentation.

When I was involved with the CFS system, they expected me to provide all kinds of professional letters—finished this course, went through this assessment, was on this medical regime. But there was no professionalism given back to me as a mother who was involved in the system. When my file was closed, in my mailbox I found a Sleep Safe Baby pamphlet issued by the Province of Manitoba. On that pamphlet was a post-it note that read my name and said, "Your file has been officially closed," and then there was the social worker's name. No official letter. No letterhead. What? A fucking post-it note.

I still have this pamphlet with the post-it note because that is my official documentation.

After I had my daughter, I took parenting programs at Thrive. I took advantage of every program they had to offer. They had a volunteer sign up, so I signed up because I wanted to start volunteering. By then my daughter was close to two years old. I was going to take her to daycare. My EIA worker had led me to believe that it was a policy that

Amy ████████
Your File Has been
closed.
████████
May 2013

ZZᶻ

Please take a few minutes
to read this important information
on safe sleep practices.

Public Health   Agence de la santé
Agency of Canada   publique du Canada   Canada

ANDREW MAHON

I had to have my kid in daycare by age two. I had no idea. I was afraid my benefits would be cut, so I did what the EIA worker told me to do. I had wanted to start doing something more anyway, because staying on assistance is hard when you're used to working.

Later, when I got talking to people in the community, I found out that the EIA worker had been hustling me. You can stay home on EIA with your kids until they are six. Then you are required to enter Educational, Employment and Training for assessment. It worked out for me, but that worker could have set me up for fucking failure. She didn't know much about me.

In hindsight, the EIA worker pushed me. Thank you. It did get the ball rolling. I ended up getting my daughter into the daycare with Thrive. When I signed up to be a volunteer someone at Thrive said, "No. We can't ask you to be a volunteer."

I was just shocked. I said, "What? What do you mean?"

"Well, you see, we'd like to hire you instead."

"What? Are you for real?"

They're like, "Yeah."

That's how I started working for Thrive. My first job there was being a community resource worker. I scheduled games and crafts and helped with resources (providing emergency food, baby bags, and community resources). That was around 2014. I also worked in the thrift store.

The staff at Thrive saw something in me. They saw *me*—someone who was determined to get back on her feet. The workers there knew what I had gone through. Thrive was my home base. I lived close by. Thrive was where I went to have coffee and to connect. Then I branched out because they're connected with other community service delivery programs. I kept looking at what was posted on their resource board and learned where their community networks were. The only way that you're going to get back on your feet is if you help yourself. If I had stayed on my couch, none of this would've came to fruition. I would still be sitting there, feeling sad.

Once I got my daughter in daycare, EIA connected me with this Education, Employment and Training program. When I went through their assessments, the worker said, "You're way too advanced for this. What's going on here?" I started telling her about my history and my schooling and what I'd been doing. I had only two years of university left to finish. I felt very vulnerable because this little well-polished lady had the decision-making power. I brought her my university transcripts and I had to sell myself. I did a very good job though, because she said, "I'm going to take a chance on you, Amy." That was in the summer of 2015 and

by the fall I was back at U of W. I did my last two years of university and I did really well. My daughter was almost three when I started back to school.

Since the time she had been a year old, we'd been living in a big house converted into rooming house apartments at 501 Young Street. There was a period where nobody was doing any kind of caretaking, so I took it on my own to keep the grounds and the building clean. When the new owner bought the house, he asked, "Who's the caretaker?"

I said, "Well, I've been doing it."

He told me he'd give me a rent discount if I continued, so I did. He started moving in questionable people with questionable habits. Then the cockroaches and the bedbugs came. That's when I first started to really understand slum landlords. They are like a disease in this city, I can tell you. Low-income housing and people and addictions—that's a whole other book in and of itself. I learned a lot about housing and slum landlords and about the different management companies that prefer EIA clients because they have that green rent form for guaranteed rent payments.

When I didn't want to live in that building anymore, I told the landlord he had to move me. I was scared that the house was going to be burned up, which actually happened two years later. The landlord had another apartment block just down the back lane so he moved me into this new one-bedroom apartment when I was just starting university.

My first night there, my brother (who helped me move) said he thought maybe something had bit him. It was 11 p.m. We turned on the flashlight on the cellphone, and there were thousands of baby bedbugs. I had moved into an infestation. That's how I started going back to university. It was awful. I had to live with those bedbugs. I couldn't sleep. I couldn't eat. Thankfully, Thrive had given me bedbug supplies before I had moved, so, I was able to combat the bugs a little bit. But it took three weeks before the owner finally sprayed my suite. I had a broomstick with fresh tape on the end that I used for picking up those bedbugs. I kept changing the tape. And that's what I did all night my first day of university.

I continued on in school though. What was I going to do, quit university because of bedbugs? I had a full course load.

That first weekend there, I had the bedbugs, and then the lady above me was jamming her music loudly, and the next morning someone on the second floor tried to jump out the window and there were nine police officers on my front lawn. That was my first weekend after starting university!

I had to make sure that my daughter didn't have bedbug bites and that we didn't take bedbugs with us when we left the apartment. So, I was doing a lot of steaming and cleaning. I had bedbug bags on certain things. I was constantly monitoring my daughter. And then I had to sit down at the end of the day and do my university work. I got through it, but I ended up developing PTSD and going on some meds, which I'm now off of. I accessed a counsellor at the university. I knew this was going to affect my schooling.

> I had the bedbugs, and then the lady above me was jamming her music loudly, and the next morning someone on the second floor tried to jump out the window and there were nine police officers on my front lawn. That was my first weekend after starting university!

I ended up failing a statistics course because of those bedbugs.

I learned that bedbugs leave an enzyme on your liver. At one point after a blood test, my doctor was concerned that my liver was fatty. The first question she asked me was, "Do you drink?"

"No," I said. "I don't drink."

"Well, do you do hard drugs?"

"No, I'm going to university right now." Then I talked to her about the bedbugs. It turns out that when they bite you, they leave an enzyme in your body that settles on your liver. (How many people living in low-income housing are getting sick from being eaten by bedbugs?) I recently had blood tests again and my doctor said my fatty liver was corrected. I had been researching about how to heal my body. One superfood is turmeric. I talked to my doctor about this. I started putting turmeric, honey, and lemon juice in my diet as one of the ways to clean my liver.

My band denied paying for my first year of university, so Employment and Training paid for my tuition and books. EIA continued to fund me with a living allowance. I also worked part-time a little bit. With EIA, you're only allowed to make $200 a month before they deduct money from your cheques. I had touched base with them about my hours to make sure that it didn't go over too much. A year later I ended up getting off assistance altogether. My band paid for my last year of school because I had proven myself, and then I was able to start working a little bit more too. I was still going to school full-time right through, even summer courses. I completed all my courses in two years.

That's when I did my practicum at First Nations Family Advocate office with Assembly of Manitoba Chiefs (AMC). They are advocates in CFS involvement. My supervisor was Cora Morgan. Cora is a knowledgeable and amazing advocate who is working tirelessly to try and fix the system. She had three different projects and she wanted me to pick one. I picked the Birth Alerts. I went back to the Women's Hospital where my daughter had been born and I spoke with this lady in charge. She ran this department and answered my questions. She told me a lot about the birth alert system in Manitoba. I learned that birth alerts are not legislative practice. This decision to apprehend babies at birth was a top-down practice decided within the CFS and hospital systems. How do you even explain that kind of decision? I was so shocked. I took this information back to Cora. They were shocked as well.

Cora had wanted me to develop a pamphlet with information about what I did when I was navigating all these systems—CFS, EIA, community resources, housing etc.—when I came back to Winnipeg pregnant and homeless. She wanted me to explain how to work through being approached by ANCR and having an open file and birth alert placed upon you and all these hoops that you have to jump through. I did what I could but time was limited when doing the practicum.

AMC offered me a job for after I graduated, but I decided not to take it. My dream was always to be a CFS advocate, but when I was finally given that opportunity, I turned it down. I know I had a lot to contribute, but I had just had enough. I didn't want to work with trauma anymore. I was tired of being constantly triggered. Also, things are so different now than when I was a kid in care. The system was sick then, but it's worse now. There's so much systemic racism ingrained within CFS and these other institutions. As I see it, the Indian Residential Schools dissolved into provincial powers. Those provincial powers created the CFS system to control the problem of all these kids in care who came from parents that the government fucked up in the residential school system. How will CFS ever become functioning? There's such a high turnover rate for child and youth care workers. So many things in the CFS system are different from even ten years ago: the kids, the trauma, the addictions, and the family dynamics. The caseloads are higher. The kids have changed because of what they go through. There's so much more substance abuse, addictions, violence, but it's because of history. It's such a compounded problem.

That's why I went to the job I'm in now.

I'm a public servant in the federal government. I went from being broke, bus-shack homeless, and pounding these streets, to working as a public servant for Canadians. I was recruited at a University of Winnipeg career fair.

This lady approached me. She said, "I've been watching you. I was too late to get a booth. I'm with the federal government."

I looked at her and said, "I don't know, lady. Everything that I've heard about the federal government to do with my people has not been good."

She said, "I get it. But this job has to do with food. Everybody eats food."

I said, "Okay. Talk to me." She told me that she was with an Inspection Agency, and that they were looking at Indigenous students. She gave me her card and asked for my resumé. I was recruited. I get it. I'm a statistic. Creator watches us in ways that we don't even know. I took the job, and it's a good job.

In 2021 I found out I was classified as a Sixties Scoop survivor. It has to do with the removal of children who were adopted out or made permanent wards. The timeline is from the '60s to 1991. The claim is loss of culture and loss of language. It's loss of everything for fuck's sakes! I was speaking my language and living in proximity to my family and my Indigenous community before they moved me. I had to wait two and a half years for my paperwork to be processed.

In 2021 I struggled for a while when they first found the 215 residential school children (unmarked graves) in Kamloops because of history and the ways the government has disrespected my people.

Me and my daughter went to the Leg. (legislature) to put down children's shoes in remembrance of those children who were found. We were driving away when she said, "Mom, how can you work for the federal government when you know that they did this to babies? If I lived then," she said, "I would have been taken away. Maybe I wouldn't have come home. How can you work for the government when you know that they've done this to us purposely?" This is an eight-year-old questioning me. My own kid.

She's at that age where the kids are being taught in school about residential schools. This is constantly an open conversation with me and my daughter, trying to understand what happened to my Chapan.

While we were at the Leg., I approached Nahanni Fontaine, a provincial government MLA, and asked her, "How do you work for the government and be okay with it?" I said, "I'm a public servant and I'm having a really hard time right now wanting to go back to work."

She said, "We need strong women like you working in government. People who are willing to stand there and still say, 'No, it wasn't okay, but you're going to give me a job so I can take care of my family.' We need to be in those spaces. We need to be a part of that agency or that department, because what we have to say is important and our backstories matter when it comes to working for the federal government." I don't know Nahanni Fontaine at all, but I had to talk with her when I saw her. She's also human and going through this experience.

Her words stayed with me—*Because we need you there*. We need to be in those spaces. Because we do belong there.

These truths that were revealed that summer have been a part of our daily lives in our communities. The Indigenous community has always known. I thank the universe that those little kids were found. Purposely exterminated! That's a real fucking harsh reality to deal with.

I took time off from my work to go to my university graduation in June 2017. It took me sixteen years, on and off, to get my four-year degree, but that's life, right? You just have to keep going back. I had my two kids in between. I graduated from Menno Simons College at the University of Winnipeg. I attained a four-year Bachelor of Arts in Conflict Resolution Studies. When I graduated, the dean of Menno Simons asked three or four of us to each give a speech. Because

ANDREW MAHON

it was a small group and we had been studying conflict resolution, which can be very personal, we all got to know our professors really well. It was a beautiful place to go to school, and a place where I met so many great people. *They knew me*. The school was proud of me and they knew how much I struggled just to finish.

My mom (my real mom) was the only one who came to my graduation. It's funny how things worked out. Other people were supposed to come; however, life happened, and they couldn't make it. My mom came into the city the day before and she stayed with me. She helped me get ready. I wore my moccasins and my ribbon skirt. I had leather in my hair and a feather on my cap. I made it known that I was Indigenous. What a feeling! As I was walking across the stage, in my heart I thought *This is for you, mom.* (I obviously did this for myself too.) To me, this was the best gift I could have given my mom, because she never got that chance to go to university herself. My mom wanted to become a teacher, but her future was stolen from her by the residential school system. It stole everything that would make a person confident in themselves.

Then I took my mom to Menno Simons, where I did my big speech. I'm not a public speaker, but get me up there and I'll win that crowd! And I did. I spoke to a room full of people, something I never thought I would ever do. I talked about how hard I had worked and some of the obstacles I faced. I spoke about Indigenous history. I thanked my mom too. I told her I was proud of her, for surviving after everything she had been through.

What am I most proud off? That I'm okay. I can recognize I'm a train wreck some days, but I'm still okay. I'm most proud of not having my children go through the system. I can sit and talk to my child and navigate parenting. I'm proud of having created a healthier family. It's something that some of us have had to relearn as Indigenous people, because the government purposely broke that. My people have suffered so much. The government and the church fucked up our family functioning systems a long time ago with the removal of children to residential schools. My generation is navigating and learning how to be traditional parents again. It's been a relearning for me, absolutely. I'm proud that I have done that.

My mom did instill in me a lot of things that I still do today. She taught me about cleanliness, about manners and being well

> My mom (my real mom) was the only one who came to my graduation. It's funny how things worked out.

groomed. She also taught me about sticking up for my brother and sister.

It sucked that our mom grew up the way that she did, because it made her a difficult parent. But I absolutely forgive her today. I can't hold her accountable for something that she learned as a child. At some point we have to grow up as adults and let that shit go. We can't keep holding things against people who were once children and who had no choice.

When my mom got hit with COVID in 2020, I had to drop the animosity and all those negative feelings. Everything. None of it mattered. I took care of her until I sent her back up North. I thought *This is my mom, this is my duty.* It's just my nature. I've always been like that. I guess that comes from understanding another person's point of view, understanding that they are managing their internal struggles and whatever they're going through as best as they can at the time. I always think about others because I know what it feels like to struggle. I believe that helping others comes back to us in different ways.

The mothering instinct of Indigenous women has been suppressed over the years. But I've become better and better at listening to myself and to that instinct because I did have many different females in my life. Diane has been the most consistent one. If it wasn't for her, honestly, I really don't know where I would be. Diane accepted me as her own. She is my special mom and will continue to be my mom.

I feel like I let my son down as a mother. But when I let him go to my mom, I was doing what I thought was the best protection for him. I don't want to say I regret it, because in a way I don't. But I also do. I wish that my mom had let him come home to me when I said that I was settled again and had my own place. But he didn't come home. He had relationships. You always want to do best for your children. I didn't want to remove him from that. I'll forever be his parent. I'm very proud of the young man he has become. He's well mannered and well behaved. I couldn't ask for a better son.

When I look into my daughter's eyes, I see a happy spirit. I see a non-traumatized child. I'm so grateful for that. She may be mad because I took away the iPad or because I didn't get her a Coffee Crisp bar, but she's not mad because I didn't feed her, or because the table is full of beer bottles and the house is messy. She will never experience what I went through. My girl doesn't know what it means to be without. She lives such a privileged life and she doesn't even know it.

Privilege is a loaded word. I don't even like the word because to be honest, I have associated it with whiteness. But privilege should not be associated with just skin colour. It can be based on money, class, where you live. It's not only white people who can be privileged. We have air conditioning; I have a new car—that's privilege! The pandemic has highlighted privilege because not everyone has had a place where they could isolate. I have to reframe the rhetoric. Now I understand what privilege is, but I also understand the different types of privilege and what they come with. I could feel privileged walking into an Indigenous ceremony when someone else doesn't feel as welcomed, or I could feel underprivileged walking into university. Knowing how to survive is a privilege too! I worked really hard to get back on my feet financially, but I always tell my girl to be grateful for what she has. It could be taken away… just like that.

Sometimes I take my daughter back to the Salvation Army's Sunrise Village. I've come back from fuck-all, bus-shack broke, homeless. I've smelled those piss-stained streets. I know what hopelessness looks and feels like. And I know what giving up on life looks like. I take her back there to remind her of the struggles we had and to remember where she came from. I remind her how hard I've worked for her and to be grateful.

Where I'm at right now is a pretty good spot for someone who's been through what I've been through in my life. I'm very grateful that I have the things that I have, even though they're minimal. Having minimal is okay. With everything I've been through in life, I know having lots of stuff is not what's important. Eventually you begin to realize that material things are just… nothing, right? What's most important are people and genuine relationships. Genuine.

> When I look into my daughter's eyes, I see a happy spirit. I see a non-traumatized child. I'm so grateful for that.

When people ask me how I find my book participants, I often say that the universe provides them, and it can even feel like a participant has dropped from the sky. This happened with Amy. In 2017 after my second book, Redemption, *launched, I was invited to a small coffee shop on Sargent to give a reading. It was an intimate group and a great evening together. Someone in the audience asked what my next book would be about, so I told them the topic of this book. As the audience was leaving, a woman named Kristy McClosky came up to tell me she knew of a very good person for me to interview—a woman named Amy whom she had worked with at Thrive. Fast-forward three years and I tracked Amy down through the staff at Thrive. Amy was generous enough to hear out my invitation and then accept it! She is a big-hearted person. Amy told me that she participated in this book wanting to send the message "You will get through this and you can become more than what you are labeled as."*

*Amy has changed the names of her foster parents for their privacy.

Marlyn

A lot of people think that because I'm a university professor, I've lived a privileged life. But they don't know my backstory. I'm the black sheep of the family because I haven't fallen prey to the colonial stereotypes that impact Indigenous people. All my siblings I'm in contact with have had substance abuse issues. I feel the after-effects of this. It's tough knowing that what my siblings experienced was the result of colonization, poverty, and all the things that have happened to us as a people, and as a family. I'm the person my siblings came to when they got into trouble. Reluctantly, I've been the rock; the one they thought could help them.

I love my siblings, and I've tried to help them as much as I could, but I couldn't fix their problems. It was a burden to know that with all my education, with all the money I make, I couldn't help them. I work in social work, and I've studied the human condition. There's a whole world out there that most people are not aware of. It's a world of survival. Many Indigenous families are fragmented—one of the insidious *gifts* that comes from being colonized. Part of that fragmentation is because of the addictions in our families, which are there because there is a lot of hurt. Before anger, the first thing

ANDREW MAHON

a person feels is hurt, and so many of our people have been hurt. Then they either hurt themselves or hurt their family members. The sad thing is that we've all been living our lives as if each of us is the only one who has had these experiences.

The earliest childhood memory I have is from when I was a baby. I remember looking up at a hole at the top of a tipi and feeling that I was lying on fur. When I shared this story with my aunt, she said, "Well, when you were a baby it was summertime, and your great-grandparents were still alive, so you were probably in their tipi outside your grandparents' house." My grandparents had two different houses over the years. First they had a log house that was just one room, and everybody slept in it. But it started to fall into disrepair, so they built a new home that was divided in three. On one side was the kitchen; another space was the living area with the wood-fire stove, and the third room was a bedroom. Everybody slept in there. Nobody had their own bedroom. Eventually they put in electricity. And I remember the swing they used to make for babies. It was like a hammock, made out of string and a blanket and then they put a pillow in it. That's

where the baby would sleep. The babies were probably my cousins; most of my cousins live on reserve.

My mom came from a large family—she had twelve siblings. There were a lot of tragic deaths amongst my mom's siblings. One of my uncles hung himself. An aunt came to live in the city when she married a non-Indigenous man. They divorced, and he took the kids away from her. I think that broke her. She frequented the hotels on Main Street. One day she drank a concoction of rubbing alcohol and it basically scrambled her brain and she subsequently died. Another one of my aunts was murdered on our reserve. Someone ran her over with a car when she was walking home late at night.

My mother had six children—two boys and four girls. This is my memory of our history. The oldest is my brother. He is older than me by three years. He didn't live with us because our family had the practice that the first-born would stay with the grandparents because they would need help. So, my brother grew up with all of his cousins as if they were his siblings. (In our culture, our cousins are considered our brothers and sisters.) We had a baby sister in between my brother and me who died in a house fire before I was born. We three have the same father. Our father was from Ebb and Flow First Nation, which is the next community north of Sandy Bay where my mom grew up. It's about an hour and a half away. We're Ojibway. I used to speak my language when I was younger.

My father was eighteen years older than my mom. My understanding is that they met in a bar in Amaranth where he and his brothers played in a fiddle band. He already had other children, so I have half brothers and sisters in Ebb and Flow. I've met only one of them, but people tell me I look so much like certain people in that family. They all knew who my dad was. I don't know what the story is between my mother and my father, but I do know that when my mom was still alive, he would often try to come and visit us and my mom wouldn't let him. So, there was always the question in my mind about why my mom wouldn't let us see him when he was our dad.

My younger sister was born closely after me—one year, less eleven days. That's when my mom married a non-Indigenous man. He was a white man with green eyes and blond hair. My sister inherited his green eyes and had reddish, auburn hair. I don't know what

happened to my mom's marriage, but at some point after my mom moved off the reserve with him, he abandoned her. I've seen photos of him, but I don't recall ever meeting him. He never came around. After that relationship ended, my mom had two more children, my youngest sister and my younger brother, who have different fathers.

When my mom married, she lost her status as an Indian. So, when their relationship ended, my mom couldn't go back to live on her reserve. That was really hard on her. At that time, according to the Indian Act, if you married outside of the community you were not allowed to live there anymore. Even if you were getting divorced, you were not allowed to go back to the reserve. That was a sign of racism.

People don't talk about the Indian Act. They don't talk about the laws and rules and policies that impact us, but we feel it right at ground level. The Indian Act is still in place today, but some sections have been removed to try and correct some of the inequality in the legislation. (For example, Bill C-31 is an amendment to remove discriminatory provisions that affected primarily Indigenous women and their children. There is a further amendment Bill C-3 that attempts to correct residual discrimination where Indigenous women were still losing their Indigenous status one generation before men did). But there is still substantial inequality regardless. There is no other group in Canada that is legislated and has to negotiate for their rights. Indigenous lawyer Pam Palmater has written extensively on how the Indian Act is being used to eradicate our rights as Indigenous people, so that at some point in the future we will be legislated out of being and the fiscal responsibility of the federal government on Indigenous lives would eventually end. Although the Indian Act is outdated, it's still a connection with the rights of Indigenous peoples.

There is no other group in Canada that is legislated and has to negotiate for their rights.

When my mom lost her status as an Indian we found ourselves here in Winnipeg. We moved to Winnipeg when I was about six years old. My mother decided that she wanted all of her kids together, so when she moved out of the community, my brother came with us. He was about ten. I felt like I met my brother for the first time when we moved to the city. He had gone to residential school in Sandy Bay. It was a day school run by nuns and priests. He was physically abused in that school, and he talked about it. My brother had some challenges trying to find his way in the world. There is research showing that many Indigenous people struggled as a result of their residential school experiences. My brother was always in trouble, even when he came to live with us. I was fortunate I didn't have to go to residential school because we were already off reserve by then.

I feel like my memory starts when we moved to the city. Although before we moved, I do have a vague memory of my younger sister and me living with someone else, so we were probably apprehended when we were younger. It happened over Christmas time, because I remember we got Christmas gifts at this home. We weren't very old; I think I must have been around four and my sister would have been around three. The home was somewhere out in the country, but I don't know where. The only things I remember are that the person was very kind to us, and that our stay was short term.

I have very few fond memories of when we lived in Winnipeg. My mom did a lot of drinking. She was an alcoholic, so we had a pretty tough life. There was a large influx of Indigenous people moving into the city then, and there was a lot of racism. It was in the way people talked to us and treated us and where we lived. I noticed the things that people would say to us about being dirty Indians. (I was a thinker. I saw the inequity and the things that I thought were wrong in my young mind.) My mother hung out at all the bars, those stereotypical places where Indigenous people are on the street corners, like The Occidental on Main Street. Indigenous people came together in those places where they felt comfortable, where they were accepted. It just happened to be in the bars. Many of them, like my mom, became alcoholics because of the inequality, the racism and the poverty at that time, and from being separated from their communities.

When our family first arrived in Winnipeg, we lived on the second floor of a house on McMillan Avenue. I went into Grade 1 at LaVérendrye School. But we moved around quite a bit. We lived out by Higgins and then in the Manitoba Housing on Doncaster. Every year we went to a different school. I was in Grade 4 when we lived on Doncaster. I went to Carpathia School. Mrs. Ford was my teacher and she encouraged us. I liked school then and I remember winning an art award. Later, when I was eleven, we lived in an apartment at the corner of Vaughn and Ellice. It's not there anymore. My mom used to make us go to Calvary Temple every Sunday. We went to church without her. I hated going because that meant when we came home, our mom would be drunk or there'd be different men there.

It seemed that our family took the Greyhound bus almost every other weekend from Winnipeg to Sandy Bay First Nation because that was my mom's home. Our aunts, uncles, cousins and grandparents were there. That's where my mom felt comfortable. That was our family. I spent a lot of time with my cousins, probably while the adults were drinking. My mom drank there; they all did. That was normal to me. We would hang out with our cousins, be out on the land. We played around and did all kinds of the things kids do. It was fun.

I don't remember if there was really any kind of connection to culture back then.

There wasn't anything much happening on reserve that was culturalized, though I do remember going to some kind of Pow Wow celebration that happened on the reserve. A lot of people were there. And we used to spend a lot of time on the land with our grandparents. They had horses, and we used to go root picking.

It's funny because now when I go home to the reserve, every once in a while I'll meet someone and they'll say, "Oh, I knew your mother." They'll kiss me on the cheek and say, "I'm your auntie so and so." It's amazing, just how many people know me, but I don't know them. They knew me as a child. That makes me feel like there's this whole side of my identity that has been ripped away. These people knew my mother. I only have a memory of my mom until a certain time. I have questions about the missing pieces of my story. That makes me think that they may know some things that I don't know. *How did things happen the way they did?*

I was in Grade 1 when my youngest brother was born, in 1969 or 1970. My mom met his dad at the lumberyard that was right beside our duplex on Logan. He worked there. I think his cultural background was Ukrainian. My siblings and I wondered where our baby brother came from. My mom had a naturally big belly, so we didn't know she was pregnant. And then one day about two months after he was born, he was gone. He was adopted out, as part of the Sixties Scoop. My understanding from my aunts is that my mother was told that he needed to be adopted because my mom was not going to get any more social assistance for another child. So that was a decision that my mom had to make. I don't know how true that is, but there were a lot of horrendous things that were done to Indigenous mothers. Things were held over their heads. I do know who his father is, and he was married. The decision to give my youngest brother up for adoption might have been made with that consideration. I don't know for sure. All I can say is that was probably a heartbreaking decision for my mom. She had to put aside her feelings. After that, my mom's drinking escalated.

We siblings spent a lot of time alone by ourselves as young kids, and oftentimes we didn't have food. We used to beg our mom not to drink. She would say, "Sure, okay." I think she loved us, but we had questions in our mind about that. My mom's alcoholism really put her girls in very precarious situations where we were at risk and vulnerable to abuse. All three of us sisters were sexually abused by my mom's Ukrainian boyfriend (my younger brother's father). I think he chose my mother because she had three girls. As well, one of my sisters was abused by other men who came into our home.

As a child I didn't understand the political realities of the day for Indigenous people. I didn't know why my mom drank. But now I think her drinking was in response to a combination of the disadvantages she faced as an Indigenous woman as well as having attended residential school as a child. My mom never talked about her time in residential school. I learned about it from her sisters (my aunts) later on, after she passed away. I went on the Truth and Reconciliation Commission's website and accessed old school records. I found her name there. As I got older, I did have anger because my mother never talked about her experience. I believe that her time at residential school informed everything about who she was. I was deprived of any of that knowledge. And, now that I'm older, I have a better understanding of why my mom was the way she was. I hold residential

ANDREW MAHON

schools accountable for all of what happened to our family. All of it. When I use the term *residential schools* it is inclusive of all those things that led to residential schools, including government legislation and outdated ways of thinking about our people. That all helps explain my mom's behaviours, our poverty, and why we didn't grow up in our community. All these factors could even explain why my mom got sick so young. My mom was diagnosed with leukemia and nine months later she died. She was only thirty-two.

I had just turned twelve when my mom got sick. I think I was in Grade 7. When my mom was in the hospital, Children's Aid didn't put us in a foster home. At that time, they had homemakers, so they put a homemaker in our home. Maybe there was an assumption that my mom would eventually get better, or at least there was a hope that she would. We had two women who came to live with us. The first one was a little French lady—Mrs. Fontaine. She was just so fabulous to us. She slept in my mom's bed and she was with us full time. There were some times on weekends where she would go home and we would have another lady. She was a Black lady with a very thick accent. She was so good to us too. There was a bit of time where our mom seemed like she was okay, so she came home from the hospital. But that was very short-lived and soon she was back in the hospital and then died shortly thereafter. It happened really fast.

I felt a sense of responsibility for my siblings. I had always taken on the mother role and had looked after my siblings before my mom got sick. I was the one who got them up and ready for school and fed them. I had to do that because when you are the child of a parent with addictions, you switch roles.

My siblings had a number of problems that I couldn't control. While my mom was sick, my older brother was in trouble for stealing cars. He stole a lot of cars and hung out with the wrong crowd. When my mother passed, he was already in the Portage Home for Boys. My younger sister tried to kill herself when our mom was dying. She was eleven. She didn't want to live if our mother was going to die. When my mother had a short remission and came home, some of her medication had been left at home. My sister OD'd on that medication, so she went into a psych ward for children. It was right across the street from the Health Sciences Centre where my mom was in the ICU. My mom never knew that one of her children was having that much mental distress as she lay dying. I suspect my sister was FASD (Fetal Alcohol Spectrum Disorder) affected. I'm not one hundred percent certain because she was never diagnosed, but she was always a bit slower and had difficulties.

My last memory of my mom is of her in the hospital, very skinny, emaciated. The bed railings were all wrapped with blankets because she could kick them and bruise herself. I do remember at that time my mom telling us that she loved us. My mother died April 9th, 1975. There was a funeral held in Sandy Bay with an open casket. I remember kissing my mother and feeling how cold and hard she was.

When we got back to Winnipeg after my mom's funeral, we stayed in the home with the homemakers but our furniture was slowly sold off. (That was probably a directive from child welfare. I don't know for sure. I was not a part of any decision-making.) It was really surreal, and it made me mad because they were taking things out of our home: our TV, tables, beds. Eventually we all had to go our separate ways. My sister was still in the psych ward. My youngest sister and I went into a foster home together where they had adopted six Indigenous children. There were three girls and three boys, plus us. The foster parents were quite elderly for foster parents—maybe in their sixties. They were white and lived in East Kildonan.

One day, shortly after we came, the rest of the family went off shopping and I was left at home alone with the man. The phone rang, but I was in mourning and I was living with strangers, so I wasn't answering their phone. It just rang and rang so I ended up answering it. It was his wife calling for him. She said, "Put him on the phone." When I went into the room to get him, he was masturbating in front of a pornography magazine. I'm sure he did that on purpose. Having been sexually abused by my mother's boyfriend, I knew this man's actions were not appropriate. I thought *Where the fuck did CFS put us? Where are we living?*

That man also used to say really sexually inappropriate things to me. I brought it up with the other girls living there and they said, "Don't worry about it. He's harmless, that'll stop." I thought it was really weird. My youngest sister was only eight years old, but there were inappropriate things that this man did to her, sexual type things. I told my social worker and he said I had an overactive imagination. Right.

Shortly after we went into this home my youngest sister and I went to camp in Ontario for two weeks. (I think the social workers must have planned that.) I loved that camp. It was really good. It was a healing thing for me, but then we came back from that camp.

This family had a son who was a farmer and we drove to their son's farm and stayed there. It was in between Sandy Bay and Ebb and Flow. We drove right past Sandy Bay and we couldn't go see our family, even though they were so close. I had no connection with any of my friends or my family. It was just me and my youngest sister. We spent the rest of the summer out at this farm. The other kids bullied me. There were a lot of hurtful things done to me.

When we came back to the city to go to school, the family had moved to a big house on Pritchard Avenue. I was so happy about that because my friend lived very close by. I asked if I could go visit her. I took my little sister with me. I told my friend about what had been going on. I told her not to tell anybody, but unbeknownst to me, she went downstairs after she heard my story and she told her mother. Her mother called Children's Aid and said, "They're not going back to that home," and we never went back. My sister and I stayed at my friend's place for a while.

Children's Aid worked to see if they could find a family we could live with. They found my aunt who lived in Calgary, so we went there. My younger sister was let out of the psych ward, so she came to live there with us too. But that didn't work out either. My aunt had her own six kids. This particular aunt and my mother never got along. She was horrible to us. I went to a Catholic school when I was there and I had a hard time making friends. I always wondered *How come me?* It seemed like my sisters were so carefree and nonchalant and that nothing ever bothered them, but everything bothered me. I felt very depressed and talked to a guidance counsellor. I told him if I didn't get out of my aunt's house, I was going to kill myself. He must've talked to somebody because my aunt was livid and sent us all back to Winnipeg. That would have been when I was in Grade 8.

When we got back to Winnipeg, we were split up again. My younger sister and I went into a group home for girls our age, and my youngest sister went into a different group home because Children's Aid said she was too young to go into a group home with older girls. My younger sister and I went to live in a great place called Pathways Group Home for Girls. It was on St. John's Avenue and then was moved to Mountain Avenue. There was one for boys too. The homes were run by John Rogers who also ran the Main Street

Project. He had responsibility for these group homes on top of all the work that he did with Indigenous and homeless people. A married couple named Bev and Barry were the group home parents. They were awesome, and so good to us.

When we lived with Bev and Barry, they had their son and their granddaughter living there too. Barry was one of these people who knew how to talk to people from all walks of life: rich or poor, addicted or homeless, a kid or a teenage girl. He was gifted in so many ways and connected with people on so many levels. Barry worked at the Main Street Project too. He eventually died of complications from diabetes. I still talk to his family.

Bev and Barry used to take us everywhere. We went shopping and had activities. Every Wednesday we went bowling or roller-skating, or to a movie or the drive-in or the park. We all learned to cook for each other. We had rules and responsibilities that we had to abide by but we had fun. It was the best place I could ever live. I absolutely loved Bev

... my sister and I went back to the same group home, but our youngest sister was adopted by this family in Pennsylvania. They took her because she looked white.

and Barry. There were eight girls total in the home. Most were Indigenous. They were intimidating at first, but once I got to know the girls, I loved them too.

But one day Bev and Barry said to us, "We're leaving. It's too hard. We're going to go run a halfway home for men coming out of prison." So, they left. Change always happens right? When that change happened, it ruined everything. There were new group home parents. They were an Indigenous couple. It just wasn't the same. They did not treat us like Bev and Barry had. They had different values. And because they were new and had not grown into their roles, they were very strict.

There was a desire to reunite us three sisters, so we went to live in a new foster placement. But the woman was extremely religious. Oh my god, it was horrible! We were like little devils to her, so that only lasted a couple of months. She didn't want to have anything to do with us.

After that my sister and I went back to the same group home, but our youngest sister was adopted by this family in Pennsylvania. They took her because she looked white. She was eleven. The social workers told us our sister would have this great life, "She's going to have everything that you guys have never had: a four-poster bed, all the toys that she wants, and she's going to be really looked after. Don't you want that for your sister? Don't you want her to have a really good life?" Of course, we said yes, but that meant they took her away.

In the group home there was one bedroom in the house that didn't have to be shared. It had a sink, and a balcony off the side. You had to work your way into having this room. It was a privilege. They had to trust you. All the other bedrooms in the house were shared. I was eventually given that room.

Shortly afterwards, I ran away and was put into the Manitoba Youth Centre. I was in Grade 9 then. It's actually quite a funny story. This Indigenous couple had their own kids who lived in the group home with us. They had this young little one who was biting everyone, so I bit him back. It was just to show him how it felt to be bitten. I did not draw blood.

Everybody said to me, "You can't do that. You'll be in trouble."

I said, "Okay, fine. I'm going to run away." I'd never done anything so crazy. I went to a friend's place. They tracked me down and the police took me to the Manitoba Youth Center. I told the police officer, "I was just trying to teach that little boy a lesson." But the group home parents wanted me in that youth center. It was scary having to go there, thinking that what I did was so bad it warranted going into a place like that. It was a prison for kids! The staff there took everything away from me because there had been instances of young people killing themselves in there with their own possessions.

I still think to this day that it was crazy that I went there. No one told me I was being charged with anything (for example assault). Nothing was explained to me. It was not like I even bit this kid viciously. He was an adorable kid, but sometimes you just give a little example back of what they're doing to people. I stayed in the youth detention centre for a month. Afterwards I went back to the group home, but they were not kind to me. I was walking on eggshells.

On the darkest and the hardest days, I used to say to myself *I'm a good person. I don't deserve this. Things will get better. This is just one day.* No matter how much people underestimated me, I have always tried to overcome that.

When I was in high school, I was part of the track team, I played in the Handbell Choir, and I was part of a musical singing group. My friends were doing all those things too so they encouraged me. It was fun. But the group home limited how many extracurricular activities I could be involved in. I had to come home from school at a certain time. We all had chores and responsibilities. I could only pick one thing, so I picked the Handbell Choir over the track team.

One of my Handbell Choir friends told me about the home she was staying at, so, near the end of Grade 11, I went there. It was my last placement. They were a couple with a young son. They treated me well, although we had some differences of opinion. I had a summer job working at a movie theatre while I lived there. I left that home a week before I turned eighteen. As a kid in care, you are constantly told that eighteen is the magic number, that you will be an adult then. I had tunnel visions about leaving. I went to live with the non-Indigenous man I was marrying. That was my way of dealing

with turning eighteen and leaving the foster system. He was a bus driver who I met while taking the bus to work at the movie theatre and we hit it off. I was too young to be married. That was March of 1981, and I graduated Grade 12 in June. It was a lot of change. It was hard.

Pretty much all my life I felt I didn't belong, because first of all I was Indigenous, right? We were just taken away from our family, our whole world. I did not understand the implications of having no mother at a young age. Then I went into homes where it wasn't my bedroom, it wasn't my furniture, they weren't my parents, these weren't my people. Sure some of them were really nice, and they tried, but I never felt like I belonged. Things were always temporary. I was never sure how long I was going to be there. I would think, *How long will these people like me? Once they find out who I really am then they won't want me anymore.*

My ex-husband and I were married for seven years before we got divorced, but we didn't have any children. The relationship actually ended around year four or five and then I moved out on my own. I was too immature to be in a relationship and to make that kind of commitment to someone.

One day early in my marriage, I saw this young woman standing on my steps and at first didn't know who she was. Then I did a double take and said, "Oh my god, that's my youngest sister." She just showed up on my doorstep. Unannounced. We used to correspond by mail, but I hadn't seen her in a long time, since she was eight years old. Her adoptive parents had just put her on a plane and sent her back to Canada. I talked to them, so I know what happened. Her adoption placement broke down when she was fifteen. She had been prostituting and doing hard drugs in the US. She didn't do these when she was first back in Winnipeg, but these behaviours eventually resumed. She lived with us for a while, but she was a wild child. I couldn't handle her. We ended up talking with Children's Aid, and they put her into independent living. She was able to live on her own with a social worker overseeing her. I've been through hell and back with that sister. She's been addicted to heroin, cocaine—you name it. She's done everything. I've been through drug withdrawal with her so many times, where she's been hospitalized. She's had a very rough life. Very rough.

After my divorce, I had a relationship with another non-Indigenous man, who was abusive. I've got the scars that remind me every day of what I will never, ever go back to. I think I had very low self-esteem at that time because I saw the erosion of my marriage as a failure. I saw myself as a failure. I was about twenty-four when I met person number two. I lived with him for maybe two years after that. At first, I thought this second relationship was a good one, but when I moved in with him, this ugly side of him came out. He was an alcoholic and like a Dr. Jekyll/Mr. Hyde. He was good and kind when he was sober, but when he was drunk, he was mean and destructive, hurtful and physically and emotionally violent. I got called every name under the sun. The ones he used the most were *dirty Indian* and *dirty squaw*. He accused me of all these heinous things that most Indigenous women get accused of, such as being a slut. At the time, I was working at a huge law firm, and he said I had gone to bed with every single male lawyer that was in the firm. I said, "I don't know if you know how law firms work, but we actually have to do work there." One night he was drunk and he struck me in the eye, and I had a huge welt and bleeding profusely. My eye was swollen and my neighbours took me in to emergency.

When I was about twenty-four I started working in that law firm as a legal secretary. The people I worked with were always encouraging and helpful. I found that healthy. When I moved out from person number two, I had two jobs. I worked full time in the law firm, and then I worked at the YMHA (Young Men's Hebrew Association) fitness facility on Hargrave Avenue. I learned a lot there and found it healing working with the Jewish community. They have been persecuted and have suffered; yet they still soldiered on and became a strong people. They didn't let what happened to them in the past define them.

I split from that second guy in 1989. I continued to work at the law firm, but I kept thinking, *I've got to do something with my life*. I wanted things, and I felt like I needed to have a shift and a change in my life, so I embarked on a journey to the University of Manitoba. That was pretty scary because no one in my family had ever been to university. I had no mentors. I'm an introvert and a quiet person, so my field of influence was very, very small. At that time, my psyche was beaten from having lived with that second man. I decided to go to university because there was something in me that felt I deserved better. I told myself I couldn't look for it in a man (as a young person you're told that your self-worth is tied up in whether you have a relationship, children, and own a home.) I was coming from a different context as an Indigenous woman who grew up in care, who had a fractured family and no strong ties with her own community. I was brave, and I said to myself, "I want this. I'm going to try it." I figured that my strength was in my wanting to learn.

My grades were average in high school. I did okay, but no one ever mentored me and said, "You know what, you should go to university." I've always loved reading, and I thought, *If I could read all these books, that must be what education is all about, because you need to read to learn*. That's exactly what reading did for me; it made me want to go on and learn.

Unfortunately, in my last year of university, I hooked back up with guy number two again. He said he had changed and that he had always loved me. Blah, blah, blah. I got sucked back into it. I was still working at the law firm and did a lot of the lawyers' work so I figured, *Hell if I can do this work for them, I can be a lawyer.* I decided to apply to all of these law schools but I didn't tell my boyfriend I was doing this. I had to save my money because it was like $50 for every university that I applied to, and I applied to twelve. That was a lot of money, but I was determined I was going to get into law school. That was a very tumultuous time because living with an abusive man was up and down, and I was trying to finish my degree. I got accepted by ten law schools.

I took a woman's studies course from Dr. Janice Ristock during the final year of my undergrad that changed my life. That course was really the linchpin for me to leave my abusive boyfriend the second time and go to law school. Reading the accounts of other women who had been abused and learning from other students who had had similar experiences taught me that it was a more common experience than I realized. When you are in a violent relationship you often feel like you're the one who has done something wrong and the one with deficits. The course helped me realize that I had to get away from my abusive relationship. I would not have done well at law school in that kind of environment.

I felt empowered. So, I moved out, put all my stuff in storage, got on a plane and moved to Ottawa to go to law school. I wanted to be as far away from this guy as I could. I took a chance getting on that plane and trying to start a new life. I had never been to Ottawa, and I didn't have a lot of savings. That was 1992.

I had no place to live, so when my plane landed in Ottawa, I found a newspaper and answered an ad for a roommate. I phoned from the airport and they came and picked me up there. It was a mother and a daughter. They were kind to me at first, but then they turned out to be terrible people and very discriminatory to me. There were certain things they did to me that were very hurtful. They opened my mail and read it (including a letter from my doctor with test results). They accused me

> When you are in a violent relationship you often feel like you're the one who has done something wrong and the one with deficits.

of horrible, stereotypical things, like being sexually promiscuous. When they realized I was Indigenous they had the locks changed. I had to ask for permission to come in or leave. I wanted to have a separate phone line in my bedroom (this was before cellphones), but they wanted it installed in the basement. They told me if I didn't like that I could leave. I lived with them for a total of fourteen days before they evicted me.

When I left, I went to the dean of the law school and said I was going to have to quit school because I had nowhere to live. He told me there was no way I was going to quit after working so hard to get there. They got me an emergency bursary and put me in the residential housing on campus. It was a really good school.

I had paid my first and last month's rent at my first residence and could not get that back. My band had only given me $650 a month to live, so I needed that rent money. There was a legal aid department at my law school so I asked them what I should do. The legal aid lawyer suggested I save money by getting a law student to help me with my case. An Indigenous female third-year law student agreed.

The mother and daughter had told me they were the owners of the townhouse and that they had the right to do whatever they wanted. But when we did a property search we found out they were not the legal owners, so they were subject to the Landlord and Tenant Act. I ended up taking them to court. When the Indigenous law student and I entered the courtroom, the judge told us we were in the wrong court, and on the wrong side. He thought we should be in a criminal law court and that we were charged with something, instead of representing ourselves. He did not think we were the appellants. I won the case in the end, but I had to wait three months for the judge's decision. Thank god for my law school colleagues. I took out a human rights complaint against that mother and daughter for their discrimination of my Indigenous status. I ended up dropping this complaint when I moved back to Winnipeg.

During my first year of law school at Ottawa U, I got pregnant. I was one of those very rare individuals who got pregnant on the pill. My daughter's father is from Australia. I met him in Ottawa. He was not planning to live here in Canada. He's a non-Indigenous man, very antigovernment, doesn't like people controlling him.

When I got pregnant, I knew I was going to be raising my child on my own, so I moved back to Winnipeg and transferred to University of Manitoba for my second year of law school. I was thirty when I gave birth to my daughter. I figured that my family was there, it would be cheaper to live in Winnipeg than in Ottawa, and I felt more comfortable in Winnipeg because I knew it well. That was probably not a very good decision because I think it was a better law school in Ottawa, but that's just my perspective.

I went back to university part time when I had my daughter in 1993. I did my second year of law school in two years. While going to university, I continued to work part-time at the law firm, and also at Child Find Manitoba. I just did what I had to do because I had a child; I had to look out for her. Even though my family was in Winnipeg and I had their love and support, I couldn't rely on them to be alone with my daughter because they had addiction issues. So, I didn't have anyone to babysit, but I was fortunate because when I was in school, I got subsidized daycare. I was able to rely on that. For the first three years

of her life, my daughter went to the same daycare so she had a lot of consistency.

My daughter also went to school with me for years. I was always in school so she was with me on that trajectory, right from the time she was born when I was in law school, then when I went on to do my master's degree and afterwards my PhD. Today, my daughter is twenty-nine. Just before she turned nineteen, she moved out to BC to go to an art school there, Vancouver Institute of Media Arts (VanArts). She lived out there for five years, and then took a job transfer to Toronto, but absolutely hated it there. She's been back in Winnipeg since 2018 and is a university student.

The start of my last year of law school I went back full time. I had one more year left, but it was just too tough to finish that off as a single mom. I left law school. I had lost interest in doing law, and as a new mom, I wasn't able to put in as much time studying as I wanted. Law school was very demanding and I just didn't have the supports to continue.

I got out of law school in '96. I took a year off from school and I worked with Myrna Dreidger at Child Find Manitoba. There were a lot of missing Indigenous children right across this country and Child Find wanted to develop a program that was geared specifically towards Indigenous people. As a mom I really gravitated to that. I only worked there for about a year and a half.

In '97 I started my master's degree in the Faculty of Arts. There was a new program at the U of M, a Master's in Indigenous Studies. Fred Shore, Emma LaRoque, and Jill Oakes were the mentors I learned from in my undergraduate degree, and they were teaching in the master's program too.

While I was working on my master's degree, I got a job working with the Assembly of Manitoba Chiefs on their Manitoba Framework Agreement Initiative. This was about implementing self-government for all of the First Nations in Manitoba. They got all this funding from the federal government, so they were beginning to work on a number of initiatives. Child welfare was one because they already had Indigenous child welfare agencies in the province. I understood the legislation of child welfare and the constitutional division of powers from my law school days. Child welfare is a provincial government responsibility, but Indigenous people are a federal government responsibility. The clash between

those two areas of responsibility impacts First Nations families. They are stuck in the middle of these two levels of government that basically fight with one another about whose responsibility it is to pay for services.

I worked out of Western Region Child and Family Services. The Assembly of Manitoba Chiefs didn't want political interference in any child welfare matters, so they wanted to make sure that we were situated outside of the political realm. In 2000, the money from the federal government dried up with the Framework Agreement Initiative, and the Aboriginal Justice Inquiry Initiative happened. I got pulled into that, and was part of all of the negotiations and the talks about what the devolution of child welfare was going to look like. (The Aboriginal Justice Inquiry Child Welfare Initiative came from the Aboriginal Justice Inquiry recommendations.) I started working at that time with the Southern Chiefs Organization.

Then a new national organization emerged: The First Nations Child and Family Caring Society of Canada. I started working on the development of this national organization. Cindy Blackstock moved from sitting on its board of directors to becoming its

Executive Director. I was the first employee. The University of Manitoba Faculty of Social Work offered us in-kind space to work for the first two years, until we moved into the community. I worked for the society from 2001 to 2013.

For my master's thesis, I looked at the role of community consultation in the move toward self-government. I interviewed all the leaders of the Child Welfare Agencies in the Southern part of Manitoba. In many respects, my thesis was, for me, the conclusion of the unfinished work of the Framework Agreement Initiative. We couldn't develop self-government in child welfare in particular, because we couldn't develop the other areas. For example, in order to have self-government and child welfare, we needed to have a court system as well as our own legislation and our own regulations and standards. None of that was in place. We still needed time to do that. I took what I had already learned and talked to people about the role of community consultation in developing self-government and in particular around child welfare. I graduated with my master's degree in 2003.

While I was working on my master's degree, I got a nice award from Indspire, a national organization that gives funding, based on need, to Indigenous students who are studying in various disciplines and trades. I believe it was 1998. They said that it could be used towards anything, including living expenses. I was a single mom then so I was thinking, *It's important that I create something stable for my daughter.* I had moved around a lot and went to a different school every year of my childhood. Nothing ever felt like home for me. I didn't want my daughter to have to go through that kind of experience. I wanted my daughter to have that feeling of safety, that this was *her home.* I used that money to put a down payment on a house. I wanted to be responsible with this money and use it wisely. That was a lot of money for me back then. Why would I pay rent and line someone else's pockets? I was fortunate to win that award.

When I worked with the Framework Agreement Initiative, there was an opportunity to learn about investing money. Investors Group came and talked to us about finances and investments. That's the power of knowledge. If every Indigenous person had an opportunity to learn what I did, would they be in the financial situations they are in? With that knowledge I was able to change my life around. I opened up an RESP for my daughter. That's how she was able to go to VanArts after high school. I had saved up all that money for her education. Investors offered mortgages as well, so I got my mortgage from Investors. Everything just sort of lined up for me. It was really good.

I bought this cute little two-bedroom house on Cambridge Street. The day I moved into that house was amazing! It was *my* home. Having that home was so important to me. I had freedom as a homeowner, and a sense of something belonging to me, myself. My daughter and I were safe. We loved it there and stayed seven years until we moved out to St. James when she was going into Grade 7. She found moving really difficult, but she stayed in our old neighbourhood for high school. I drove her to school every day, so she was still with her friends. I wanted to ensure that she had some consistency in her life. Those things are important, right? We moved because I had been dating a man for six years who was in the military, and we decided to get a home together. The new neighbourhood was close to the air force base. But he and I didn't last. I think we were together a year

after we moved into that house. I just paid him out his share of the house and he went his way.

I took some time off before my PhD. I continued working with the Caring Society. I started my PhD in 2008 and finished it in 2016. I got another nice award when I did my PhD. I received one of the Joseph-Armand Bombardier Canada Graduate Scholarships Awards from the Social Sciences Humanities Research Council of Canada (SSHRC). It's the second highest award for PhD students. It was $105,000 ($35,000 tax-free for three years). It is given based on academic excellence, research potential, and communications skills. My area of specialty is youth leaving the foster care system (aging out, emerging adulthood).

Doing my research, all of the youth I worked with were Indigenous, struggling and unemployed. I used digital storytelling for my research. I did not want to tell their stories; I wanted to give them the power to tell their own stories. They learned skills and capacity building from using the software (film, video), because they could use it beyond their project with me. Using their own voices lent authenticity to their stories and was a creative outlet for them. I really got to know the young people who participated.

We are failing our youth in care. There needs to be more of a safety net available for them when they emerge from care at age eighteen. They need a home, because a lot of youth are homeless after they leave care. A home is really important for a sense of belonging—not just belonging in this world, but belonging to yourself. You need to claim ownership over yourself, and when you have a home you can do that. I also learned about their disconnection from the land. Because these youth grew up in care they had never been to the community that they have membership with, so there was a huge disconnection from the land. I also learned that these young people make their own meaningful families, many not based on blood.

When I finished my PhD, I was hopeful that I would get a job teaching at a university somewhere. I knew about the University of Manitoba's Master of Social Work based in Indigenous Knowledges Program because I had worked with Michael Hart while I was working on my PhD. He's an Indigenous scholar who used to be part of our faculty. I'd helped him with finding literature that contributed to the development of that program a little bit. (There are all kinds of research opportunities when you're a student.) So, I knew the faculty would be hiring. When the U of M finally posted the job for two academics, I applied for the position and was thrilled to get the job.

It was an amazing opportunity because I focused on Indigenous issues and taught with Indigenous knowledge holders. The graduates of the Master of Social Work based in Indigenous Knowledges Program learn about Indigenous knowledge and can then incorporate this knowledge into the models of service delivery at their organization. It has been proven that our Indigenous cultural ways are healing and result in better outcomes for Indigenous clients. I learned a lot in the six years I oversaw this program.

In the summer of 2022 I moved to the University of Calgary as a Canadian Research Chair in Indigenous Child Wellbeing. I had no plans to leave the U of M, but I was approached about this new job and they were persistent. I wanted to focus not on the deficits of Indigenous people, but on their wellbeing. As Indigenous people we have answers to what it means to live well, so I created a program that looks positively at Indigenous experiences that we can learn from. A diverse group of people is participating in land-based gatherings to collaborate, create, and develop stories about Indigenous wellbeing that are child- and youth-centered. Individuals are guided through storytelling circles and land- and arts-based activities as they learn to craft stories digitally. Indigenous ways are incorporated into the program. It will serve children and youth in advancing healing, wellbeing, and successful pathways to adulthood informed by Indigenous ways of knowing, being, doing, and feeling. I am excited to do something innovative.

One of the things my first husband always told me was that I was nothing and I would amount to nothing. When our relationship ended, part of the pushback for me was to say, "I'm not nothing, and I'm going to show you I'm not nothing." I knew I was capable of doing more. People would say I am stubborn. Also, I believe in myself. I came from nothing and I went through shit in my life, but I persevered. It wasn't easy going to school; I struggled. I've had bouts of low self-esteem. Sometimes I struggle with Imposter's Syndrome (doubting my accomplishments and illogically thinking I will be exposed as a fraud). I work with so many amazing people that it's hard not to be in awe of what other people have done and to compare myself. But I remind myself that we are all different people, with our own paths and experiences. I'm just like everybody else, who once in a while has to fight the demons that crop up saying I am not good enough. Generally, I do know I am capable.

I remember when my mom was still alive and we first moved to the city, she used to always say to us, "Yes, we're Indians, but you know what? We're good people, we're strong people, be proud of who you are." I've always let that be my mantra. I'm a good person and I'm Indigenous and that makes me who I am. I am not ashamed to say that; I am proud.

Today I live with my partner, Mike. We met in 2005 and have been together for fifteen years. Mike is my best friend. He knows everything about me, and I know everything about him. He is loud and brash and totally opposite to me. Mike is Métis. He was adopted and did not know anything about his birth family and cultural background until a few years ago. He has learned to love Indigenous people. Mike is a very friendly person, the kindest man ever. He would give you the shirt off his back even if it was his only shirt. That's just the way he is.

My connections to my siblings have been strong; however, I have not yet connected with my youngest brother who was adopted out as a baby. I did put my name into the post-adoption registry to find him. The registry did not respond for fifteen years, and when they finally contacted me they told me that they had found my brother but he was not interested in connecting with me. I respect that. It's his decision. But even though he doesn't want to know us, he is still my family.

My younger sister died in 2013 and my youngest sister died in 2021. My youngest sister had breast cancer and decided not to take treatment. Her cancer metastasized and spread. Even though she died, she made a choice. She had always said to me that she would exit the world on her terms, not on anyone else's. So people may be sad about the way my sister passed, but I feel she had a lot of strength. I do think both my sisters' addictions had a lot to do with their deaths because they both died earlier than they should have.

I had to make the arrangements and pay for each of their funerals.

My older brother and my youngest sister did live together until she passed. They lived in a world that was really hard for me to fathom. My youngest sister used to live in a hotel on Main Street. She survived the best way she could with what she'd been given. I want to honour the hardships that she experienced. How she lived is a reality for many of our Indigenous population. She once explained to me that she took substances because missing her sons hurt, and she wanted to forget. Years ago my sister moved back to the US and met a man in Florida. They got married and had two boys but their relationship broke down. She came to Canada with her two sons but her husband travelled up here with his wealthy brother and took the boys back to the US and she never saw them again. There was a Sixties Scoop class-action lawsuit and my sister received a portion of her settlement (because it's still not definite how many people will receive funds). The lawsuit is for any Indigenous children who were adopted or in long-term foster care as part of the Sixties Scoop. (I got a payment too.)

My brother is doing well since he received his day school settlement. He has plans to develop a small business creating Indigenous-focused headstones. He has been spending his money in a responsible way. He is drinking responsibly and taking better care of himself. I think my brother is relieved that my sister has passed. He saw how she suffered. She is now free from the pain and he has peace in his heart that she is not hurting.

When I lived in the group home, I saw girls who experimented with drugs and alcohol, and I saw what it did to them and the trouble they got into. I witnessed how this influenced the way they acted when under these influences and it made me very angry. I just don't like seeing people out of it. I tried alcohol as a young person and have gotten drunk—everybody explores these things—but it was just never my thing. I never liked losing control and I don't find anything attractive about alcohol. I tried marijuana once too, but I would never touch any other types of drugs. Alcohol and drugs don't feed your brain or your body. I value my mind and see it as a gift to have a healthy brain. It is one of my greatest assets. It allows me to feel and experience and acknowledge the world around me. I am thankful that my mom was healthy when I was growing in her womb. She was living a good life for me.

It's really hard to reconcile that my life has been very different from that of my siblings. I cannot fathom that how they have lived is the way we are meant to live our lives. People look for ways to cope with their situations. They self-medicate. I can only guess that my sisters didn't want to feel anything so they chose substances to numb out their emotions, whereas I don't.

I'm the type of person who has to feel all my emotions so I can understand what they are. I intellectually dissect my emotional experiences. I really analyze myself. I ask myself, *Is the way I'm looking at this because of the way I'm thinking, or the way I'm feeling?* Sometimes that's a burden, but I want to feel the full force and effect of my hurt, because then I understand the true breadth of what that means for me. I don't want to numb it, because I don't want

> Alcohol and drugs don't feed your brain or your body. I value my mind and see it as a gift to have a healthy brain. It is one of my greatest assets.

to ever have to feel it again. For me, that's healing. Whereas when people try to numb their feelings with alcohol, the moment that alcohol dissipates, those feelings come back again. Then they have to pick up the bottle and drink more. I want to get these feelings over with.

When things are bad, I try to be as positive as I can. I don't know where that comes from. Maybe it comes from my dad. My dad was a positive guy. I finally met him in 1996, long after my mom died. He tracked my brother down and then I met him too. He was a lovely man. It was a positive experience meeting him. My dad was a wanderer. He travelled back and forth, all across North America. He couldn't set his feet down anywhere. We spent time together for about a year, but still, he wasn't always here during that time. He had a daughter in BC, another daughter in South Indian Lake in Northern Manitoba, and he went home to Ebb and Flow because he had all those kids there too. He died shortly thereafter, so I really got to know him for only a little while. I didn't get the whole story from him about what had happened with him and my mom. I guess it's just the nature of relationships; they break down. There were so many questions that I had, but I never got a chance to ask him.

Sometimes when it's really hard to understand my feelings, I like to be busy but allow those thoughts to come through. I do that a lot with my artwork. There was a time when my brother's adult child lived with us while transitioning to a man. He did really well when he was with us but the moment he left our home, he went off his hormone therapy for reasons we don't yet know or understand. I think there might have also been the possible onset of schizophrenia. All the signs were there, but at the time I didn't understand them. Since he chose to exit this world by taking his own life, my entire family is living with a lot of survivor guilt. I use my art to channel that hurt.

When my nephew died I painted ten rocks. I went to the land, put my tobacco down, and picked up these beautiful rocks that were gifts just sitting on the shores of our rivers. To me, rocks have the spirit of our ancestors, because these lands belong to the Indigenous people, and they're the spirit of mother earth. So, there are lots of healing elements in picking up a rock and feeling that spirit come through it and working with those feelings at the time. I like to do a type of art called pointillism that consists entirely of dots. Every dot represented a feeling or a memory of my nephew. That was a very cathartic experience. Some people use alcohol; I use art.

I did art when I was a teenager too. It's just one of those innate gifts that has been given to me. My older brother has the gift of being an artist too. He is a very skilled stone carver. I'm proud that one of his pieces was gifted to Prime Minister Justin Trudeau.

I've also been through neurofeedback training. That really helped me with channeling my hurt and pain. Our bodies tell us when we're hurt, or sleepy, or hungry, but our brains rarely give us feedback on how they're doing. But our brains can get sick too. I did some research back in 2010 for The Biocybernaut Institute of Canada in BC. They needed an Indigenous woman to do research with them on a project they were doing with troubled youth in a community in Saskatchewan. They were trying to understand and interrupt the way that Indigenous people thought about themselves. When I was first involved in the study, I asked to experience the training for myself in order to understand it. I needed to know what this was going to be like for those young people. Through this experience, I learned about the forgiveness protocol. Learning to forgive is something so fundamentally important for all of us.

To go through that forgiveness protocol, I had to choose something that had impacted my life and understand why I chose it. Then I had to create a courtroom in my imagination and choose four *impeachable* beings (personal symbols that are strong and would do no wrong to me). I chose things that were very culturally specific, like an old grandmother holding the moon and a wolf and a moose (mine shifted into a unicorn). They became my judges. Then I had to bring someone into the court who had to be charged. For me it was my mother. I had to work through being angry with my mom for dying. I had to feel the pain and the anger. Everything. Then I was asked, "Now that you know what you know, what did you learn from it?" I learned that there are things I am powerless to change. I had to accept my mother's path and her destiny. Unfortunately, it impacted me too. And I had to understand that she was powerless over what happened to her. Getting cancer was what was handed to her. I was powerless to help her because

I was a child, but she was equally powerless, because who can stop cancer? I had to learn to let go and accept that. I connected the dots and had the realization that to some extent, I can't control what happens in my life, so how could I control what happened in my mother's life? And how could I be mad at her when she couldn't control any of that? There were so many other teachings that came with that because there were all the other things that she couldn't control too—being born an Indigenous woman in that era and being affected by racist laws and assimilation. She had no power over any of that. Then I learned to forgive and let go.

There's a science to the forgiveness protocol, but there's a mystery to it as well. It's a very spiritual experience. I've been able to use that training to understand some of the experiences I've had in my life. I wish everyone could have that training. It helped me channel a lot of things that I have come to understand about myself and my brain. Our brains are really here to assist us. They are one of our greatest gifts, if we know how to tap into that and listen to our own inner voice we can learn to be kinder to ourselves. When you're a young person, you start to internalize the really negative things about yourself. When you think about what has happened to Indigenous people, a lot of those things we've had no power over. But yet, we internalize them and blame ourselves for a lot of things that have happened to us.

This forgiveness protocol would be a very helpful tool for reconciliation and healing, but the price is out of reach for most people. It is $15,000 for one session, and some are even more expensive. This is one way to heal, but not the only way. Our Indigenous practices are another way. The right Indigenous teacher can teach you how to forgive and move forward. An Indigenous Elder will help you if you give them a gift of tobacco.

Sometimes I can feel anger like anybody else does. It gets a hold of me, and it just comes out and I can't stop it. I'm particularly angry at the circumstances my siblings have faced and still face. We all come from the same place, but why am I doing so much better than they are (on my scale of doing better)? I have survivor's guilt. I wish they could have a good life and not have to struggle. It seems like my siblings are happy, but I think you grow to accept where you are in your life, so you become happy with less.

The key to the future is reclaiming who we are as Indigenous people. I am lucky that I had a yearning for education. I went to school, got educated and learned about settler laws and about the history of oppression. Not everybody is interested in going to school, and that's okay too. There are other ways to learn. The thing that is really important is for young Indigenous people to connect with someone who knows our Indigenous culture and can help them to connect to their own Indigeneity.

I tell young Indigenous people to find something to love about our Indigenous culture because when they find those things, they find meaning and purpose for their existence. Once they understand who they are as Indigenous people (and what has been done to their families), then they can reclaim their pride, dignity, and the willpower to effect change for themselves. What can weather them through the inequalities they may be experiencing is a strong sense of who they are and of the beauty and resilience of our culture. What I have learned from reclaiming who I am as an Indigenous woman is that once you are proud of who you are, then you allow other people to be who they are. Different worldviews, different faiths, different cultures can all co-exist. None of them are wrong.

There's still lots I have to learn about what it means to be Indigenous. And we have conflict in our communities just like in other ethnic groups. But there is a lot of beauty, a lot of strength in our Indigenous culture, and once you begin to see that I think that it can give a person a sense of purpose, strength, and direction.

When I was a little girl, I felt sad because I was embarrassed by my mom. I was also angry with her for drinking, and then for dying, and somehow, I made her responsible for our poverty. I didn't understand why we lived in poverty and I certainly wasn't aware of the forces beyond my mother's control that dictated where we were in our life. I didn't understand my mom's backstory. I didn't know how our people had been subjugated. And I didn't understand racism or why my mom was not able to get a job. I just saw the after-effects of all of that. Today I hold this racist society responsible for the things that hurt my mom, my family, and my people. I think that we are marinating in (excuse my words) white supremacy.

People learn to live with racism any way they can. I don't know if my sister or my brother thought about it, but they have felt the effects of it. People would probably take a wide berth around my brother and sister if they saw them on the streets. But again, they're just like my mother—they have had lots of hurts in their lives, and they might not have been as strong as I was. They chose to cope in ways that weren't always very healthy for them. But underneath all of that, they've been good and loving people. They have the capacity to love and care. But they didn't have a lot of money, and there weren't safe spaces for them.

When my sister tried to leave that kind of world behind, we had difficulty finding an apartment for her. We found a really nice one, but when we called, the guy said the application was online. My sister didn't have a cellphone then so she couldn't apply online, or leave a deposit. The next best thing was to go down physically to the place, to submit an application and put a damage deposit down. But, the moment we walked into that place…well, we faced challenges. I'm visibly Indigenous, and even though they knew nothing about who I was, they likely judged me because of my race. My sister is a little bit less visibly Indigenous, but people can tell she's not white by the way she talks, and people will discriminate against her, right? So, it was hard getting a new place for her to live.

Racism has been prevalent in my life too. When I got married to my first husband, we bought a used Jaguar and it was registered in my name. I was pulled over by police so many times and there were assumptions made that I was a prostitute and I had stolen a john's car. People are astounded when they hear that, but that really happened to me. And, I still experience that type of discrimination but in different subtle ways that are equally troubling. It doesn't matter how much education I have, people will look at me and see an Indigenous person and automatically make assumptions based on stereotypes, not knowing who Indigenous people *really* are. My education hasn't sheltered me from racism.

When I was older, in my twenties, I took lots of time to reflect on *Who was my mom?* But, I really didn't know my mom. I only knew her for a short span of time and what I did know of her, that wasn't my *real mom*. There was more to her. I know that she had deficits in her ability to show love, but she had a lot of resilience too. I don't want to forget that there was resilience in everything my mother did, even in just giving us life.

As I thought about her drinking and her death and wondered, *Did my mom love us?* I came to understand that people with addictions show love in many different ways. If we are open, we'll see the love that they are giving out. I realized, of course my mom loved us.

Because my mom was an alcoholic, I was responsible for getting my sisters up for school. But there were days when she actually got up and made us breakfast instead of me having to do that. She wasn't under the influence then. She always made porridge, which was a staple in residential schools. When my mom made us porridge, those were probably the best moments of my life. My mom was awake and coherent. She was feeding us, giving us sustenance. But what I never realized at that moment was that she was also feeding us with love. So, for me, the act of making porridge was an act of love that sustains me to this day.

A mutual friend introduced me to Marlyn in 2017. He thought she would be a knowledgeable person to talk to during the research phase of this book because of her area of academic expertise. Marlyn spoke with such passion and insight about her work with youth aging out of care. When we met I did not know that she had once been in care herself. I interviewed Marlyn at the home she and Mike share. It is a cozy and peaceful spot, with large amounts of her art and a beautiful backyard. I can see how much she values their home. Mike and Marlyn have an easy rapport, and I felt very comfortable with them. They have gifted me with Indigenous medicines, homemade smudge, great conversations about life, and lots of laughs. I feel welcomed in their home.

Karlii

It was a hundred percent harder to be a kid in CFS than it was to come out as transgender. Coming out and being transgender was a breeze in comparison. I was born biologically male, but I always wanted to explore being a girl because I feel more comfortable being identified as a female. Me not really caring what people think has a huge part to play in my coming out and going through transition. If a person is insecure and cares too much about what others think, this would be a really tough journey. It could be very different for someone who is beaten down by other people who don't support them.

Being a woman makes me happier. And I am proud that I can wake up every day and be myself. It was the best decision I've ever made!

As a child, I felt that my mom loved us; she told us she loved us every day. She still does. She never says "bye" without saying "I love you." My mom is affectionate, and a hugger too. I lived with her and my older sister, Carmel, until I was three. Carmel's a year and three weeks older than me. I'm technically the fifth of five siblings. My two older siblings, Tyrone and Shantelle, lived with their dads. Tyrone is two and a half years older, and Shantelle is three and a half years older. And

ANDREW MAHON

then Devin, who is my father's kid with another woman, is thirteen years older. My mother came into the picture after he was born.

We lived in a small, small town up north outside of a reserve. My dad passed away from cancer when I was six months old. My mom took my dad's death really hard. There was no help for her. She didn't have access to antidepressants or therapy, so she dealt with it in her own way. She turned to alcohol.

My mom and dad both came from Indigenous backgrounds; however, my maternal grandmother is the white one who married into our Indigenous family. I got my white skin from her.

My earliest childhood memory is a dark one. I was about three years old and one of my siblings was crying while being held upside down by the ankles by their dad and his girlfriend. I was outside and looked inside the house through the window. I probably wasn't supposed to see. It was scary to watch.

And then there's another vivid memory, less scary, from when I was about three and we had just moved to a new house. Me and my older sister were having fun rearranging the living room furniture. We were home alone so we could do whatever we wanted.

We pushed the coffee table and the sofa into the hallway.

Things started to get especially bad when my mom's depression started affecting her judgment. I ended up going to live with my dad's sister and her husband from age three till about ten. I was an impulsive kid. I had undiagnosed ADHD and impulse control disorder. None of the adults in my life understood my behavior. They thought they could discipline me and possibly make my behavior better. The discipline started out as a small innocent pat on the butt, but then it got worse and happened more often until it became out of control. My back or my legs would be purple from being physically abused. I finally worked up the courage to run away.

I ran away to my mom's because I found out where she lived. I saw that she had the space for me. I thought, *I'm not going to be abused almost every day.* I told my mom everything that happened and she told the police. CFS decided my mom was stable enough to take care of me, so they said I could stay with her.

Her drinking wasn't heavy at first, but then my sister and I started noticing she was gone more often than she should have been.

She did have a job at the bar just two streets away. My sister and I were fine. Our granny Florna (She is actually my grandma's sister and was an Elder in town. All the kids called her granny) lived next door, so we could just run to her if there was ever anything wrong. She was literally the mother hen of the town. Our auntie (my mom's sister) also lived across the field. It was a small town so we knew who lived in every single house. Anytime our mom was at the bar, we were either at my cousin's or at granny's. But then there were times where our mom wasn't home at night. Maybe we fell asleep really early and she came home later, but we didn't see her. Some nights I didn't even think I had a mom. After living with my mom for about a year, I could see that she was still going through something. She obviously had not seen a doctor or a therapist to get things off her chest.

My mom never really had any parenting skills. We just kind of did whatever we wanted. I started noticing patterns: there was never any set dinner or breakfast time, and there was no routine or structure. I knew this was an issue. There was always food, because my great-grandma would have killed my mom if there hadn't been any food.

I also could see that my mom was a really angry person.

This one time my mom hit me on the back. It was the first time I think, but she didn't understand the circumstances I'd already been in as a kid. I told her, "I don't want to live here. I'm going to call my great-aunt. I don't feel safe." She was a social worker with CFS and I had her number on hand. My mom told me to go ahead and call her. So I did. My mindset was to just get out. I knew there must be somewhere else that would be safer. I hoped she could get me the security I needed: living in a stable home and going to school. My great-aunt took me to CFS. They got involved and apprehended me from my mom's. That was 2010. I was twelve years old.

My great-aunt tried to keep me in the same school that I had been going to, which was on reserve up north. I bounced around CFS a bit. There were two or three homes on the reserve that were emergency placements. I don't really remember much about them. I do remember going to live with a woman who was married, had a home, and two sons and a daughter. I felt safe, but there were just too many kids for me. I wanted someone who paid more attention to me and my needs. I wanted to be someplace where I could learn properly. It was hard to focus in school. Everything would distract me. I knew something wasn't right, but I didn't know what it was. You can't work on something like ADHD when you're in a small town. You're just labeled as a problem child. Moving to the city was my only option.

Living in Portage was a possibility because my sister was living there, but I preferred Winnipeg. Obviously it would be a lot easier to access a university or college from Winnipeg. That was my thought process.

I moved to Winnipeg around 2011 when I was thirteen. I started living with my foster parents, Bob and Trudy. When I got to Trudy and Bob's place, it looked great. It was your average North End bungalow home…perfect. I had my own room, too. I was just so happy to be there.

I went to Andrew Mynarski School, which is a middle school on McPhillips. I had a guidance counsellor there, who I remember vividly because every time I got into trouble, I would have to go to her office. It wasn't major trouble, just typical new kid stuff. I got sent to the principal's office only once or twice. But they were watching me like a hawk. I knew I had an attention disorder but I didn't know what it was called or what to do about it. I wasn't on any medication. While I was going there, I explained to Trudy that I couldn't focus. She took me to my family doctor and I was diagnosed with ADHD and impulse control disorder. I was put on a dose of ADHD medication—108 mg—that most doctors would probably say no to. I just remember not wanting to do anything because of how the meds made me feel. I was overmedicated. Sedated all day.

While I was going to Andrew Mynarski, we moved, so I had to switch schools. My new junior high was H.C. Avery and, oh my word, did they ever label me as a problem child. As soon as I walked in the doors that very first day, the principal greeted me, walked me to my class, and then the teacher walked me to my desk. I couldn't go to the bathroom alone. Nothing. I think that what set them off was me being on such a high dose of ADHD medication. At H.C. Avery I

I just remember not wanting to do anything because of how the meds made me feel. I was overmedicated. Sedated all day.

was put on strict supervision. Someone was constantly beside me to make sure I was sitting still and doing only schoolwork. The person would follow me around all the time and report back to the principal. When I wanted to hang out with friends at recess, it was like, *Hey guys, it's me and my supervisor joining you in your friend group.* I didn't want to go to class and sit next to this person who is kind of just *there*. I wanted a tutor, not an usher.

In Grade 9, I started turning into a rebel: skipping school and getting high smoking weed. I would go to school, take my lunch, but then leave for the day. My foster parents owned a business, so they never answered their home phone and didn't even know what was going on for the longest time. I skipped school for about two months under their noses. I would go to my friend Delaney's house. She was a ginger so she was really picked on and bullied, too. We would get high in her upstairs loft.

That's when I decided to come out as gay. Delaney was the very first person I told. I never really wanted to date because I didn't feel attracted to girls. I thought it was strange, but that maybe when I hit puberty I'd become interested, but that wasn't the case. It was just… boys. Delaney told me it was okay. She made me realize that people judge only because they're uneducated about something and it frustrates them. When I thought about that, I was like, *Maybe I could just tell my foster parents and they wouldn't tell anybody.* Right?

So I told Trudy one day and she was like, "Oh, well, honey, I already knew." I had this surprise, but she already knew the surprise! I hated the fact that she said that to me, rather than just letting the moment happen. It kind of ruined it for me. But, on the other hand, Trudy and I started having this bond because I was being more honest and open with her. I felt like she thought I was maturing. I was trusting her more and opening up to her, so she became more lenient when it came to punishments, bedtimes, curfew—stuff like that.

I came out to Trudy and Bob about a year and a half after being with them. I feel like today's society is really based around sex, and I was just trying to find out who I was, right? There were kids who were openly gay in junior high, so I thought, *If I'm interested in boys, why can't I just say so?* Like what would it lead to?

Trudy and Bob's business really picked up. It got so busy for them that I'd come home and there'd be dinner made and on the stove, but we weren't sitting down and having a family dinner like we used to. Then it just started to feel like living there was like living in a hotel, and there wasn't really any parental supervision. I wasn't getting any reaction or empathy from them. I thought my only route was to do something to get their attention. What I did next, I regret it to this day.

Trudy always cleaned her glass-top stove with these straight-razor blades. I knew where she kept them. So one day I took one and started trying to make myself bleed. This was not an attempt to end my life; I have impulse control disorder and I wanted their attention. Using the razor was something that popped into my head and I just did it. That's the way the disorder works; it can be something completely irrational. It can make sense to me at the time, but then later on seem irrational. I made slits all up and down my wrists. It looked horrible and the cuts were so hard to cover up. I didn't think it would look as bad as it did. At one point I thought, *Was this even worth it?* I realized that it was a big mistake and doing it for attention was not the right idea. I didn't have to go to the hospital. It wasn't that bad. But it was bad enough that I still have the scars.

I wanted to hide the cuts because I knew Trudy and Bob would be upset with me. I wore only long-sleeve shirts and hoodies for weeks. Then one night I reached for something at dinner and Trudy saw my wrists and that's when everything went upside down. I didn't know what to say. It ended up getting their *full* attention, right? Trudy started a suicide prevention case with Macdonald Youth Services. They were trying to reduce the conflict of interest within the case, since Trudy knew that my great-aunt was my social worker. My clinical case manager started coming for visits every now and then.

That's when all the trust between me and my foster parents just went out the window. I had a curfew and I started receiving a smaller allowance. I remember trying to convince everybody that I wasn't suicidal, I wasn't going to run away from home, and I would be safe. It was just so hard to convince everybody. I understand that now as an adult, but back then things started to get to the point where Trudy was just so worried that she almost kept me a prisoner inside the home.

I thought, *Enough's enough. I need to get out of here.* So I called my social worker one night. She came and picked me up with all my stuff. We drove to Portage la Prairie, where I stayed with a relative for a couple nights while my social worker prepared my file for the Knowles Centre.

It was March 2012 when I went to the Knowles Centre. I was fourteen. I begged not to go to this place. I cried in the office. I sat there for hours just not wanting to go. But when I got in there, it wasn't as bad as I thought it was going to be. It's a locked facility. The bedroom doors were locked from the outside, so somebody would have to let you back in your room. If you were misbehaving, they could lock you in, but that never happened to me. You could go outside, but when you came back in they locked your shoes up so you couldn't bring your shoes inside and get out the fire escape. There was TV, but no internet. It's not a place for people who are weak, that's for sure!

The locked facility was really traumatizing because the staff there were allowed to restrain kids and put them into a room with padded walls. Nothing else, just a light. The light was obviously secured, but it was spooky. So prison-like. If a kid started spazzing out and beating up staff members, they'd restrain the kid and put them in this padded room. I was never put in it, but I've seen it. I had to clean it once. They made us do chores. Oh my god, they made us clean that place spotless.

After staying in the locked facility for a short time, I was allowed to go into the open facility because I was being good and following the rules. Knowles also had an open facility, which is considered a group home. There were no locked doors and we got our own key to our room. We had access to TV and internet and a bigger allowance. I remember there was a dance class once a week. I lived for that! We also had this thing called Quiet Time. It was an hour of sitting alone, locked in our rooms while there was shift change. I don't understand why they didn't have us doing something else that occupied our minds.

About six months into living at Knowles, I noticed I hadn't heard from my social worker the whole time I'd been there. I think I was a permanent ward already. (I know now that my file shows that she missed multiple meetings from 2012 to 2014.) I started trying to get ahold of her to see what was going on. *Like what's my plan?*

I had heard about this independent living program where you can live on your own when you turn eighteen. I wanted to get some more information about it. When I finally asked my social worker about it, she ignored me. I felt she didn't care about my future. Apparently the program was really expensive, and honestly, by the sounds of it, CFS would have rather just discharged me. I started to get worried about aging out of care even though it wasn't for a few years. *Where would I live? Could I go to school? Was I going to have to get a job?* I don't think any kid should ever have to worry about what it's going to be like after aging out of CFS care.

My social worker was my great-aunt so she had a conflict of interest. I thought she was using her authority to punish me, but I couldn't talk to her supervisor because she was her frickin' cousin! Everybody was related at that agency office.

I didn't know who I could call, so I started looking at the posters all over the wall in the locked facility, and there was a poster for the Children's Advocate (now called the Manitoba Advocates for Children and Youth—MACY). The poster said something along the lines of, *Let your voice be heard,* so I called them. The Children's Advocate Act protects children and their rights and prevents them from being neglected. In any situation where there is neglect, they have the right to step in and flex their authority.

I talked to an advocate named Rosie. She said, "I'll come and see you right away." I think she came the same day (if not, it was the next day) and she met with me privately. She listened to everything I had to say from start to finish. From the very beginning she made me feel like she was going to get something done. And, that's what made me want to keep working with her. Rosie taught me that all I had to do was ask.

After working with Rosie, I asked for a new social worker because of being neglected. Transferring my files should have been done quickly, but it took way too long, and I was basically in between social workers and didn't have one. So, I got in touch with MACY again and let them know. Rosie was on vacation, so I met with Gerald, who was a colleague of Rosie's. He expedited my transfer to get me a new social worker. But my new social worker was basically just a 2.0 version of my first one. So this is when I started cracking down. I stopped going to my social worker, and I started going to advocates instead. I said to Rosie and Gerald, "If I need something, do you mind if I just go through you guys as a third party, because I know that you have authority over my social worker?"

They said, "We can do that. But obviously, if you just want to do something like change a class at school, you're going to have to go through a social worker for that on your own." So, I started working with Rosie. She was my advocate for about two years. We started looking at things like me getting my driver's license and getting into my independent living program, but then Rosie retired. There was another advocate, but I was not eager to work with her. Being in CFS, there is always, always, always a new adult who you have to deal with. I was assessed with having Adjustment Disorder from being in the system. I developed anxiety and depression during times of adjustment (emergency placements, for example). I didn't want to meet yet another person. This was one of those situations where it was about me, not about her. Once Rosie retired, everything with CFS fell apart. My experience of working with MACY was short-lived, but it was great.

ANDREW MAHON

While I was at Knowles, I left for a while to live in a town called Langruth. It's a small town on the west side of Lake Manitoba. I lived there with a very distant relative and my sister Carmel too. I went to school in Sandy Bay on the reserve. I didn't like it in Langruth though. While I was there, I got blamed for arson when a bunch of kids burned an elementary school playground. They broke into the school and stole a bunch of laptops and all of those charges stuck on me because one of the older people that lived nearby saw me leaving the playground earlier that day. The RCMP came to the home that I was placed in and arrested me. After that I got sent back to Knowles. I had to do community service, write an apology letter to the principal, and follow a curfew and conditions by law because I was in an undertaking (meaning the charges were pending and still under investigation). I was such a rebel that I breached my conditions regularly. I was never home for my curfew. The police would take me to the Manitoba Youth Centre for a night or two. I would meet with the judge and agree to follow my conditions, but then breach them again. It was fun to have some freedom. It didn't matter to me where I was locked up. Then the police discovered that I was not guilty of arson. No one ever wrote me an apology letter to me! What about compensation for me?

Knowles is a military-style structure, but honestly, it works. It's a place where kids go when they need to learn how to follow rules and instructions. I understand why I went there. I was a devil child, and I honestly don't think I would be where I am today if I didn't have that type of structure. I was at that facility on and off for about three years.

When I got admitted to Knowles I started experimenting more with makeup. I had come out as gay before then, but I wasn't full-on transitioning. Now that I'm older, I understand what I was feeling then. I just wanted to be a girl, and I was attracted to boys. But I had not explored my sexuality yet. I was kind of in the closet, putting on makeup in the bathroom and washing it off. That was another reason I begged not to go to this locked facility, because it was all male. I had told my social worker, "I want to transition eventually." But, she told me to just *be gay*. I wanted to get rid of her after that. I never really went to her for any type of support or advice.

When I was young, I always played with dolls and everything was pink because I had older sisters. I was more interested in girl things and they were available for me to explore. That's what helped me to find what I was more comfortable with. My mom did introduce me to video games and action figures and cars but I didn't have any interest in them. My sister's toys were a lot better! I could explore my interest in being a girl. That feeling was always just *there*.

What inspired me to be transgender was that one of my cousins lied to me and told me that Lady Gaga was once a man. That would have been in about Grade 5. I frigging believed him. I was like, *Wow, that's crazy. I could be a woman!* The desire to be a woman was inside me, and seeing Lady Gaga became my inspiration. I would never have become a female if I was going to be an ugly one! I thought I could be a beautiful woman like her. Lady Gaga would always have these really exotic music videos and this dramatic and unique wardrobe. She just did what she wanted and didn't care what people would think. I loved that!

I knew that I was already attracted to boys at that age. I didn't want to say anything to anyone. I was like, *Okay, I see what's happening.* Then when I lived with Trudy and Bob and told them that I was interested in guys, they were way more open and honest and accepting about it than my social worker. I didn't find out that Lady Gaga wasn't transgender and was biologically a woman until I was fourteen, fifteen.

When I got into the facility, they started doing monthly clothing shopping with me at Giant Tiger. This one time I told the staff that I wanted to go shopping for girls' clothes. I started wearing some girls' clothes publicly;

because it was skinny jeans, they didn't really look like girls' clothes. I was wearing yellow, green, blue, red skinny jeans. They probably didn't really look girly, but to me, they were girls' pants, and that was all I needed. Those jeans felt much different than the boot-cut jeans I had been wearing. Basically, I just felt hotter. Having the sex appeal of a woman is what I wanted to achieve. And I got it.

My hair came first. I shaved all around the sides, but I left a lot of long hair on the top. It was down on one side. I dyed it, kind of like a Cruella DeVille style. It was streaky looking—blonde and a dark brown.

Then came the makeup when I was about fifteen. One of the facility's staff members, Tara, had to do my Christmas shopping for me—the agency gave her $100 to buy the gifts I would open up for Christmas day. Tara is one of the greatest support workers I've ever met in my life. I'd give her a list of what I wanted. (It was makeup or a cellphone, but my grandfather gifted me $200, so I went and bought a cellphone myself.)

That Christmas I was in the open facility (some kids went home for Christmas) so we celebrated and got our gifts early. The first time I wore makeup publicly I went to the

Kildonan Place Mall close to where I was living. It was a test of my confidence. I think I followed a Jeffrey Star makeup tutorial online. I wore foundation with some powder and some eyeshadow with eyeliner, eyebrows, and eyelashes. I asked for these specific eyelashes that were the bushiest of bushy eyelashes. Those things looked like caterpillars. I thought it was the greatest thing ever! Now I would never, ever, ever wear those again, but back then—oh my gosh!

When I first put that makeup on publicly it was so weird because obviously no one had ever seen me with makeup on. I was trying to explore people's reactions. Thinking about it now, nobody gave a shit I was wearing makeup. Nobody cared. Being ADHD as I am, I tested limits, tested patience, tested almost everything that you could test, basically. I just wanted to see how far I could go with everything. So, that's where a lot of my fearlessness and confidence came from.

There were obviously the bullies but those have never ever bothered me because I knew the staff at Knowles would protect me. If anyone made fun of me, there'd be punishment for them. There was no name-calling or discrimination allowed. I think that was a good lesson to be respectful to people no matter who they are. I also had a friend who was gay in the facility. We were a duo. That's another thing that helped me come out. He always supported me.

After that, there wasn't anything that I did without makeup on. I went to school with a full face of makeup. I did my chores with makeup on. Everything. I remember telling everybody that there would never be a time when they would see me in public without makeup. It was true for the most part. The makeup was the finishing touch, but I'm pretty sure everybody knew before the makeup that I wanted to be Karlii.

I was probably about sixteen when I started taking my estrogen hormones, because I know there was something parents had to sign if you were younger than sixteen. I went with a support worker to get the letter from my family doctor so I could then go to the psychologist to get the approval to start hormones. The first time I ever took estrogen was when I knew *this is happening.* The psychologist specifically told me "You can't go back on this." Part of me had a little bit of anxiety, yes. It was not a question of *Am I this person?* but mostly from wondering what if something went wrong along the way? But that's normal anxiety. I also felt so excited. The year I started taking estrogen was one of the best years of my life. That's when everything just took off. I felt completed. Reaching my peak through my transition was one of the best moments of my life. That's when Karl became Karlii. Nobody knew Karl at all; everybody just knew Karlii. That was just the greatest feeling ever, honestly.

Even family members that I hadn't seen for a while were like, "Hey, Karlii." I felt accepted. Okay, *Hello!*

Around the time I started taking hormones, I left Knowles for the last time to live with Joseph and Tammy in Portage la Prairie. Joseph is the father of two of my siblings. He is the guy in one of my early memories who was shaking one of my siblings upside down. I agreed to be placed there because all my friends lived in Portage. I lived there for about two months, but then the family moved to MacGregor (which is between Portage la Prairie and Brandon). I stayed with Joseph and Tammy in MacGregor for about six or seven months.

I wanted to get out of that home really badly. I was verbally abused, poorly treated, and belittled for being transgender. When I had asked my social worker to move me, he said I was being difficult and would say anything to get out of anywhere he placed me. He also said that I should just stay and be happy there. The CFS agency handled it all very poorly and I am currently seeking justice and compensation related to this. I cannot comment about this lawsuit.

I had to contact someone. Again, I was looking for advocacy options but couldn't contact Rosie because she was already retired, so that's when Voices came into my life. It's an organization that works specifically with kids in and from CFS care, ages twelve to twenty-nine. I wanted to find a place that understood the Child and Family Services Act. I emailed the program director, Marie, and told her a bit about what was going on. I explained that I was worried about where I was living, and also about not being able to get into the independent living program with CFS when I turned eighteen (I had just turned seventeen). I was really lost. She told me that anytime I wanted, I could come down to the office to talk, or if I just needed a place to go hang out for the day, I should come by. And, I did.

After I got in touch with Marie on email, I ran away from Joseph and Tammy's home. It was late at night in the middle of January and it was cold. I took a backpack with two changes of clothes, my cellphone, and that was it. Throughout my entire life, I tend to run away from really terrible situations or terrible adults. That's why I knew that I could walk down Highway 1 and make it. I was walking along the highway towards Winnipeg, and these two really sweet guys in a semi-truck picked me up. I let them know what was going on, and they took me safely to Winnipeg. They understood. They had a friend pick me up and take me wherever I wanted to go. That night, I had walked for about fifteen minutes on the highway. It wasn't a long walk, but I don't think any kid should ever have to go through that.

I stayed with my cousin Brittany. I got in contact with my social worker to let him know that I was safe. I wanted to tell him everything, but I didn't think he would believe me because of what he had said to me about trying to get out of everywhere that he placed me. I called his supervisor and told him that I didn't want a foster parent anymore, and I wanted my CFS cheques to be directly deposited to me. My social worker said that I needed a stable foster home or guardian because I was seventeen.

My friend's mom asked me what was going on, and I explained everything to her. She told me that I could stay with them, which was really nice. She was willing to take on that guardianship (for some rent, obviously). I stayed with them for about six, seven months. I was going to school, and I got a job at a restaurant in Charleswood doing dishes. Then this friend and I had a falling out—he liked me, but I didn't like him—so I moved back in with Brittany for the winter and continued to go to high school.

I wanted to get a better education so I enrolled myself into the University of Winnipeg Collegiate and took law, psychology, and another course. The school had a number of tuition waivers for Aboriginal kids, and I got the last one that year. I was already thinking about my future and my career. Everybody thought I was a partier but I hadn't been to an actual party. I hadn't had sex either. I was a good kid. I went to the Collegiate because I wanted to take courses that would help me get into university.

I spent a lot of time at Voices. I did schoolwork there and hung out with the staff. It's not your typical organization. The office is completely open and it doesn't feel like an office when you walk in, but it also feels private. I felt more of an actual connection to the people that I was working with there than at other organizations. Voices is welcoming, but it's also a professional environment. It's a place where people can go, knowing that they won't be judged at all. Marie the ED is the mother hen of Black women, honestly. When I think of *mother*, Marie is who comes to mind: she actually cares about others and puts them before herself. She looks past a lot of things in people (like addiction) to help them. She treats people all the same. A lot of people, including social workers, don't really know about Voices.

I began living on my own in the spring. I wanted to start making decisions on my own. I didn't like CFS telling me what to do. I had just turned eighteen, and *I wanted* to be eighteen. I wanted to go to school. I wanted to be able to just hang out with my friends and find out what I wanted to do for a career. Originally I wanted CFS to put me into the independent living program. I wanted to

learn about how to live on my own and pay bills and stuff like that. I didn't know how to pay bills except a cellphone bill. I didn't even know how insurance worked. I asked that I live wherever I wanted and receive my cheques from CFS. But because I lived on my own, I no longer qualified for any help from my social worker. They said they would only help me get my own apartment and sign my lease. At that point, I was already discharged from CFS. When I asked them to discharge me, they said it was a bad idea; however, they showed me no reason that it was a good idea to stay with them.

Then I was on my own. I had no furniture. Nothing. I was using my basic living allowance of $850 a month for my rent. If I had gone on social assistance I would have received a maximum of only $773 a month. I didn't want to have to work a full-time job, but I had to. I had switched jobs to work at Hat Tricks at the Ho Jo (Howard Johnson). My shift was from 6 p.m. to 2 a.m. every day. I had already gotten promoted up to kitchen manager, but that job was a lot of work!

Things started to fall apart because I didn't know I had bills due. I had got a furniture loan from Aaron's Furniture Store that was $300 a month. I missed a payment and two days later they came and got all the furniture while I was at work. My friend, who was staying at my apartment when the landlord let the furniture company in, called me and said, "Yo, your furniture is all gone." Because I was young, the store owner had no confidence in me and was ready to take the furniture back the minute I made a mistake.

My apartment was empty and I didn't want to live there, so I quit school, quit work, and cancelled everything. There was this boy in Brandon that I just had to move for. I met him at my sister's graduation. I packed my bags, packed my kitchen and bathroom up, and moved to Brandon. And that was that. I moved there in the beginning of 2017. I lived in Brandon for five years. That relationship didn't work out, but we stayed friends. Life goes on. I moved into my next apartment with a different boy and that didn't work out either, so I lived by myself with some roomates after that.

My confidence lies in being a woman. I think of myself as just a regular woman. That's it. I don't see myself as a minority. I don't try to take advantage of that either. If somebody tells me off, I don't think, *Oh my God, you told me off 'cause I'm transgender.* That's what a lot of people do if they identify as transgender. I understand that people handle oppression differently, but I am a very strong person and it's not something that I would automatically do. I just take it as constructive criticism.

I am not oppressed by any of this. The only time people's comments bug me are when they act ignorantly in a professional setting. If you want to be a jerk at the convenience store, I don't give a fuck; I can walk away from that. But if you are an asshole to me while working at the bank, then there's a line that has been crossed. That's when I get upset about being oppressed.

I have the privilege of looking like another person. Having "the look" is the biggest thing ever. If I didn't? Whew, I would not be able to pick myself up if that was the case. If you could see my Adam's apple, if you could tell at first glance I had been born a guy, my confidence wouldn't be as high as it is. But if you hear my voice, you can tell that I was biologically a male. It's still deep and very flamboyant. Nasally. I live with that insecurity.

Some people don't understand me. Being uneducated about something can frustrate somebody. I know it really irks me when I'm not educated about something and I just want to learn about it. Sometimes, that's all people want to do when they're frustrated with the LGBT community. They're acting out because they don't know. If they are engaging with me, they must just want to learn. That's all it is. As a teenager, I understood that. I have compassion for people who don't understand me or don't understand what being transgender is all about. I feel sorry for them. I want to be the person to tell them what this life is like, what I have to face, why I'm going through all of this. And just help them understand. Being transgendered comes from the brain, so it's just how people's brains are wired.

As transgender, I find it hard to *defend* myself against someone who is uneducated. I'll wear makeup, do my hair, wear girl clothes, but at the end of the day there's no real solid answer as to why I am transgender. It's just *there*. It's not something that I want for attention, or because transgender people are treated differently. It's something that I discovered about myself, because I could explore it and so it fell into place, just as it was meant to. It's like the same way we have a favourite colour or favourite music. Sometimes you just like the colour green and you don't know why. You can't control what's in your brain. It's just the way feelings work.

I haven't legally changed my name on my birth certificate yet. I kind of don't want to, because Karl was my dad's name. My name isn't something that I care about. It's not a trigger for me (but that might be different for other people.) My mom told me that my dad wanted to name me Axel. That would have been a shitty name to transition from! Using the name Karlii was my idea. I wanted to add the ii at the end of my name. It's the aesthetic.

When I'm meeting a person, my gender is never ever the highlight. My gender is definitely not something I'll lead with when talking about myself. I'm like, "Hi, I'm Karlii." That's it. (But obviously, when dating, that's something else I should mention.) I understand it's a huge journey for some people, but for me, it's just my lifestyle. If I'm vegan, I don't say, "Hi, I'm Karlii, I'm vegan." Being vegan is a lifestyle, right? That's exactly how I look at being transgender: it's just a lifestyle.

Anyone who wants to know more about genders and sexualities can visit OK2BME.ca.

Gender and sexuality are two different things. That website explains the terms, who they are specific to, and the associated feelings. The website says the full abbreviation is LGBTTTQQIAA. So it's lesbian, gay, bisexual, transgender, transsexual, two-spirited, queer, questioning, intersexual, asexual, ally. There's also pansexual, agender, genderqueer, bigender, gender-variant and pangender. I just say LGBT or my gay friends. Nobody's going to cancel you for that.

A lot of people also ask about pronouns after a little while, because they start to get a little confused. I give them the pronouns she/her. When people ask me, do I care about pronouns, I really don't, because I think people see you the way you see yourself. If someone wants to go into detail about my gender, that's a whole other conversation, right?

When I came out, I was really confused about who I should talk to first. Should I tell my social worker or my foster parents? Should everybody know or would I need to tell just one person? I am planning to give some workshops about these questions with CFS youth, through Voices.

Some people are really lucky and do have a good bond with their social workers, but some kids don't even know who their social workers are. That's appalling. How do you survive if you don't know who your social worker is? That's your person, who controls all your money and everything. I know that a lot of social workers tell foster parents (especially new ones) not to get too attached to their foster kids because they might move or go back to their families. This makes me so angry, because it's not good for the overall foster experience. The foster parent should be allowed to form a parental bond with a child. That's where my commitment to advocacy comes from.

When you are having your hardest times, oh god, honestly, I don't think there is anything you can say to yourself to make yourself feel better. Crying helps. Even to this day, sometimes late at night I think about what happened to me growing up and I let out as many tears as I possibly can. I have that time by myself. It's definitely a satisfying way of getting a lot of emotions out.

When you hit rock bottom, you're at *rock bottom*, so you just have to rely on the people around you more than yourself. Relying on yourself is what led you to where you are, right? My biggest supporters are Rosie and Marie. There's also my cousin Skye, who is a social worker. While I was in care, I went along with her to her work. She works at an Indigenous agency called Wahbung Abinoonjiiag. It's an agency in Winnipeg that focuses on women in poverty, women with kids specifically. There were a few of us who volunteered there preparing feasts for the mothers and their little ones and operating the food bank. This is when my advocacy took off because I started advocating for these women that came to Wahbung. Anytime they had an issue, we would talk about it and I'd give my input about what to do. We were all about the same age.

I like to describe myself as a self-proclaimed advocate. I advocate daily for other people. I've never been scared to say what I want to say. I am mostly an advocate for youth in care, helping them find solutions to some systemic problems. I've lived through those challenges and it's an experience that I don't want any other kid to ever have to live through.

I have a basic understanding of the Charter of Rights in Canada and acts like the CFS Act, Ombudsman Act, and the Children's Advocate Act. They all exist to protect people and their rights. I also understand some basic policing legislation. Provincially legislated jobs like social work and those in CFS and the police department have rules. I find out what those rules are. I do a lot of work with The Manitoba Advocates for Children and Youth (MACY).

My work with Voices has given me the credentials and representation I need to do my advocacy work. I have taken advocacy workshops with them going back to 2014 and I helped host a big one they had in Brandon in 2017. My lived experience of going through my own systemic problems is also part of my credentials.

I am not at all shy to pick up the phone. I have a social network of people who are specialists, government ministers, and directors of different organizations like, for example, the Residential Tenancy Branch. Knowing these people allows me to find out information and get things done. When I need to know something I can also call MACY. They have endless advice. I've been doing advocacy work for six years. I'll do it for anybody who wants my help—friends and even a few strangers who have heard about what I've done.

One of my more memorable advocacy experiences was when a really good friend of mine got a $1,000 ticket from the RCMP for driving without her insurance. People in positions of authority are supposed to take into account the story leading up to the situation. My friend had explained to the cops that she was being abused and trying to get away from the guy when the officer had asked her what happened and why she didn't have insurance. When she told me that the officer still issued her a ticket, I thought this was not right. So I called the officer's supervisor and asked if I could file a complaint, but they said the person who got the ticket would have to do that. I called my friend and told her how to make the complaint and what she needed to tell them. I told her to make sure they really understand how she felt. People in power are always going to take into consideration how you felt at the time. Her ticket was cancelled. I also called the Civilian Review and Complaints Commission for the RCMP to make a complaint. It's an organization where you can file a complaint about any RCMP officers or dispatchers. I encouraged them to put the police officer under review.

When I'm advocating for people in CFS, a lot of the complaints are because CFS workers have not been educated enough and just don't have experience with their jobs. Their inexperience can turn into neglect for those in CFS care. This is where a lot of systemic problems are created. Another thing that I do is help foster parents and respite workers who are mistreated by CFS social workers or supervisors. I make sure that these social workers are doing their jobs because they are working under a policy and have a job description. Being a kid in the CFS system taught me that, unfortunately, a lot of social workers are lazy. A good social worker is rare. They will try to leave you on hold as long as they can. These people are taking children who are coming from very, very harsh backgrounds and essentially becoming their guardians. If they're just going to show up every three months, what's the point? You might as well just let these kids live with their mothers.

Honestly, doing this advocacy work is relieving, because it is hopefully helping make people do better work. It's also about helping people understand how someone else feels when something happens. So many people don't voice how they feel. There's a huge tension between social workers and advocates, because social workers don't really like being told how to do their jobs.

In 2021 I started digging around to try to get my CFS file. I wanted my documents from schools and guidance counsellors. I also requested medical records and information about my ADHD treatments, mostly for my physician. (I am currently on antidepressants. I've been dying to try them. So far, it's been a great coping mechanism.) I wanted to be able to piece together much of what happened when I was at Knowles specifically. My time there was pretty blurry. I contacted a social worker a few times over several months but heard nothing back. So I called the acting ED at the CFS agency and she said she'd look into it. Months went by. I understand there's a process, but at least they could keep me in the loop. I called the CEO of their CFS Authority and told them I was trying to get a release of information and I wasn't getting it.

Her assistant asked me why I wanted the information. I said, "Because it's my right." CFS is under FIPPA (Freedom of Information and Protection of Privacy Act). FIPPA provides a right to access records held by public bodies.

Basically any provincially legislated body is under that act—hospitals, police stations, treatment centers, CFS agencies—because they all collect information on you.

When she asked me why I wanted the file, I knew something was up. I eventually started making *promises* of what I would do if they continued to do nothing. They finally told me that the hard copy of my file had burned in a fire, but I requested the rest of my file from CFSIS (the CFS Information System). The assistant to the CEO of the Southern Authority withheld my file from me. It was Francine (an aunt of mine who is a CFS social worker) who brought me my file to look at. She had been authorized by the supervisor. She couldn't give it to me to keep. When I saw my file I knew immediately why they did not want me to see it. It was only like fifteen pages long. It was missing four years of reporting (medical records, schooling, and my whole treatment process) from my time at Knowles. The whole section about Knowles, my first foster placement, my information about ADHD medication were missing. There was almost nothing in there about my transition. There was a small comment saying that in 2012 I asked to be referred to as she/her instead of he/

him. But throughout the entire file, the social worker refers to me as he/him regardless.

I now have a copy of two of the four years that were missing. They had been electronically vaulted at Knowles Centre. I called the Centre directly to ask for these documents. I said that if anyone else calls for this information, deny them. It has information about my psychiatric therapy sessions. I was diagnosed with cluster B traits: bipolar, borderline personality disorder. I was not aware of any of that. Apparently I had depression and was suicidal (not from my time with Trudy and Bob). Apparently I had anger issues as well and had to go to group therapy. I also had an Addictions Foundation of Manitoba assessment. None of this was true. They were trying to pin on me that I was crazy, and that I had an addiction. That's hilarious. I had some of the best grades in the facility. I don't know why they didn't see my full potential and put it to use. Now that I see these files, I want to call the people and tell them *Look at me now!* Fuck!

I did a lot of research into advocacy as a career. I learned that you're allowed only twelve years as a government advocate (two

six-year terms). I would rather look for something longer term. So my career mindset is advocacy and social work together. That's where it's been for the past six years now. My cousin Skye basically led me on this path. Until I volunteered with her, my idea of a social worker had been the social workers that worked with me, right? She showed me a different way to be a social worker. Skye told me there are so many more ways that I can use a social work degree. She said I don't have to be taking kids out of homes and placing them into emergency placements. I could take funding from the government and spread it where it needs to be. I just think of helping people. I want to have a Master's in Social Work by the time I'm thirty.

I don't have my high school equivalency, so I'm taking four courses that are going to finish it. I'm also taking an Indigenous course that is a prerequisite that I need to get into social work. I found a three-year social work program that's all online. If you're in my situation where you did leave school at an early age, (maybe because of CFS), there are adult programs in Winnipeg that allow you to get a Grade 12 diploma. That's what I'm doing right now. It's through Kaakiyow Li Moond

Likol, an Adult Learning Centre located inside the Turtle Island Neighbourhood Centre on King St. They've emailed the entire course to me. I get to work at my own pace. I can finish a whole course in a week if I decide to.

My goal with my social work degree would be to do advocacy work in the Band office, on the reserve. The government and MACY only have jurisdiction to advocate for kids on reserves when requested by the kids themselves. I want to work advocating for kids without them having to ask. I want to start some type of organization that would get resources for all kids who live on reserves (tutoring, online study resources and peer groups, stuff like that). Getting kids involved so they have a better life. I want to do better for them. I know what it's like to grow up on a reserve. A lot of people can be really ignorant. I ran away from that. I've gained from my lived experience in foster care. I can apply it to my work, right? What I've lived through and learned is not something that you can just teach. It's special. It motivates me to get work done for kids. I've become a better person because of my experiences. I am not ashamed of anything.

Karlii was candid and very patient with me when I asked her many questions about her gender. I was the recipient of the compassion she talks about giving to others. I am grateful to her. Karlii had gender reassignment surgery in 2022 shortly after we completed this story.

Karlii would have preferred her coming out as transgender to be revealed in her story over time. ("A plot twist!" she said.) This detail begins her story only so that the reader isn't confused as her story unfolds. I am very conscious that Karlii does not want to be identified only by her gender. Karlii told me, "That automatically makes me a minority, and I get treated differently. That puts that negativity onto me. I don't want to claim oppression. I just want to live my life as me." I thank her for her generosity to the readers.

L-R: Melissa and Rachel

Rachel and Melissa

(nijiimens, nimise /my younger sister, my older sister)

Rachel: I am the second oldest in my family of five kids. I'm a mother to three children and I also care for our younger sister. She's lived with me since 2016 when she was in Grade 5.

Melissa: I am the oldest of our five siblings. After Rachel we have two brothers and then our youngest sister. We are keeping their names anonymous. That is the most respectful thing we can do for them. They have their own journey and will have their own time and place to be heard. I really cherish my siblings. I helped raise my siblings for most of their lives.

R: I co-parent my kids with my ex. I do my best to provide for them the life that I was never given, and I see them flourishing. My two older children have taken on hockey as a lifestyle, so I'm a hockey mom, which I love! I'm also a full-time university student in my last year now. I'm working on my Bachelor of Arts, double majoring in History and Indigenous Studies. I don't know what I want to do when I finish university. I don't know if I'm going to end up back working in the child welfare system or if my education will lead me somewhere else.

I first started university when I was twenty-one, but I didn't finish my degree then. I was already a mom and then my second child came shortly after. I was also working full-time as a case manager with a for-profit foster home organization that served CFS. The demands of working full-time and going to school were too much. I worked at that job until I had my youngest child six years ago. That was 2016.

I wanted to go back to university because I knew that I needed more education to be able to make more of a difference. If I didn't have a diploma, nobody was going to listen to me. So that was a factor in deciding to go back to school. And too, after a number of years, the kids were getting older, and I sat with myself and said, *if I don't have that degree who am I to tell my kids that they need to go to university and get further educated after high school?* So I made the decision to go back to university when I was thirty-four, two years after having my youngest child.

For the past twelve years I have also worked casually for an organization that oversees group homes and places where family visits are supervised. That was my side job because working full-time as a case manager didn't always pay the bills. After leaving my full-time job, I told my part-time employer that I wanted to keep working because I needed something to tide me over. They were super.

I was born in Winnipeg, but my maternal family is from Rainy River First Nations. The other name is Manitou Rapids. It sits on the border of the US and Canada.

M: Our maternal grandmother went to Indian residential school and so did our mother. On my paternal side it was my grandfather who attended Indian residential

> I wanted to go back to university because I knew that I needed more education to be able to make more of a difference. If I didn't have a diploma, nobody was going to listen to me. —RACHEL

school. A lot of that history, that darkness and woundedness, is still present in me today. But I don't let that define who I am. I try to honour their experiences by being and walking in a good way in the present. When I say *honour it*, what I mean is that I try to find peace with that trauma and all that woundedness and loss that my grandparents and my mom experienced. I do my best to lead, to continue that healing journey and to correct what's broken in our family. I put a lot of energy into that.

I also put a lot of energy into being a mom to my beautiful teenage daughter. (I am separated from her father.) My daughter is such an incredible blessing to my life and to our whole family. She is my everything. I'm so incredibly thankful that she chose me to be her mom. Me and Rachel always share with our kids, people choose their families and you chose us. We were taught by my grandma Brown that before our souls come down to earth from out there in the stars we select where we are going. *I'm going to be that person.* And so they go down and become that person. And so all our kids were once up there in the universe and they said, "you know what—"

R:—"these guys look cool."

M: Yeah. "I choose them." I'm so thankful that my daughter chose me because I know she really completes me. Women are the givers of life, and it was an honour to carry and birth her. It is also an honour to guide her and support and love her. I've taken care of my siblings and worked with young people, but nothing is the same as raising your own child. My daughter has helped me in every way: spiritually, mentally, emotionally. *Everything.* I'm so grateful to be mother to such a wonderful young human being. She's beautiful, intelligent, humorous, and so caring.

R: Melissa's daughter has got the biggest heart ever! She'll do the kindest things for Melissa. It's unreal sometimes.

M: And then I'm an aunt to Rachel's kids. I absolutely love those kids. They've also played a big role (just like my daughter) in helping me become the person I am today. I do whatever I can to love and to lead and to support all these young people in our lives.

I'm a very involved, very present auntie. That just goes back to my relationship with my siblings. I was more of a mom than a sister sometimes. We're all close, but if you were to ask any of our siblings who the closest are, they would say me and Rachel.

R: One thing that you have to understand is that our family is very close. There isn't a celebration that we aren't all together. Our mom's a part of it when she's able to be. We're making peace with how we were brought up, so we don't exclude her from our celebrations or even dinners.

One of the things that I'm very blessed with is that my siblings have helped me raise my children, especially my youngest. Before COVID, she was never home. She would be at Melissa's for a night, and then one of my brothers would call and say, "Oh, it's been a few days since we've seen her, can you drop her off for a couple hours?" (One of the things that we had to adjust to during the early pandemic was her not being able to go visit so freely.)

Because of the way we've raised all our kids together along with our younger sister, she is more of a sibling than an aunt. My youngest daughter has a really close bond with her and with Melissa's daughter.

M: My daughter is the oldest, then it's our younger sister, and then Rachel's oldest. They'll actually all be sixteen for—

R:—I think it's like twenty-seven days.

M: Yeah. That's one hat my daughter wears very proudly, that she's the oldest.

I've worked for Manitoba Justice going on ten years now. It's a good job. I was a probation officer, and then I started a new position there in January 2021 as a cultural advisor. I'm so excited to have been selected as the first cultural advisor for the Restorative Justice Branch.

But sometimes I struggle working for a very colonial system because it's based on settler laws and it's just so far removed from our pre-contact Indigenous justice system. Restorative Justice is the approach that the Indigenous have always taken; let's come to together, involve everyone, even the people who have not been directly impacted but are part of the community because there is a ripple effect.

I walk in both those worlds now: Western and Indigenous. It's a hybrid system for me. Indigenous people will never be able to go back to a pre-settler contact way of life. I used to struggle; I was frustrated and angry. But I've found a balance in how to be successful in the western world's hierarchy, but also how to be true to that traditional Indigenous, holistic way of life. It can be done.

It hurts my heart to work with individuals who continue to be imbedded in a system that's not there to really support them. On probation, youth can get put into programming to address issues, but people's trauma is so deep-rooted that it needs more than a twenty-hour program. It needs a healing journey.

I also work casually at the same organization as Rachel. I hate going to their office on Main Street because it always triggers flashbacks in me. It was a CFS building (back then it was called Children's Aid) when I was a kid. That office was the place I went the first time I can remember being apprehended. I experience vicarious trauma in my job to this day. I hate when parents are saying goodbye after a visit. Do you know how much that triggers flashbacks from my history? It's so incredibly hard. Fucking exhausting.

I was born in the town of Emo, Ontario, which is right next to the Rainy River First Nation. I can't remember my early, early childhood. I don't know if it's something I've blocked out or I just don't recall that part of my life.

R: While our mom was pregnant with Melissa, Melissa's dad died by suicide. Our mom decided to come to Winnipeg, but we were never sure why. Our mom's whole family was in Ontario so she had no support system in Winnipeg.

M: I don't remember Rachel being born at all. She was born in 1984. I think I was spending a lot of time in Ontario with my grandma and grandpaiban Brown. There was me and my cousin Richardiban, who I loved and who really was a brother to me.

R: When you say *iban*, they've moved on to the spirit world. It's an Anishinaabe word where you're honouring them.

M: It was like my mom had shipped me off to my grandparents after she had met Rachel's dad. Rachel was probably born shortly after that. I was four and a half when she was born. And then I don't even know how old I was when I came back to live with my mom. I do remember that Rachel was a tiny toddler then.

One of my earliest memories involves Rachel's father. I was living in Winnipeg. One morning I got up early and Rachel's dad was there with my mom. I remember thinking, *Who is this man?* He was a curiosity. I'd never seen him before. Unfortunately I don't recall many positive experiences from my childhood. We did experience some abuse, as well as extreme poverty. We were often hungry because our mom had no money to feed us. (Rachel's dad Garryiban would refuse to provide our mom with any assistance.) It was horrific because it deeply scarred me.

Sometimes we didn't even have clean clothes. I remember I found an old, white washboard in the garbage and I was so happy. That's how I used to wash me and Rachel's clothes. I filled the bathtub with water and rubbed our clothes with dish soap or even bar soap. I rinsed them and hung them up to dry. It was more Rachel's clothes than my own because I wanted her to have clean clothes. I remember as far back as I can, always trying to be the best for Rachel. I just wanted to protect her and love her and teach her. I did everything I possibly could. I'd bathe her and feed her. I was probably five or six and Rachel was one or two. I was just so proud of her and loved her so, so much.

> Sometimes we didn't even have clean clothes. I remember I found an old, white washboard in the garbage and I was so happy. That's how I used to wash me and Rachel's clothes. —MELISSA

We were living in this apartment right on the corner of Sherbrook and Cumberland. That's the first place I remember. I want to say that it was in '85, '86. I would have been in French immersion at Ecole Sacré Coeur. I think I went there for kindergarten or Grade 1 because that's when Rachel was probably one. She was a really cute little baby. I was so cute too when I was little.

R: Yeah, she was.

M: We got apprehended there. I think Rachel was old enough to be walking. I have a flashback of Rachel walking, dressed in her blue snowsuit and big ugly white chunky boots.

My mom was out, and Rachel's dad was babysitting. I don't know if she went to bingo, or what. Maybe she didn't come home. I'm not sure what happened, but I remember Rachel's dad got up and left, and Rachel and I were alone. Later I found out that he had called CFS. I don't think he ever lived with us because he lived with his aunt. But he would come and stay, especially for the weekends. He called CFS because he was a fucking asshole and wanted to hurt our mom. If he knew we were alone, why not come and watch us instead? Looking back, Rachel's dad used to do that when he wanted to get back at our mom for something. The landlord had to let the cops and two CFS workers in because I remember them going through the door. They were asking where Mom was. I don't even remember what I said. They took us to that office on Main Street. Main and Bannerman.

We went to stay with a white family. I slept in the basement. (I don't remember quite where you slept, Rachel.) They didn't like me because they were calling me *Indian girl,* but they liked Rachel because she was light skinned. They treated her really differently. I remember feeling so scared and missing Mom and not knowing what was going to happen.

L-R: Melissa and Rachel

ANDREW MAHON

That was a horrific experience for me, but they loved Rachel. They doted on her. She was happy.

I know we were there long enough for those people to make me not like myself. They kept referring to me as *that dirty little Indian girl* and *not cute like this one.* Certain things are just ingrained in your memory.

This one time, they gave me a new tooth-brush and said, "Go brush your teeth." I remember scrubbing my hand and arm, trying to make my skin lighter like Rachel's so those people would be nice to me too. They started banging on the bathroom door shouting, "What are you doing in there?" They were so mean to me, so awful.

That time in my life is kind of a blur... I went back and forth between my mom and my grandparents. I went back to live with grandma and grandpaiban Brown for the majority of Grade 1. (They lived in Manitou Rapids First Nation, Ontario). At some point I came back to school in Winnipeg. I failed Grade 1 there because I had missed so much school. I had to do that grade again. But I know I was happy going back to Winnipeg because I knew I would be with Rachel.

I went to Fort Rouge School until the beginning of Grade 2. Ken and Kathy were my workers in the after-school daycare program and they took me under their wings. *They knew*. Sometimes I went to visit at Kathy's house. Rachel didn't come, but I don't know why. I admire all those teachers and daycare staff who work with so many broken children. Just thinking now about our situation and our history, I think *Holy Crap*. I liked visiting with her because it was a safe place. Kathy cared about me, she was so nice to me. She fed me, and we did things together like crafts. It brought me peace when I visited her. That was a time for me to check out of the reality back home. I don't quite remember how I even got there. Did mom just drop me off? I don't know.

R:—Like how the hell did Mom let you go to her house?

M: Yah, I know. I do know I was in Ontario when I was seven and my younger brother was born. That was June 1987. I remember I was already done school for the summer, and I ran up to the Grey Goose bus and my mom came off carrying him in one of those baby carriers and I was so happy. I already had so much love for Rachel, and right as soon as I saw him, I loved him too.

R: I don't have any memory of my younger brother being born. I was only two and a half. I don't have a lot of early childhood memories either. I think one of the things that I've done to keep myself from re-traumatizing is I've blocked out a lot of my childhood. One of my earliest memories would be walking to and from Sister MacNamara School with Melissa. I must've been in kindergarten. So I would have been five or six? I remember doing that walk from—what street was that, Melissa?

M: We lived at Young and Portage.

R: We did that walk four times a day. I remember waiting outside my classroom door for Melissa to pick me up and we'd walk back home for lunch. A lot of times we'd have next to nothing to eat there, so walking back to the school we were still hungry. But we didn't stay at the school during lunch because Melissa didn't want us to be around kids that were eating since it would make us even more hungry. In the winter it was really cold and Melissa was always saying, "Hurry up," or "Where are you?" when she was crossing the street.

Melissa played school with me before I was in kindergarten. When I started school I could read and write simple words, and I could do my name really well. I remember my teacher really praising me, and me thinking, *I like how this feels. It makes me feel good about myself.*

M: In Grade 3, I went to Sister Mac. I had Mrs. Okemaw for my teacher. She is an Indigenous woman. She was very special to me and I know I was special to her too. She really cared for me.

R: Remember, Melissa, you were a hoop dancer?

M: Oh yeah, Mrs. Okemaw made sure that I learned. We did hoop dancing at school. We got to go to a couple of Pow Wows too. I totally admired Mrs. Okemaw. I remember thinking, *Man, I don't have to be poor!* I had never seen an Indigenous woman who was a teacher. She was educated. She was a symbol that I could be somebody.

In the inner city, I had seen tons of Indigenous people living in poverty. Even from a very young age, I knew what poor meant because I could not have what other people had. Poverty was horrible. Horrible! Thinking about it makes me cry. I don't know what I did when we had no food.

R: That just triggered something for me. I remember throwing up and nothing coming out except stomach bile. I can't remember what we did for food either, but I remember that's how bad it got sometimes.

Even to this day, if I'm low on food, I get this sense of anxiety where I feel like I'm not doing my job as a parent. The pandemic made it even worse. I bought a small freezer and it's in the basement. If I see that we're down to just three loaves of bread, I get a sense of panic. So I'll make a point of going to the store the next day and getting, like, six loaves of bread. Then I can breathe again.

M: When Rachel goes shopping, she's buying for a frigging pandemic (even when there isn't one!) and it all stems from what we experienced as kids.

I don't know what I did emotionally or even physically as a kid to overcome that feeling of hunger. I just remember, it was always me and Rach for the longest time until our younger brother was born. And it kills me to think, *What happened with Rachel when I was with my grandparents and wasn't there? Who took care of her?* Looking back now, I'd say that's when her dad was present instead of me.

R: I don't think my dad was around regularly. I just remember him being in and out, but not consistent. I have the same dad as my two brothers, but not as my younger sister. I got treated a lot better than my brothers.

If Melissa hadn't been there to raise me, holy shit, I think I would have had ten kids that were all in care! (I'm not being dramatic.) If I didn't have my sister telling me that I could do better, be better, or am better than what society expected of me, then I would never have found the self love I needed in order to do my best and be my best.

I think us kids would have all grown up in care if it wasn't for Melissa. I remember there were quite a few times when people would come and bang on the door and Melissa would put us in the closet, and we'd have to wait for the people to go away. A lot of times, she saved us from going back into care. That couldn't have been easy.

M: It was actually really awful to have to tell the kids to go hide and be extremely quiet. Sometimes I'd even have to hold their mouths with my hands because I was so scared they'd be heard. I knew CFS was at the door. I'd wait for the feet to leave from underneath the door, but I still wouldn't go get the kids from the closet or the bedroom, because I'd be worried that CFS was only pretending to leave. I'd make my siblings wait in the bedroom to avoid being heard, until I was sure the people were really gone. I was afraid they'd come back with the police and get the caretaker to open the door and take us back to foster care.

R: Melissa, remember when we would go to school, we would leave early to get to the breakfast program? It'd be so cold and still dark outside. You would say, "Hurry up. You got to be faster so that we can get there so we don't miss breakfast." We were like babies—Grade 3 and kindergarten.

M: We were definitely in care while we went to Sister Mac because I remember a CFS support worker carrying my brother and picking us up at school. I think they were short apprehensions. The three of us kids got apprehended shortly after I started Grade 3 there. Rachel's dad had called CFS again. I think all our CFS encounters stem from him calling CFS. It was me, Rachel, and our younger brother. We must have gone to a CFS house. The reason I know it was a CFS house now is because of working with children in the CFS system. It must've been an emergency placement or a shelter home. I recall it was somewhere not too far off Portage. Those houses are cold and very unwelcoming (even to present day). It was just a basic home with a couch, a table. There was a white lady. She was fairly young.

Sharing a bed with our siblings was common. Probably lots of families do it, right? Either me and Rachel together, or sometimes we'd sleep with our mom. I remember there was no way this CFS woman was going to allow us to sleep together. I was so scared, so lonely; I had trouble falling asleep. My brother had to sleep in another room with the worker. He didn't know her. I heard him crying in the middle of the night because he was so scared. I tried to go to him and take care of him but the worker told me to go back to my room. I remember going back to my room and crying. Hearing my brother cry that night has forever scarred me.

One night we ate and then we went outside to play. We had sidewalk chalk so

> I was so scared, so lonely, I had trouble falling asleep.—**MELISSA**

I wrote our names on the sidewalk. Later, when we went back home with our mom, she said, "I know where you were because I saw the names you wrote on the sidewalk." My mom and my auntie must've known that was a CFS house and walked by when we were there. I wondered why she wouldn't have just knocked on the door and tried to see us? And I think about how I didn't even know my mom was passing by at that point. It hurt me so much but now I think about how much it must have hurt my mom too.

R: I honestly don't remember. But I do remember that time when you had a mark on your face and Miss Penner asked you about it.

M: Miss Penner was another teacher who I looked up to a lot and who I felt very safe with. I had her for Grade 4 and Grade 6.

R: I remember our mom being really angry with Melissa.

M: One day me and my best friend went home from school for lunch, and I saw my mom's cheque was there. It could have been a welfare or child tax credit cheque—I don't know. But I knew she was waiting for it, so we took it and went to find her at the Adult Ed School she was attending. When we got there, my mom wasn't at the school, so we left and walked back to our school. I saw my mom on Balmoral Street, so I crossed the street to get to her. She was livid and yelled at me and asked me why I had taken the cheque from the mail. Then she hit me in the face with her shoe.

R; My mom used to take a lot out on Melissa.

M: It was a pretty big deal. It was the side of my face. The shoe left an indent. CFS was called and came to see my mom. She was angry afterwards.

R: I don't think that we were apprehended though.

M: I specifically remember lying to Miss Penner. She asked me how it happened and I said I fell down and scraped my face. I never told anyone my mom hit me.

CFS came to visit my mom and afterwards I went back to my grandparents in Emo. There was a pattern that after CFS would come to our house, I'd be shipped back to my grandparents. I'm pretty sure that was our last encounter with CFS, because after that I was at the age where I could babysit.

R: *Legally* babysit.

M: There were definitely lots of times when I took care of the kids and couldn't tell anyone because I was not old enough to babysit yet. Mom went to bingo a lot.

But I think Rachel was probably in care a few more times as a child because it was her father's mentality that whenever my mom would piss him off, he'd call CFS.

R: I don't know. Like I said, I've blocked lots out. When Melissa talks, some memories are triggered, but I think forgetting is just how I'm able to cope with how we were brought up.

M: After Grade 6 all of us moved to Onigaming First Nation in Ontario. Onigaming is my father's community.

R: Our mom's sister married a community member from there. So that's where our cousins are from as well.

M: Our mom's sister had lost her daughter in a car accident and so my mom went there to support her. We were there for like a year.

R: Melissa, you were twelve or thirteen when we moved to Ontario. That's when Melissa went wild. She'd take off and go partying when we lived on the reserve. Our mom was gone a lot too.

M: At that point, our mom's being gone wasn't so much about alcohol. It was more about gambling. She would take off to the casino.

R: Our mom would be gone for a night or two and Melissa would be gone too. That's when I started being in charge. I hated living there because I started having to take care of myself and my brother.

One time I remember me and my brother went to bed hungry on the couch and watched a VHS tape of *Charlotte's Web*. (To this day, I will not watch that movie.) I put that on for him and told him to go to bed. I woke up at two or three in the morning and it was the end of the movie and the credits were playing. There was a wooden stove in the house and it must've gone out because it was getting cold. I remember feeling like I just wanted to die. I must've been eight or nine. I was overwhelmed, being hungry and not knowing where everyone was.

I had to try to start a fire in the wooden stove so that it wouldn't be so cold in the house. I told myself that as soon as it started to get light outside, I'd get my brother dressed and we'd just go walk down the hill to our auntie's place. I don't even know when or if we got fed that day.

M: I just hate hearing that so much. It was just this ugly, nasty, repetitive cycle. I had no idea they were hurting like that. I am so ashamed of this because all my life I've taken care of them.

I was running around the community doing stupid stuff. While we lived there I tried to OD. Twice I tried to kill myself. The local child welfare authority became involved after that. I was probably twelve or thirteen, because my great-grandma was still around and she came to see me in the hospital.

> I remember feeling like I just wanted to die. I must've been eight or nine. I was overwhelmed, being hungry and not knowing where everyone was.—RACHEL

R: That's when you took the pills, right Melissa?

M: Yeah. I don't even know what I took. It's crazy. They were auntie's pills. I don't think I wanted to die, but I did not want to feel pain and hurt. I think I was just so depressed and so lost. My spirit was broken and I did not engage in good behavior. I just wanted to forget.

Around then my mom took off with us to Calgary, because CFS had gotten involved again. We weren't in Calgary long at all. Maybe half a year—

R:—Six months, yeah. I remember smoking for the first time in Calgary. I think I even tried pot there. I hung out with this one girl and she was not a good influence. I was supposed to go home but then she said, "No, let's just go smoke." We got high and then all of a sudden my mom pulled up and shouted, "What the hell are you doing over here? Get in this fucking car." I was super embarrassed, but then scared she was going to hit me. My mom is a really small woman, but I was always terrified of her from seeing what she did to Melissa. I was eleven, maybe.

M: No, Rach, you were probably even younger.

R: I think we all had an apartment of our own because I remember we had literally *nothing* in it.

M: Calgary was a very sad and depressing time. I think CFS was still in contact with us because I remember talking to this awful social worker we had back in Ontario. But I don't think Calgary CFS got involved.

R: And then mom pawned all of her fucking CDs and that's when we moved back home to Winnipeg. Calgary is a blur for me. I don't remember a lot.

M: When we came back to Winnipeg I went to Grant Park and Rachel was at Montrose School.

R: I hated Montrose because there were these really racist girls there. They were so mean to me. I wore the same dress for the first day of school, picture day, Christmas concert (any special things that we had) and they would taunt me for it. I hated that.

Our baby brother was born in February of '96 while I was in grade six.

M: His birth kind of breathed life back into our lives. Our home was filled with negativity, poverty, and not a lot of love. He wasn't just my baby, the way Rachel and my other brother had been; our baby brother was Rachel's baby too. We loved him so much.

R: Yeah. We wanted to protect him. He was literally *our baby*. I remember boiling his bottles and feeding him and burping him.

M: We adored him and took care of him. That's about the age when we started working, so we bought him the baby stuff that he needed. We got him the best clothes and toys we could. He was our baby.

At Grant Park High School I was obviously designated as one of the *poor people*. I never fit in with the popular group, but I had my little group of misfits and we were fine and content. It was a predominantly white school so that was not the best experience.

I never graduated. In Grade 12, I needed only three or four more credits but I quit because I needed to work to provide for myself and the kids. I need to go back and get my diploma. Ever since I started working, I've never stopped. I was never, ever going to go without again.

At this point, our mom was mainly with her boyfriend who would later be our youngest sister's dad. Our mom wasn't around much, but she did make sure we had a roof over our heads and she brought us groceries or take-out food.

R: When I turned twelve I started working too. Me and my mom would sometimes go for lunch to a restaurant close to our house. The owner hired me for the summer. My mom had charged up a bunch of takeout food and said she'd pay for it, but then she didn't. The owner kept my pay. I was super hurt by that because my mom had cost me my income and my job.

M: But the money wasn't even really for us. We would buy things for our brothers.

R: Yeah, and food.

M: It was pretty fucking sad.

R: And then there would even be times when the water or the hydro would be cut off.

M: Ever since I've moved out, paying bills is so important to me, because I could never have a repeat of what happened to us.

R: Just thinking about that makes me feel sick. When I look back at those times growing up, I think *How the fuck did we live through that?* We were just kids.

M: We were resilient.

R: Growing up poor, you don't think education is going to get you anywhere. (That was what we thought, anyways.) It wasn't important to go on in school.

M: My mom took me for my first welfare appointment. I got $76 and I thought, *Screw this.* So I just started working. I worked doing youth programming at a community centre and retail work. I sold men's shirts and ties. I tried going back to school, but it was just not in my life plan. I couldn't do work and school.

When I turned eighteen, I stayed with my mom after I quit school because I was taking care of the kids and working. Our baby brother was so tiny and I just couldn't leave him. Our younger brother was about twelve and he had started engaging in some unhealthy behaviors and skipping school. CFS didn't come around as much at that point because I was now a legal adult and could take responsibility for the kids. My mom sort of checked out of parenting at that point in our lives.

R: She was never around because we could all take care of each other.

M: And we did.

M: We ended up moving out because we'd just had enough. I left home at twenty.

R: I was sixteen when I moved out with Melissa. We had a two-bedroom apartment.

M: We left our baby brother with our mom, but he was over at our place all the time anyway. Sometimes we would go get him, or our mom would just drop him off. Our younger brother didn't stay with us though.

R: He and my mom are closer. Out of all of us kids, he has been with our mom the most.

R: At that time I went to Argyle School but I didn't graduate then. I was on welfare when I was in high school and I got $80 a month. I was so depressed because I couldn't even afford to buy myself the basic things I needed, like shampoo and feminine products. I thought *This isn't the way I want to live my life.*

M: After we moved out on our own, Rachel and I got kicked out of our house because we partied too hard, so we all moved in with our mom and brothers. I thought, *I guess we could live with my mom again and make this work.* My mom lived with us, but wasn't around much.

CFS became involved with our baby brother when we lived there. He was in kindergarten or grade 1. He wasn't in care all that long, maybe eight weeks, but it was really traumatic for us because we thought of him as our baby. My heart was so, so broken. I hated it.

R: My mom, my brothers, and me moved to Ontario again when I was eighteen or nineteen. Our mom got a job at the band office.

M: I stayed in Winnipeg. I said, "I ain't going back to Ontario." My mom told me to take over the house on Goulding.

R: I only lasted out in Ontario for the summer. Melissa was in Winnipeg and I didn't want her to be alone. I didn't want to be that far away from her. Me and my younger brother came back and moved in with Melissa.

M: That's when I got pregnant. I had my daughter in 2005 when we lived on Jubilee—

R: It was me and Melissa (Our younger brother had left to be with our mom) and then our baby brother started living with us there. Melissa had raised me and our younger brother, and then she raised our baby brother too.

M: I completely took over the care of my youngest brother from the time my daughter was born. (Rachel's always been present too.) He never returned to my mom's care. My mom was pregnant with our youngest sister at that time. I remember one picture of him sitting in the kitchen holding my daughter while he's eating his cereal. He was nine when he came to live with us.

R: I started working part-time at the Community Centre at River and Osborne. I had to wake up at 6 a.m. to open the doors there for the yoga classes. I was twenty when I graduated from high school. I went to Adult Ed. I was a couple of months pregnant with my first baby when I graduated. My first baby was born in 2006.

My kids' father and I lived together for a few years and then we decided to separate. When the kids were with their dad on the weekends, I started doing a lot of partying. I would get into drinking on Friday and Saturday and then sobering up on Sunday when they came home.

M: I lived with my daughter's father for a little bit, but not very long.

R: When Melissa's relationship with her daughter's dad started to disintegrate, she came to me and said, "Why don't we look for a four or five-bedroom house and move in together. We'll help raise each other's kids. We'll live there for at least five years so we have enough time to each save for a house." We moved in together in 2010.

M: My daughter was five then.

R: And my oldest two must've been four and two. We signed a five-year lease with the owner. The first couple of years living there, my partying was very controlled, but then I started going back to my old habits, partying every other weekend when the kids weren't home.

Melissa was doing a lot of the parenting. Melissa finally said to me, "If you don't stop the way that you're living and get help for yourself, then I'm going to go to your kids' dad and tell him exactly what you've been up to. I know that it's not just drinking for you anymore. You're getting into other shit." She said, "I know that you're better than this and your kids deserve better than this."

I knew Melissa was right. My last year living there, I got sober.

That was the summer I started sundancing, and that was a big turn-around for me. I partied pretty much up until the day before we left to go down to the Sundance. I danced and fasted for those four days (that included not having any water). I remember coming out of the fast and thinking, *If I can do that for four days, then I don't need drugs or alcohol to get rid of the pain that I'm carrying from all of the stuff I've been through.*

It was early August. I told myself I wasn't going to have a drink until my birthday, which is in December. When my birthday came I didn't really feel like drinking, so I told myself I'd wait till Christmas. And then Christmas came along and I just didn't feel like I needed it. All of a sudden it was six months later, and I thought *Holy shit, I haven't had a drink or done any drugs in six months.* Six months turned into a year and so on. I literally quit everything cold turkey.

When I was abusing drugs and alcohol, I wasn't seeing things clearly. But as soon as I gave all of those things up, I was able to feel that love for my kids again. It was such a beautiful feeling. The love that I have for my kids is so amazing. I knew that my kids deserved a parent who would see and think clearly.

I'll have my bad days parenting, but then my little four-year-old will tell me she loves me a hundred times that day. Just hearing

M: Rachel and I do this unspoken thing where we always take care of each other, no matter what, right? So ever since our younger sister was born, we do what we've got to do to make sure she's okay: that she has a roof over her head, food, clothing, and is going to school. We do everything within our power, especially Rachel. Rachel does such a good job taking care of our sister.

I really don't know where I learned to be a mother. I ask myself that all the time. As a child, I just remember loving Rachel so much and feeling blessed that she was there. I wanted her to be loved and not alone. I just knew instinctively that I had to care for her and protect her, at all cost. I knew that very, very early.

My mom did teach me that no matter what; it's always your family. She used to tell me to take care of my siblings and watch over them. I heard this right from a young age so therefore I learned that my family is everything to me. She also taught me how to be a strong woman against all obstacles, but as to being motherly, she didn't teach me those kinds of qualities.

My grandma Brown taught me how to love. Even though she wasn't physically

those words and knowing that this beautiful little girl loves me like that, I don't even miss any of the booze or drugs.

I had to do what I had to do to break that cycle. I know that I'm not fully healed from my past, but I know that I'm doing something to prevent my kids from feeling the pain that I felt growing up. I feel so good about myself because I had to do that in order for my kids to live the life that they're leading.

Our younger sister ended up coming to live with me in 2016, when she was in Grade 5. It was in our sister's best interest.

affectionate, you knew you were loved and cared for. And my grandma Margaret (my dad's mom) always found ways to show her love too, especially on birthdays and holidays.

R: I don't always see my little sister as my little sister. I see her more as a daughter. I try really hard not to think of her that way, but since she's the age of some of our oldest kids, that's where we place her a lot of the time. Since I'm her guardian I have to guide her through life and provide for her the way I do for my kids. I always do my best to include her with the family unit, because she is a part of it.

Even my brothers can think of her as a daughter too. I think our youngest brother feels protective of her and like he needs to be this father figure to her.

M: Yeah, that's how I feel with our sister too. Sometimes I feel like she's just *one of our kids*. And I do feel more maternal with my baby brother because I raised him for so long.

R: I don't think our sister considers either of us to be like her mom. She doesn't call us mom or anything.

M: She's very protective of the relationship she has with our mom.

R: Sometimes she's almost loyal to a fault, but I know what that feels like. I think every kid has that loyalty to their parent, no matter what happens to them. I see that a lot working in the child welfare system. No matter what a mom or dad does to you; they're always going to be number one.

Melissa is just like another mom to my kids.

M: I won't cook!

R: Melissa will call me at the beginning of the week and say, "Send me your schedule for the week so that I know when and how I need to help you out." (Especially for my youngest.) When Melissa bought her townhouse, immediately she made my youngest a beautiful little bedroom in her house.

M: I am most proud of where I am in life and the success I've had because I wasn't expected to be where I am today. From a societal perspective, I was likely to be dependent on social assistance, pregnant at a young age, incarcerated, an addict, someone isolated in a community where I had no future, or even possibly murdered. But I am a contributing member of society and I have a good job. However, I'm always trying to prove my worth because Indigenous people have been stereotyped and viewed negatively as the lazy uneducated Indian.

R:—*She must be lazy.*

M: Unfortunately, that mentality is still there in present-day society. I'm employed, I own my own home, drive my own vehicle, take my daughter on vacations, provide for her. We don't starve. I pay my bills.

That reminds me of my first encounter with one of the young men on my caseload. He comes to the office and he's got this look of confusion. I said to him "What's wrong?"

He says to me, "What are you doing over there? Do you work here? Because you're Indigenous, and I don't understand this. You're not supposed to be working here."

I said, "Yeah, I do. I'm actually your worker."

I do my best to empower the young people that I work with and let them know that their past will not define what their future can be, because right now they are in control, despite any obstacles.

R: Melissa says it so well. I'm really proud of my kids and of the way that I am as a mother. The relationship that I have with my kids is something that I yearned for with my own mom. I can laugh and joke around with them and tell them when they're doing something wrong. We talk about how they're going to correct it or do better next time. And I think that they listen to me. That trust is there with my kids. I love the fact that I have that relationship with my younger sister and niece as well.

I love that I am able to hug my kids and kiss them and tell them that I love them, because growing up our mom never did that. The fact that I can show love so openly with my kids is the most beautiful thing that I've experienced. They know that they're loved. Hearing "I love you" breathes fresh air into your body and your spirit.

One of my friends said that I'm really good at keeping my home fires burning. I'm really, really proud of everything that I put into my own home to make it my home and to make it a safe haven for my children. Growing up, that's not how I felt. I didn't always want to go home.

My kids never go without. If I have to go above and beyond to provide for them, then I do that. I'll take on side jobs or contracts here and there. It means I am exhausted sometimes. There are times when I'm working every other weekend because my son wants certain skates or one of their birthdays are coming up or we have a vacation that we're planning.

M: About six years ago, before I moved out of the house I had shared with Rachel, I did have a bit of a breakdown. That's when I finally decided to really love myself and heal.

I had spent the majority of my life taking care of Rachel and my siblings, and even my mom. I just gave and gave and gave. So I told them, "You guys have to be responsible for taking care of yourselves. I'm tired and I can't do it no more." It wasn't that I was pushing them away, but I was older and I wanted to put all my energy into loving and supporting my daughter, Rachel's kids, and our younger sister. I had this beautiful little spunky daughter and I wanted to focus all my energy

on her, and give her everything I didn't have growing up.

It was so incredibly hard to have that conversation with my siblings. They were *my babies*, but I know that they needed to hear it too. I am happy that I had that conversation with them. I was still their biggest supporter, but verbally saying it was healing for me.

Also around that time my mom was having a harder time and it was just all too much for me. I talked to my mom then too and told her she needed to live her life however that was. I thought *I can't do this no more.*

This was around the time when Sundancing became a big part of my life and I was on my healing journey. Being a sundancer is one of the most profound achievements in my life.

My earliest recollection of anything to do with who we are as Anishinaabe is my grand-paiban Brown. I have early recollections of his hand drum and him singing. My grandma Brown walks in both worlds. (She's still alive.) After her experience in Indian residential school she carried on as a Catholic. She prays and has her rosaries, but at the same time, she is a very traditional woman. My grandparents were always talking Anishinaabemowin.

My grandma Brown's medicine bag had such a great significance for me. It hung on her bedroom wall. She took great care of it and she'd bring it down only at certain times. It was black, and it had beaded florals on the front. It was so beautiful. She had her tobacco and cedar in there.

I also remember my grandma's jingle dress. It was green and just so beautiful. She wore it when she danced at Pow Wows. She did the old traditional two-step. I wanted to be a jingle dress dancer too. So my grandparents got me a little jingle dress made and I danced with her at Pow Wows. I was little, little. I also remember smudging with my grandparents.

R: I think my earliest cultural memory would be smudging at my grandparents too. When we were little kids, we would go back to Ontario for a week or two in the summertime.

We have a family drum. The story behind it is that there's seven of them, and they're all sister drums. I think three of them were in Canada and four of them were in the States, probably in communities that were closely connected to ours. Our family drum is called the Bwaanidewe'igan, which means Sioux Drum.

And then fast forward to the first actual connection that I made with my culture after that would definitely be when I started Sundancing when I was twenty-seven. I had gone for two or three years to support Melissa before I started dancing. 2020 would have been my sixth or seventh year dancing, but due to COVID we made the decision not to go. Melissa and I both attend Sundances with our Lakota relatives in Rosebud, South Dakota.

When you go down to a Sundance, it is an absolutely beautiful experience that you can't put into words. You're just incredibly blessed with the people and the prayers that are all around you. I'm also a pipe carrier. I was gifted a pipe three years ago. So that was an honour.

M: My first year dancing was in 2009. I would have been twenty-nine.

R: My spirit name is Kaagigegiizhigook. It is Everlasting Sky Woman. I was very fortunate to receive my spirit name from my uncle Wab.

We were down at Sundance one summer and I had told myself that I was going to ask for my spirit name. On our second day of dancing, it was about to rain or it was spitting. I had said to Wab earlier that day, that before I go to dance I'll pray for rain while I'm sitting in the sweats (sweat lodge), so we won't die of heat when we're out there dancing. When it started spitting rain I said, "Oh, my God, I prayed for rain and Creator listened to me!"

It feels like when I pray for certain things when I'm out there dancing, Creator listens to me. So I think that when Wab was giving me my spirit name, he gave me that connection to the sky. I don't have a say in how the weather goes... but I just kind of feel heard when I'm praying. It's really amazing.

M: My spirit name is Siigasiige, which translates to The Rays of the Sun. When the rays from the sun come through the clouds, that's what this refers to. For me, this name is about being very, very powerful. The sun is a powerful force. My spirit name is about breaking through whatever hurdle or barrier I am experiencing and remaining strong while I overcome whatever I am facing.

> My spirit name is about breaking through whatever hurdle or barrier I am experiencing and remaining strong while I overcome whatever I am facing. **–MELISSA**

All my life I've had to be strong. Yellow is actually one of my colours (yellow and bronze). And every time I see the sun's rays break through the cloud, such peacefulness overcomes me. I just smile with pride and I have happiness in my heart.

My paternal grandfather, Tobasonakwutiban, gave my name to me maybe ten years ago. I was very happy. It would have been so beautiful to have a name from my maternal grandfather too. (You can be a carrier of more than one name.) I love my spirit name.

M: The Red Road is about living a good life, a healthy life. Mino Bimaadiziwin. That is about living and following the Anishinaabe principles. They were gifted to us as humans through spirit. Our ancestors did all the work and planned this life for us (our language, our teachings, the way we act, think, and choose to live and be). This is how Mino Bimaadiziwin was taught to me.

R: No drugs, no alcohol. That's the way I see it.

M: It's living life incorporating the simplest things like smudging or going to ceremony with our kids. We want to instill that way of life into our kids' lives.

I did experience drugs many years ago; however, it was for a very short time and I am drug free. Interpreting how to live the Red Road is up to the individual. I do like the occasional social cup of wine here and there, but I feel I am able to walk the Red Road because I'm not abusing alcohol. I am still able to have a pipe and be a Sundancer.

R: Unlike Melissa, I used to drink to blackout. I used to go on binges. I have experimented with drugs. I think that those are the things that I had to go through in order to become the person I am today. Now I know what it's like to live a clean, sober life and live my life on the Red Road. I can say no to drugs and alcohol because I know what it feels like to use them and be at my very lowest point. Leaving that lifestyle showed me what I could get through to be where I am today. It has also given me a sense of humility that I need when I am working with families that are struggling with addictions so that I'm not judging them. I think, *I've been there. I know what it's like to want to drink Friday to Sunday. I know what it's like to spend your last forty bucks on drugs.* That all plays into the person I am today. Despite overcoming my addictions, I continue to encounter struggles in life, but not using helps me to deal with them in a healthier way.

Walking the Red Road is about treating people like human beings and not judging them. For example looking at somebody that's homeless and wondering what happened for them to be in that situation.

As I'm growing into who I'm becoming, I want to teach my kids. I want them to volunteer more and understand how fortunate they are because of the changes that I've made in order for them—

M:—I reiterate to the kids, "I want you to be grateful and appreciate what you have in your life, and *who*. You have a roof over your heads, clothes, food, access to things. You're probably never going to experience *being without*. Respect it." We teach the kids to be humble about their lives, and to be kind. Our kids have already started creating their own sacred bundles and are all living the Red Road in their own way. I always tell the kids

"Spirit is watching, so be the best version that you can possibly be of yourself."

R: I don't think I really grew up and was an adult until I was twenty-seven when I made that decision to start Sundancing. That's when I thought *I need to not take my life for granted*. I suffered and I prayed for those four days. Afterwards I was able to walk away from alcohol and drugs.

Walking on that Red Road allows me to understand that everybody has their own backstory. So I am trying to be a kinder person. I am doing my best to live my life on the Red Road and by the Seven Sacred Teachings. I'm also being more mindful of when I allow somebody else's opinions or thoughts to affect me. If someone talks bad about me, it's not a reflection on me. It's a reflection on the things that they've gone through.

M: The Seven Sacred Teachings, as well as walking the Red Road, contribute to living a good life (Mino Bimaadiziwin).

R: I want to continue my journey because I love being a Sundancer and what it means, and the life that it's shown me. One day, I'm going to be an Elder.

Melissa, our younger sister, and I just recently committed ourselves to the Midewewin Lodge (Medicine Society). This is the next step in my healing journey. I have found the strength that's inside me. It is also the next step in our growth as Anishinaabeg. I never want to stop growing and learning our way of life. Committing to the Midewewin Lodge is naturally the next step to leading a good life. I know we are doing the right thing. I am meant to do this at that time and place.

M: We are learning what our commitment to the Midewewin Lodge means.

R: I have a long, long ways to go. I'm literally in my baby years of becoming who I'm meant to be, but I think that ultimately all ties back into walking the Red Road and living by those morals and values.

M: Ceremony is who we are as Anishinaabeg people. I want to understand all the ceremonies because one day I am going to be a Kookoo (grandma) and it will be my responsibility to ensure our traditions, our language and medicines get passed down to my grandchildren.

One aspect of the Midewewin Lodge is addressing one's loss and grief. Losing my father to suicide two months before I was born has left a void in my heart. I never got to properly grieve him.

R: There is a connection between the grieving and the healing I am talking about. Everything is connected somehow.

Our relationship with our mom? Well...

M: Don't get me wrong, no matter what, I love my mom. She's my mom. But I don't have a lot of patience with her. Now, knowing what I know about how you can overcome and heal things and you can't blame—

R:—or dwell on things—

M:—but you *can* heal. I feel that our mom has not committed to starting her healing

> I want to understand all the ceremonies because one day I am going to be a Kookoo (grandma) and it will be my responsibility to ensure our traditions, our language and medicines get passed down to my grandchildren. **–MELISSA**

journey yet. I understand my mom's gone through a lot of horrific events in her life: from the results of colonization, to her mother attending Indian residential school. That began the breakdown of our mom's family. Then our mom attended Indian residential school too. That robbed her of everything. Losing my dad to suicide and then being in unhealthy, unstable relationships have all been very traumatic for her. And then there's the continued oppression and poverty.

Our mom's spirit broke as a child. That little girl is still inside my mom and it so badly wants to be loved and cared for. It never was. Never. I think that was the most horrific thing—that little girl never being able to be loved for who she was. She was never nurtured and cared for.

I just wish that my mom could heal and move forward because she has a beautiful life. Rachel breaks it down really well for her: you have happy children providing for their children, beautiful grandchildren, and you are alive!

R: Our mom's been through a lot. I agree with everything Melissa says. We always have to remind ourselves about what our mom has suffered through in order for us to get to the empathy and understanding she deserves. Being able to give her that is also a part of our healing. If we continue to be angry, we will never move forward. Our mom needs that empathy and understanding from us in order to heal.

M: I know our mom does want to heal, but I think she is afraid of that journey. And I want nothing more than for her to heal. That's what I pray for and ultimately what I wish for, for our mom.

R: As much as I wish things could have been different growing up, still all the things that we went through as children and young adults have shown me how resilient I can be and how many things I can overcome. My history has made me resilient.

M: Rachel pretty much nailed it home with her comments about resilience. There has been intergenerational trauma, but there's also been intergenerational resilience. Definitely my experiences (and my mother's and grandmother's experiences) have impacted me. I can complain about my mom and be angry at her, but I recognize that she and grandma Brown have really taught me resilience. They taught me to be that strong Ikwe (female) and that no matter what you've been through, you're going to get up and keep living. I know that even more now as a mother and as an auntie. But somehow I think I did have some understanding of that as soon as Rachel came into my life when I was a young girl.

We, especially as Indigenous women, are not expected to be successful. We're thought to be *less than* by society. The worst was that that attitude also came from our family while we were growing up. We were pitied: living in poverty, having a mom who was a single parent. But I can see now that my mom was resilient. She would always find a way to get us Christmas presents and the things we wanted, like my MC Hammer pants or special toys for Rachel. In those ways, she was a good mom; she did the best she could. She always taught us to take care of each other.

To this day, she's such a little fighter. She's so feisty. To see and hear about all the issues she's encountered and endured in her life. I think, *Holy shit, man, my mom really should have been dead.*

R: Still, never being hugged or told that you're loved on a daily basis really affects you. Maybe our mom didn't do those things because her mom didn't do them too. I think that Indian residential school robbed us of that sense of kinship.

Indian residential schools also broke the ties to all of these things that our roots are connected to: language, spirituality, culture, community, parents, and our sense of self. That intergenerational trauma had such an effect on our upbringing. It makes me sick to my stomach. I pray almost daily that it stops with Melissa and me and that the cycle is broken with the next generation.

I still see the intergenerational effects of Indian residential schools today in the CFS system. I started working in the system when I was eighteen. I remember working with a youth in a group home and then, ten years later, I ran into the same girl who was now a mom whose baby was in care. And her mom had been a kid in care too. That circle doesn't stop. It's so eye opening. Those effects are still prevalent today.

M: CFS has a lot of power. Indigenous children have been taken away from their parents and families for years and years and years. I echo what Rachel said.

R: Indian residential schools even affected our kinship. Our mom never had a relationship with her sisters. I pity my mom because she doesn't know what it's like to have a sister the way I do. And I know that there are times when my mom yearns for that.

M: That loss really does have that ripple effect on us. The damage that Indian residential schools did was just horrendous.

My grandma would ask, "Can I do this? What do you think?" She was always asking permission. Our mom does the same thing. Me and Rachel do it too. It's more than just wanting someone else's opinion. It's definitely way deeper than that.

R: It's doubting your ability to make a decision for yourself and needing to ask for permission to make simple decisions. I don't trust myself. It's so hard to explain.

M: It's psychological, and it's been passed down. My daughter has done the same thing. So that's four generations. Did that happen unconsciously?

R: I think our grandmother learned in Indian residential school that you weren't allowed to think for yourself. I'm guilty of that too. I feel like I need that validation from others.

M: For my grandma and my mom, Indian residential schools really instilled in them that our Indigenous ways were bad.

R: Growing up, I had times when I was scared of authorities and sharing things. That's another thing that ties into the effects of Indian residential schools. I remember while growing up being told never to tell that there's no food at home, never to tell that there's no running water or hydro because then CFS would come and take us away. And I remember being terrified of sharing anything like that.

M: Me too. I used to be really ashamed to share my story and talk about my experiences because I was scared I would be judged. Now I tell young women I work with to be cautious, but never be afraid to share their story, especially as women. That's how we are going to heal and move forward. That's also how we are going to be the role models: the moms and the sisters and the aunties for the next generation to come.

R: Sharing our story in this book makes me so proud of who we are today. If we hadn't gone through all these things, then maybe we wouldn't be the people we are.

M: Talking about our lives is totally heavy, but it's good to share because it's really part of my healing journey. I've come so far that now I can talk about it and it feels good afterwards. Whereas maybe ten years ago, I probably would have shut down for a while after talking about these times in my life.

R: Like Melissa said, the more we talk about our stories, the more we cry and then we can let those things go and they aren't inside of us anymore. It's healing. And again, I'm in a place where I don't need to use substances to heal or soothe anything. That's really huge.

These memories trigger me, but at the same time, I look at myself and I know where I am today and I know how loved the next generation is in our family. My kids, my niece, and our sister are never, ever going to know what those things feel like. That allows me to think *I survived what I had to.* Deep down I know that I'm okay. I have that strength and resilience in me. Talking about my struggles without holding it in and having it eat away at me—that's a gift.

M: I love my sister lots, but sometimes we do disagree and get pissed off at each other.

R: Oh my god, yeah! And then we reach out to the brothers. We team up on each other. It's so funny because usually Melissa will go to our baby brother, and I'll go to our younger brother. But we don't stay mad at each other for very long, maybe a couple of days, and then one of us will usually give in.

M: Our younger sister stays neutral.

R: Yeah, she knows better.
Me and Melissa always joke that we're going to end up old together sitting on a

porch and it's just going to be the two of us. Melissa is my best friend. I can't make a decision without getting her advice. I do that because I know that she loves me and wants the best for me, so any advice she's going to give me is out of pure support and love for me. But I rely on her almost to a fault sometimes. I'm thirty-seven years old, and it's in the last few years that I've said, "No, Melissa, I'm going to do it my way."

M: Rachel is my best friend, but really she's more than just my best friend, she's like my partner in life. And I know that's maybe not healthy, but I don't care how other people—

R:—perceive it or see it.

M: Yeah. I don't know what my life would have been like without Rachel. Sometimes I don't think she realizes her worth in all this. She's definitely my rock and my biggest supporter. I'm so grateful that she chose me to be her big sister. Rachel's youngest daughter named our family The Carer Club.

R: It's all of us: our mom, sister and brothers, and our kids. My youngest started calling us this after watching the *Care Bears* on TV. She'll say, "Are we doing a movie night with our whole Carer Club?" Or "Is the whole Carer Club coming for my birthday?" My youngest just lights up when we are all together. One of the things all our family has in common is how much we love the kids. My youngest daughter is the heart of the Carer Club. She reminds us of the love we all have for one another.

I was amazed at the deep connection between Rachel and Melissa. I don't have a sister, so I don't know that kind of relationship. It was evident how incredibly close they are and how much they love each other. They are a force! They told me that sharing their stories required them to unpack some things they have not thought about or talked about in a long time. As Melissa told me, "Thinking about our lives takes up a large thinking space." We laughed together, cried together, and smudged together. It was a privilege to document their shared story.

Jenna

Boozhoo, tansi, aniin ndinaway maganadook. Away-Ganam-Gamoot Ndihznikas. Makwa dodem gaga indojiniag indoodnjang.
(Hello, all my relations. My name is The One Who Sings With The Grandmothers. I am Bear Clan. I come from Long Plain First Nation.)

My spirit name is *Away-Ganam-Gamoot* (The One Who Sings With The Grandmothers). Knowledge Keeper Chickadee Richard gave it to me in 2017. When I received my name I felt powerful. I finally knew who I was as an Indigenous person and felt that I had a place in society. My culture means everything to me now. I am Aniishinabe. I come from these lands on the banks of the Red River. I want other young Indigenous people to find themselves—their identity, their culture, their spirit—at a younger age than I did, so they don't have to fucking go around wandering and wondering; wandering the streets; wandering in their life; wondering who they are as people because the whiteness of the *system* fucking stripped that from them. You know? So yeah, my culture means everything to me.

The mom I talk about, she was my adopted mother. She adopted me when I was eight days old because my birth mom didn't want me. My birth mother had an affair with my birth dad. I don't know him. He was married. My birth mom's husband was in jail at the time she got pregnant with me. She needed to get rid of me before he got out of jail, so she gave me away to my adoptive mother, who wasn't able to have her own babies. My two moms were drinking buddies. My adoption was never legal; there were no papers involved or anything like that. I have an older brother, but he is no blood relation. He was adopted three years before me. He's the oldest, and then I'm next.

The very first memory I have of my childhood is of me being sexually exploited in a house right behind the Safeway on the corner of Sargent and Sherbrook. I was with a babysitter named Joey. I was probably three years old. He said that he would give me 7-Up if I sucked his dick. I remember doing that act. I also remember lying down after on the couch and drinking from the 7-Up bottle like it was a baby bottle, 7-Up spilling down my face.

Honestly, I was so neglected. When I became a teenager, people from my mother's past who took care of me as a kid told me they were surprised I was still alive. They told me that I didn't get my diaper changed enough and there was often sour milk in my bottle. My mom would take my brother to the babysitter in the duplex upstairs, but she would leave me alone in our house below. I was little, like about four years old. I had to take care of myself. One time I remember waking up, going to the fridge, getting lunch meat, and sitting down all alone and watching *Goosebumps* on TV.

One day around that time, I remember the cops and CFS banging on my front door. Being Indigenous, we were always told never to answer the door for cops. Ever. So I didn't answer the door. I said, "I'm not allowed."

I could hear a woman who must have been a social worker say, "It's okay. Open the door."

I said, "I don't know." Then they came to the back and shouted, "Open the door, open the door." They kicked down the door.

Someone must have called CFS. I've never really thought about that before. Wow. Where was my brother when I was taken? Who was caring about me and knew I was home alone? Or maybe someone wanted me to be taken away from my mom? (Some people call CFS on each other.) Maybe my neighbour upstairs called. I don't know.

They took me to a building at the bottom of the Salter Street Bridge, where Seed Winnipeg is now. I remember that they had put blue stockings on me and that I was wearing a nightgown with a picture of a Canadian goose on it. I was put in a room where there was a TV and some toys. I remember just sitting there in that room looking at the TV, and I was cold.

After that, I went into a foster home, but it wasn't good. I stayed there about six months. Then I went into another foster home with a lesbian couple so I had two moms. They were super nice. The only good memories I have of my childhood are with those women. I stayed with them about a year. I remember I liked Play-Doh, so I was always playing with Play-Doh. I had my own room. I felt safe and cared for. They were two white women. One's name was Sally, and the other was Teresa. Sally was a paramedic. I don't know what Teresa did. I still keep in touch with Teresa from time to time.

But my adoptive mom didn't like that they were lesbians, so she made me tell a lie to a CFS worker to get me home. Then from age five or six, to age eleven, I stayed with her. I stayed with her until the middle of Grade 7. I don't think I should have been given back to my adoptive mom at age five. I wish I would have just stayed in that foster home with the two moms while also having a cultural care component.

Living with my adoptive mom was horrible. I was abused in every single way—spiritually, mentally, emotionally, physically, sexually. I was sexually abused and exploited by her and by my brother and his friends too. They would use me as currency. *You can do this with my sister if…* Yeah.

School was my haven. But I wish that someone who must have seen the black eyes, the bruises, the tell-tale signs of abuse would have done something to help me. I recall that one guidance counsellor—her name was Jackie—did bring me to her office one day and said, "Who gave you that black eye?" I didn't say anything, right? Obviously not. She's like, "Was it someone that you don't want to get in trouble?"

I said, "Yeah." Right then and there she should have called someone. I was in Grade 4 at the time. That was a fucking betrayal.

After that I didn't like the counsellor. I wonder where she is now.

By Grade 7, I was bigger than my mother, and I decided not to take her shit anymore. The very last time she hit me, I slapped away her hand and said, "You're not fucking hitting me. You're not laying another hand on me ever again."

I ran away a lot. I started drinking. Started hanging around with people who did drugs. That was just normal to me, you know? I also started smoking weed. Back then I never stayed anywhere for more than a month or two. I can't give you specific times or dates. It's all a blur. I stayed at group homes, foster homes. I stayed at Ndinawe Safe House. I also stayed at Marymound—that's a stabilization unit for girls. And then, there were also the hotels…

That was a time when foster kids were living in hotels. I stayed in the Best Western. I was there for a good two months, and then I ran away. I remember also being placed at the Howard Johnson's on Portage Avenue by the Perimeter. Those were the two main hotels where I stayed.

At the time, I thought living in the hotels was the best because we had a lot of freedom. CFS hired a company called Complete Care to look after us. Complete Care hired newcomers who didn't know English and who had no experience whatsoever. We'd get a random worker who was Native and knew her shit. There was this one worker—you couldn't pull off anything on her.

Today I would say there was sexual exploitation while we stayed at the hotels. We could persuade workers to do trades to have sex with us. Sexual exploitation can be about getting money, but it can also be about getting something for sex, like drugs, food, shelter, or protection.

Those guys were naïve. We needed the money. (But I don't want any victim blaming.) We were doing the best we could to survive at that time. We Indigenous women are born into this lifestyle of survival. We just know how to survive, and that is part of sexual exploitation. The workers didn't know any better. We told them we were seventeen or eighteen. But they were exploiting us—having sex with underage kids.

> Back then I never stayed anywhere for more than a month or two. I can't give you specific times or dates. It's all a blur.

I stayed anywhere I could because once I got kicked out of foster homes and group homes where was I gonna go? Who would take care of me? The streets would. I'd go to gangs; they would take care of me. Sometimes I'd go to trap houses (we used to call them crack houses), or my friends' houses. A trap house is like a drug house, or a gang house; a place where people sell drugs. Some people sleep there. We'd drink and do drugs and sleep on the floor. That was normal for us, you know?

I lived on the streets on and off during my teenage-hood. But mostly my time running around on the street was from age twelve and fifteen. I was also sexually exploited on the street. I had no john. For me it was about survival. I needed the money.

I wouldn't even listen to my social workers. One of my social workers got fired because she told me to just stay out on the streets and call her when I was ready to go back to a foster placement. I was like, *Uh, that's fucked up.* The streets were addicting. It was freedom.

The first time I spent the night outside, it was winter. There was snow on the ground. At nighttime me and my friends needed a place to sleep, so we were checking car doors, and when we found one open all six of us slept in that car overnight. I remember my toes, they were in so much pain from the cold. In the morning we walked all the way to the Robin's Donuts on Selkirk. That's where we warmed up until Ndinawe (Youth Resource Centre) opened. At the time, it was only open from three o'clock till eleven o'clock. So until it opened, we would roam the streets and find things to do. Mostly get in trouble.

Honestly, a lot of the time I wanted to kill myself. I would self-harm by cutting myself, slitting my wrists, hoping that one day I would bleed out and finally be gone. I tried that often. Self-harm is categorized as physical self-sabotage. If all your life you are told that you are nothing, that you are shit, you start believing that. It starts to get to you. And then you start to physically harm yourself. But if you tell a kid they are the best, loving and kind, they will start to believe that and then they do become the best they are. I don't know what the fuck kept me going. Maybe just my next fix. I was either high on weed or high on pills every single day. Drinking, smoking weed. Yeah, all of it.

I had two really serious attempts at ending my life. I had one at seventeen after my birth sister died and a second two years later when another birth sister killed herself. I always knew I had blood relations from my birth mom. I have four birth siblings left. It was really painful when my two sisters died. Even though I wasn't raised with them, I got to know them a bit as a teenager. It was good to know that I had sisters out there that I could probably confide in later in life. Knowing about them gave me hope for the future. Today I just have contact with my baby sister.

Age fifteen came around, and I was houseless. (I prefer the word *houseless* more than *homeless*. If you talk to people who are "homeless" they say that they're not homeless, they're houseless. They have homes, they have a community like a family, but it's out on the street. They don't want to be a part of the system. They don't want to go by any rules.) I used to sleep at the corner of Selkirk and Powers. Right where the basketball hoop is. That used to be an amphitheater, all stone with concrete seating. Sometimes I would get old furniture from the garbage (one time it was a loveseat and a chair) to put right in the middle of the amphitheater, and I'd sleep on it at nighttime when Ndinawe closed. (I think that's why I'm so obsessed with old furniture. I started an Instagram account of photos of furniture on the streets. It's called *Furniture of Winnipeg*.) All my friends would come and chill. We didn't care if the furniture was dirty or not. We were fucking dirty.

So I was there sleeping at the amphitheatre for about two weeks on and off. I was hungry. I was tired. I called my CFS agency, and they said, "Oh. You have a new social worker now." (I knew my former social worker had been fired.)

I'm like, "Well, can you put me through?"

That new social worker, Mary Anne, said, "Yeah, where you at? I'll come to you right now."

I was like, "What? You're going to come to me right now?"

She's like, "Yeah, I'll take you for lunch. Where are you?"

I'm like, "I'm on Selkirk and Powers." So she came. She bought me a four-dollar poutine from Junie's right across the street. That poutine changed my life. I was like, *Who is this white woman spending her own money on me?* That showed me that working with me wasn't just a job to her. She was so nice, so kind. Non-judgmental. I was like, *Okay, I'll open up to her.*

She's like, "Are you willing to come with me? We'll get you sleeping in a safe place tonight."

I'm like, "Okay." I thought, *This is what the Creator wants for me.*

Mary Anne was so trustable because she stuck to her word. When she couldn't do something, she would explain that in a way I would understand. She was just so kind and so real. I felt like I was being listened to, and that someone actually cared. Like, truly fucking cared. She was just there. I still talk to her to this day. I call Mary Anne my angel. And I call her Ma. Because Mary Anne, M-A, Ma. Mary Anne helped me save myself.

Mary Anne saw the tell-tale signs of exploitation, so she got me into a program called TERF (Transition Education Resources for Females). That got me off the streets. The other girls at TERF told me about a group home called Little Sisters. It's for exploited girls. It was good. I stayed there for about two years, other than when I got kicked out of Little Sisters twice for fighting. (It's a girl-eat-girl world when you are a teenager!)

At TERF I started with the Skills Building program, which got me off the streets and ready for school. Then I did the Just Program,

ANDREW MAHON

which is run by TERF in collaboration with Gordon Bell High School's off-campus program. Going to school was kind of hard. I think I did Grade 9 about three times. But

I went to school every day. After I graduated from TERF I went to Gordon Bell off-campus, where I was able to get credits. Then I graduated from Gordon Bell High School when I was nineteen. I celebrated. I invited everyone. Mary Anne came. It's still one of the happiest moments of my life because I didn't expect to even be alive past sixteen.

When I graduated from Gordon Bell, the graduates did a graduation walk all the way down to the Westminster Church on Maryland and Broadway. That's where they had the graduation. Because my last name starts with W, I was at the end. The pride I felt walking down Maryland! All the cars were honking. Oh my God, it just makes me tear up. I was wearing a white tux. I spent my own money on it. I bought it from Michael's Tux, where Bear Clan sits now. And there was a pink bow tie. After the graduation I went to the Red River Ex with my date. I didn't go to the dance or whatever because I was too cool. Yeah.

When I was nineteen, after I finished high school, I ran away from CFS and never looked back. I didn't know what to do with my life. I took a certificate program from Red River College. It was the Ndinawe Child and Youth Care Practitioner Course, an experiential program. I was houseless, just going from place to place. Then I ended up living in a trap house. There was always traffic coming in and out. There were five, six people sleeping on a bed. Sometimes I'd have to sleep on the floor. And the fucking house was cold. I was just sick of that lifestyle, and I called up my friend Michael, and I was like, *Yo, I can't do this anymore.* I asked to sleep on his floor.

I had met Michael Redhead Champagne when I was twelve or thirteen. He was my youth care worker when I was living at Ndinawe Safe House. It was his first shift and I was all fucked up on pills. He had to keep me alive, keep me awake all night. No one else wanted to take care of me. They were all scared of me. I was just a little shit. I didn't listen to anyone, right? So that's how we met. Back in the day, there was the old weather station on TV. It had a green and red pattern on the TV screen and it played music. I remember that night the song by The Fray, "How to Save a Life," was playing on it. That's been our song ever since.

When I met Michael, for some reason I didn't like him. But then I didn't like most people in those days. My friends and I gave him a pretty hard time for a while. I think I didn't like him in the beginning because I thought he was white. But then he brought me his treaty card. After that I had respect for him and started liking him. My friends and I would listen to him. I started to become friends with Michael when I was probably sixteen or seventeen. He was still working at the Ndinawe Resource Center then.

Another person who has been a huge positive force in my life is Knowledge Keeper Chickadee Richard. (A knowledge keeper is an Indigenous person who has acquired an extensive knowledge throughout their life.) I don't remember the first time I met her. She was always just there, as a grandmother. She's a very grand woman. Very wise, and loving and kind. But I do remember the first time I met Chickadee's son Ninoondawa. Ninoondawa Mushcode-Biizhiguy. (That's his name. *I Hear The Buffalo Calling.* I think it took me about a year to learn his name.) Yeah, it was in September 2009. I was seventeen. It was the very first time I got on the back of a truck at a Grandmothers' March. Ninoondawa and I met there and became really good friends.

It was at that same Grandmothers' March that I drummed for the first time, and it blew my mind. Yeah. I was on the back of a truck with other women (mostly grandmothers) on my way to the march. The women were drumming, and I tried it. I felt the need for people to hear my voice because my whole life my voice was silenced. I had been severely abused and had been in and out of foster homes and group homes, running around on the street, houseless. No one heard me. That first time I drummed, I felt powerful. It felt like a release. Finally. I was healing. I could just yell at the top of my lungs and sing with a group of women. It felt amazing and powerful. It felt like I was connecting with something greater than myself, like I was connecting with my ancestors. Those songs! Yeah.

At that point, I didn't have no connection with my culture. My whole life, I was yearning to know who I was as an Indigenous woman. Every time I went to Chickadee's house and visited Ninoondawa—we were never allowed to be under the influence of drugs or alcohol—I felt like I was one step closer to becoming the person I needed to be. Chickadee has always inspired me to stop using.

Me and Michael used to sit with the grandmothers, and they would tell us about the movement back in their day—the Native Youth Movement and the American Indian Movement—and they'd talk about the way they used to be. Another Knowledge Keeper, Mae Louise Campbell, would often be there. I met Mae Louise along the way at the grandmothers' marches. I loved hearing the stories she and Chickadee would tell. The grandmothers didn't have no TVs in their living rooms, so we'd just have to sit there and listen. We'd listen to their songs too.

I had a lot of learning from Chickadee and Mae Louise. When I was with them I felt like I belonged and people heard me. Like, for the first time in my life, I was loved. They were super nonjudgmental, and I loved being around them. I want to pass on their teachings and have Chickadee and Mae Louise be proud of me.

Michael and I reconnected when I was about eighteen or nineteen. He was no longer working at Ndinawe by then. We co-founded Aboriginal Youth Opportunities (AYO) in 2011. AYO provided inner-city youth a sense of hope. It was our passionate

work until 2020 when Michael and I stepped away from AYO. AYO has since disbanded. The purpose of AYO was to help Indigenous young people feel like they belong and to provide hope, meaning, and purpose. Those four things, we kind of adopted from 13 Moons, a movement or a way of life that focuses on returning to culture and traditions to heal from substance abuse. That's what we were trying to help all our peers with so that they wouldn't have to use drugs. But then we started applying those teachings to everything we did and, honestly, it provided a family-like structure. So, essentially, we were a group of young volunteers in the community who worked to provide Indigenous young people with a way to find their voices and to help them use their voices to achieve their goals. AYO was kind of like a gang. And it's a greeting—Ayyyooo!

It was Michael who started the idea for AYO. He had been working at Ndinawe but quit. He said he wanted to keep the relationships that he had with the young people there. So he told all of us that there was going to be an event at Thunderbird House. He invited thirty of us, and he bought a bunch of pizzas. There was a whole bunch of job opportunities listed on papers, jobs we could apply for if we wanted. He called that one event Aboriginal Youth Opportunities. The thirty of us who were there that night signed a paper, and we said we were going to commit. There were maybe five members from that day that stayed strong. So we were the five co-founders, I guess. But me and Michael were the two active ones, every single day, every single night, 24/7, 365. Always reachable by cellphone, social media, everything. We got all different kinds of calls.

From our AYO community we knew young people just wanted to be involved. So we told them to come down to what we called Meet Me at the Bell Tower, every Friday night at six o'clock to join us and get involved in the community. On Selkirk Avenue at the cross street of Powers there sits an old City Hall bell. That is where we met. Yeah, it worked out pretty good.

Meet Me at the Bell Tower started because there was an influx of gang activity. AYO had been around for like one year at that point. I was working at Ndinawe for a little bit in a gang-prevention program called Triple T. It was a work-placement program. On my last day there I'd seen my really good friend, Sean

Hunt, climbing up the bell tower close by on Selkirk Ave. In my twenty years of living around there, I had never heard the bell tower ring, so I had an idea. I thought, *Hey, if I can liberate an extension cord from the Ndinawe (because it's my last day), I could give it to Sean, and then he could put it on the bell to ring it at eleven o'clock at nighttime, when all the staff are gone home.* So we locked up the community center and I gave him the extension cord. Told him to tie it on to the bell and ring the bell, and so he did. I think that was in 2011—maybe around September. A couple of months later, Sean completed suicide. That was a big surprise to me, and the community.

Then my bro Clarky Stevenson got stabbed on the corner of College and Aikins, and he died. The next day a group of us were hanging around with some gang members we knew from the 'hood. Those gang members hit us up. They're like, "Jenna, we want to do this vigil for Clarky, so let's do it." So we did the vigil and called our rally Stop The Violence. We rallied all the way to the legislative building to tell them that we were going to stop the violence in our own 'hood; that we didn't need the government's support. Soon after that, we really wanted to show the community that we were serious, so we rallied again. We decided to put out an invitation to meet at the bell tower. So we put a call out on Facebook, and forty people came that day, even though it was minus 40°C. Yeah, and then we rang the bell. So we rallied and we marched down the street, forty of us, and we said we're going to take back our neighbourhood.

In our first year of the Meet Me at the Bell Tower initiative—the ringing of the bell every Friday night at six o'clock—we got the violent crime rate to go down 18.9% in our two-block radius. (I think that number came from a Winnipeg Police Services safety report.) Meet Me At The Bell Tower went on for nine years until the pandemic of 2020 came, and Michael and I stepped away. The average number of people who came out each Friday was around twenty to thirty. When we were having a big event, probably a hundred were there.

In the beginning we used to rally and walk around the neighbourhood. When the Merchants Hotel and beer vendor on Selkirk was still open, we used to march there shouting, "No more violence!" And so we got that shut down through community rallying

and support, with the help of the North End Community Renewal Corporation (NECRC). That was cool. Today, if it's winter we gather inside, and only the deadlies go outside and they ring the bell. (The word *deadlies* is a slang word that describes people who are fearless and put their all into everything. They will put their lives on the line and sacrifice for something.)

With Meet Me At The Bell Tower, first timers would get to ring the bell. First, we would go outside and hang the hope banner. (It was actually a photo of Michael's hands spelling out the word H-O-P-E, just like gangs have their signs with their hands.) We'd talk about what was going on in the neighbourhood, how we started, and then we would give others (like our guests) a chance to speak. After that we took our family picture, rang the bell, then went to the Indigenous Family Centre across the street on Selkirk. Inside, anyone who wanted to would talk about their initiative (for example a community event). We'd have a draw for little trinkets and prizes, which was fun, and then we'd all eat together and clean up. Usually at the end, only the younger AYOs would drum and sing. I felt almost like the grandmother of the group because I taught them all of their songs. After that we would just go home, or some of us would hang out and go somewhere later. We met from 6 until 8 or 8:30. Meet Me At The Bell Tower was a way to start the weekend off. Together.

Too many of my friends for me to count have died. I can't even fathom the number. Today what matters the most to me is keeping my friends alive because a lot of them are currently using substances or are alcoholics—including myself, because I'm currently fighting an alcohol addiction. We've seen an influx in violent crime again, and we're like, *Why is this happening?* People have addictions. They are doing crime because they need to feed their drug habits.

But the "meth crisis" has been sensationalized. People have always been using drugs, and people who are doing meth now were doing different drugs before meth. They just changed to meth. There are more potent drugs than meth out there, but meth has been sensationalized because of systemic oppression. People want to make the crime that comes with substance use into something, just to victim-blame users of that substance, so

people can put more money into the institutions that oppress us Indigenous people.

The whole bigger system is making money off the poor. There is an economy of Indigenous misery. Social workers, the police, correctional officers, nurses and doctors (for example) all benefit financially from the oppression of the Indigenous in white society. These people are all part of *the institutions*. If you look at the Health Canada stats at the Health Sciences Centre, you see that a big percentage of people coming into the hospital are Indigenous. So there's that link to colonialism. Indigenous people are also overrepresented in areas like CFS, jails, and addictions.

There's not a "meth crisis". There are other real crises… there's a media crisis and in the past few years it has become clearer that there are police intimidation tactics, and we have a colonial policing crisis. And then there's the upholding the status quo crisis. But we now have the beginning of the breaking of the status quo. It is being questioned and challenged. It's not one big crack yet, but there's many small ones. The system is slowly breaking in front of our eyes. With the Black Lives Matter movement and the criticism of policing, the status quo is now in crisis. The government is trying to uphold the status quo, but society is breaking this system by questioning the upholding of whiteness. The belief that *White is right*. People of colour are being oppressed, but we are woke and awakening. We have found our voice and our strength. There's a race war happening. I feel a shifting right now.

One way I tried to make a difference was through the 13 Moons initiative, which was a peer-to-peer, harm-reduction, culturally based program out of AYO, partnering with Ka Ni Kanichihk, Manitoba Harm Reduction Network and the Winnipeg Regional Health Authority. Unfortunately, in 2020 the funding ended for the program. One of the reasons Michael and I created 13 Moons was that we were really scared; we didn't want to see any more of our friends dying. (The phrase 13 Moons refers to the phases of the moon, like the phases of addiction. As well the moon and addiction are both in the dark.) 13 Moons had a peer advisory circle that was made up of people who actually used drugs. Those peers in the circle were the ones I reached out to and asked, *How can we help you? What do you need? Do you need to go to ceremony? Do you need an Elder?*

The other reason we started 13 Moons was that one of my friends had killed herself. She hung herself in the parking lot of a clinic in the North End. It was at like seven or eight o'clock in the morning, before it opened. She was pregnant, and she was fucked up on meth. She was scared that CFS was going to take her baby. She already had kids that had been taken away. If she'd had access to my phone number or anyone else's, she could have reached out before she killed herself. She could still be alive.

Throughout the two years I was involved with 13 Moons, we hired six people, if you count our supervisor. I was the lead outreach worker. 13 Moons went out on the street and handed out clean needles, safe crack kits, and safe meth kits to help people reduce harm to themselves when they were using substances. Sometimes people—usually our houseless relatives—would call me or message me in the middle of night needing clean needles so I'd go deliver them. I didn't sleep much at night. (I use the word *relatives* here because in our culture we are taught that everyone is family.)

The biggest part of my job for 13 Moons was to be on social media, supporting people. A lot of people are in really sad places. Dark places. I'd answer messages in a timely fashion. Being fast to answer them is super important with young people. I feel that they need to feel heard and not neglected. So we always tried to be on top of all of our social media. Instagram, Facebook, and then texts too. I had cards with my cell number on them. People would text me just to see what was up, or to ask about resources. People still contact me through Facebook. All the time. I support these people informally because our vision of AYO was a people-first movement and not a money-first movement. We never let money get in the way.

We need to redirect the resources in Winnipeg. Winnipeg must defund the police and redirect those resources back to the community. The community needs funding for workers with experience in areas such as food sustainability, housing, mental health care, mediation, domestic abuse, and childcare.

We need the city leaders to address the root causes of the challenges our people face—to *acknowledge* colonialism, *acknowledge* genocide, *acknowledge* systemic racism. Acknowledging it is one thing, but then these things need to be changed. We need to address the root causes and then allocate the resources to be used in the way our people want to heal. Resources need to be focused on original Indigenous ways of knowing and being. For example the healing of trauma needs to honour ceremonial ways, like sweat lodges.

I don't feel like I'm giving a lot of myself because I feel it's reciprocal—other people support me when I need it too. And when I help people, it helps me. I can empathize with that person in need of support because I know what it's like, that feeling of helplessness, and I don't want the person to feel that way. It boosts some kind of positive feeling within myself when I give.

My compassion comes from not having had any given to me by other people until I was an adult. I overcompensate and want

> Resources need to be focused on original Indigenous ways of knowing and being. For example the healing of trauma needs to honour ceremonial ways, like sweat lodges.

everyone to have it. My compassion comes from me being angry most of my life and growing up without compassion. Then, I was given these new things called kindness and respect and compassion, which didn't cause me to have negative feelings, but nice feelings. I first experienced them from Michael, Chickadee, Mae Louise, and Mary Anne for example, and also from my friend Wayne. Wayne was another youth care worker of mine when I first met Michael at Ndinawe. Michael and Wayne worked together. Wayne taught me how to play basketball and how to be kind. I want to be like Michael and Wayne. Everyone loves them. Just recently Wayne passed on to the spirit world.

Two-spirit—that's me. When I was probably thirteen or fourteen, and I first started to go around my culture drumming and singing for the first time, I heard this term, *two-spirit*. That's also around the time I met my friend Ninoondawa. I saw that he was a two-spirit person. I didn't identify as two-spirit at that time in my life. I didn't yet know who I was. I wondered, *What is two-spirit? Does it mean you're gay?* No, it doesn't mean you're gay.

It means that you have two spirits; you honour both male and female. You're neither, but you're both, together. Whether your gender is female and you dress like a guy, or your gender is male and you dress like a woman, you can be both. You don't have to conform to either/or. (The term *two-spirit* was actually coined back in 1991 by a whole bunch of Indigenous Elders including Albert McLeod and Myra Laramee.)

I am a woman, but I dress like a guy. Some days, I'll be a woman. Some days I'll be a man because someone will call me a boy or a guy. I'm okay with that. And if people aren't sure about pronouns, just ask. *What pronouns do you use?* Be progressive about it. I use the pronoun *she*.

So if you're a young person reading this, I want you to accept who you are. You don't have to conform to any gender norms. If you want to choose to honour your feminine side, or your masculine side, go ahead. You can just be a spirit. Right?

I would call myself an advocate. There's no negative connotations to the word advocate. I'm an advocate for the land, the people, the water, the sun, the moon. And the Indigenous knowledge I have been given is not my knowledge to hold onto. The young people, those younger than me, need the teachings too. And when they get to be my age they need to pass it on too, so it just keeps going and going. I think that in that *passing on*, there is wisdom and connection as well. Connection to Creator. Connection to our ancestors. Connection to pride. Connection to having made it through genocide.

That genocide goes back five hundred years to when the first ships came to our land and "discovered" us. There was already a thriving population of Indigenous folk here. So that is the genocide that I'm talking about. Residential schools are another form of that genocide. The timeline of genocide probably goes from smallpox blankets, to buffalo hunt, to Wounded Knee, to the banning of all of our ceremonies, to residential schools, to missing and murdered Indigenous woman, to the millennial scoop, and then to the current CFS system that we are in today and the upholding of the police and RCMP state. Those are the major ones.

It is common knowledge that CFS is an ongoing part of the current genocide. We have to fight against the colonial system, the colonial state. CFS today is the modern-day version of the residential school. I believe that's the case because the government (where all the power and control is) needed a new and flashy way to colonize our people, to "take the Indian out of the child." They're still saying that we're unfit to parent our kids. Meanwhile, some of us are fighting addiction and poverty, just struggling to survive, but that's all because of colonialism.

Instead, children should go back to their parents or families, and if the home is not safe, safety measures should be provided. CFS is doing this new thing where they don't take the children out of the home, they take the parent(s) out. This is promising. CFS is no longer putting out birth alerts (to my knowledge). CFS is getting some parents the help and support they need by using a wraparound approach.

I feel conflicted between the choices of safety and culture. When I was a little girl, I would have liked to be in a family where I felt safe. I felt safe with those two white lesbian moms. But I would also have liked to be in a home that was culturally woke (aware), so I could have learned about my culture. Then I could have grown up knowing I am supposed to sing with the grandmothers. That access would have helped me to know where I came from so I could go on in a good way. Mino Bimaadiziwin (Live that good life). The best home for an Indigenous child is a safe Indigenous home, and the next best home is a safe non-Indigenous home with access to Indigenous culture.

All in all, if there wasn't colonialism, then we would have our land, our waters, our own food, and there would be no poverty. Back in the day, when there was no white man, there was no poverty. Everyone had a house. No one went hungry. But then flash forward five hundred years and all Indigenous people are oppressed. Why is that? Colonialism—because the white man (the government) wants to take our land and our resources.

You are about to get some truth! I hate the word reconciliation. When people use the word reconciliation I don't believe them. Reconciliation is for white people. What do we, as Indigenous people have to reconcile? We didn't create the problem, or ask for all this. Reconciliation is dead.

Lateral violence is another result of colonialism. It is real in our communities. But if my brown brothers or sisters are hating on me, I try to remember that they are in the same system that oppresses me. I have to try not to hate on them. They are trying to heal from their traumas too. I try to focus on the fact that we are all in this together. We are all trying to get through the same oppression. I can empathize, even though it can be really hard. Everyone heals at their own pace. People may be early in their healing journey, full of hate or envy, and they need to learn to let that go. I understand that it's not me. People will come back around when their heart is better, and I will be there for them. That's the kind of person I was raised to be by my elders. I want people to be happy in life. I'm not trying to be fucking generic; I'm being fucking human.

Some people have called me resilient. That word is a sick, sadistic word. It puts labels on us. When people use that to describe me, I think they are making fun of me. *You "survived" this colonial state and all these institutions and look at you go!* I shouldn't have had to be resilient in the first place.

The turning point in my life came when I got my spirit name, just a few years ago. Away-Ganam-Gamoot. *The One Who Sings With The Grandmothers.* I learned my purpose in life.

I took Chickadee out to Ottawa to a national Elder and youth gathering. While there, she took me to a ceremony at this white woman's house. She was Chickadee's friend. She was an old woman herself. I was like, "Chickadee. What is this? She's white!" (Today I have a totally different opinion.) But we were in her living room having ceremony. We're drumming and singing, and this white woman drummed a song that we knew here in Manitoba, but she was singing it differently. They were doctoring (enabling healing for) each other, and then all of a sudden I could see red lights blink on and off, like fireflies outside in the dark. And I could see white lights, then blue ones. Chickadee was seeing them too. I looked at Chickadee, and she was nodding her head. She knew that I was seeing them too. I thought *Oh my goodness, what is happening?*

Then that white woman stopped singing the song, and she said to me, "Okay, your turn my girl." So I sang the exact same song, but the way we sing it in Manitoba. After, both of the women said, "I hear grandmothers singing with you." I had a cloth, and I gifted it to the ceremony.

Chickadee said, "This is your spirit name: The One Who Sings With The Grandmothers." Thinking of me with the grandmothers and what it meant to be with them, oh my god, it makes me cry. I was looking at Chickadee and the white woman. They're both grandmothers. From that day on I learned not to judge white people by the colour of their skin, only by their character and how they treat me.

They say that when you get your spirit name and you get your clan, you know your way in life. Knowing my name, I knew who I was as a person, and I knew my destiny. I knew who I needed to be. I wish I would have known that when I was a very young kid, so I could walk in that good way, like Ninoondawa does. He doesn't drink or smoke weed. I really aspire to be like him.

When I got my spirit name I knew that I needed to be a medicine person when I got older. A medicine person is someone who knows the traditional medicines of our people and doctors people who are sick. I'm kind of already doing that, but in a colonial, urban setting. I am trying to decolonize by gathering resources from my culture that our people can access when they are in need of healing. It's not so much a physical healing: medicine goes beyond that to include providing food, and shelter. It's more than just the colonial idea of medicine.

That day in ceremony was the very first time I saw spirits. Still to this day I'm a visionary. I see things before they happen. I see things in front of me sometimes, like you see things in sweat lodges.

I'm still young, and I need to kick this alcohol addiction. I am battling my inner healing journey by using substances to cope. But Chickadee always tells me, "Go at your own pace. Don't rush yourself." I aspire to be like Chickadee because she said that she stopped drinking at the age of twenty-eight. I'm thirty now. So I'm trying really hard. Trying really hard to reduce my harms and drinking.

After living a life of being severely abused and called down every day of my childhood (during critical developmental stages), that's all I hear in my head as an adult. I have to rewire my brain, my synapses, and neurons firing back and forth. That's what I'm learning to do on my healing journey.

So sometimes I'm just grieving and in pain, and would like the pain to stop. Now that I have become older, I'm starting to understand that suicidal ideation has become less physical and more about the pain I am feeling. I want to escape from the person that I was, but not the person I am today. I still want to be physically alive and live a fulfilling life. I don't want to kill myself, because I love myself and I love my friends. I just don't want the pain anymore.

I don't think anybody wants to fucking kill themselves. If they had to choose between having the pain stop or killing themselves, I think they would just want the pain to stop. You know? It's an ongoing battle. My friend Kelly, she just killed herself on Christmas Eve, so I'm still grieving that, to this minute. We're planning a vigil for her tomorrow. I have to go drum and sing for her. When the pain is at its worst, it helps to drum or talk to friends. When I feel destructive or like sabotaging myself, I try to use my healthy coping mechanisms. But when all is said and done, if I'm still feeling bad, that's when I drink.

It's been like ten years since I was addicted to using hard drugs, but I still drink so I don't have to feel the heartache. I try not to do drugs anymore, but this healing journey is not linear. It is not a competition. It's a journey.

Part of living with the pain and moving forward is not being so hard on myself. I just wish that I could always acknowledge the pain so it can help me do better instead of doing worse. I want to use it to fuel my fire instead of putting myself on oxygen.

When I start to feel down on my darkest days, I say one of two things to myself. One is kind of childish. You know Dory, the cartoon fish in *Finding Nemo*? She sings *Just keep swimming, just keep swimming, just keep swimming, swimming, swimming.* I sing that when I'm trying to block out negative thoughts. That's one. Or I'll repeat to myself the words from the movie *The Help*: *You is kind, you is smart, you is important* (with a southern accent!). I'll also try to remember the nice comments that people have told me. Sometimes I go on Facebook and reread people's comments because I forget the good things that people say.

Telling my story, I'm ripping off the scab of my wound, if I look at it from a deficit point of view. How I feel about telling my story all depends on the relationship to the person I am telling it to. But telling my story is also a form of healing. Every time someone tells a part of their story, they understand it a bit more. Now I take a solutions-based approach and focus on the positive.

This is not the only time I've told my story. I've learned throughout the years that, yeah, it's fucking triggering. So I need to put those healthy coping mechanisms in place. I've already planned for this interview today. I have already taken steps to reach out to people. Tomorrow I will be going to a sweat and I will be drumming. I will take my feelings and everything that I have stirred up today and put them into my work.

The reason I want to be in the book is that I want to be able to share my voice and have my story written down. My story has been told before, but only in very small snippets. I want to be able to help others who are in my position, to show them that, hey, somebody else was there, might still be there, but she made it out. You know? I've made it out, and this is how I'm healing. You can do the same.

I feel stronger after sharing my story. Even though I've gone through all this shit in my life and feel vulnerable sharing about it, I am not *vulnerable*. I'm a strong, Indigenous, Aniishinabe woman.

Speaking for myself, from what I've learned from others, there is a point in your healing journey where you don't identify as a survivor anymore. You are trying to thrive, to live your life beyond just being a survivor. I want to have the opportunity to thrive, not just the opportunity to survive. Now that's *deadly!*

Sometimes you take steps forward, sometimes you take steps back, but that doesn't mean you aren't healing. It just means that there's still something more out there for you. Your success in healing doesn't need to be compared to others, and shouldn't be. You are your own self. You are healing at the rate Creator wants you to heal and needs you to heal. Try not to feel shame, or guilt, for having a slip or experiencing a trigger or anything like that.

In the fall of 2020 I got a great job as a lead researcher in Winnipeg for someone doing national research on homelessness at the University of Toronto. I can't believe my lived experience has gotten me somewhere in life! I have a PhD from the streets.

I want to encourage people to keep going and always remember not to be too hard on themselves. I can be very hard on myself. Before 13 Moons started I was so ashamed and so full of guilt because I kept on slipping up on substances and alcohol. I would go on benders and say that I'm not good enough.

But then I would come back to my teachings, and I would come back to my elders, and they would wrap their arms around me and tell me, "It's okay. It's okay, you're healing." It's going to take forever. But just know that you're healing.

One day driving together in my car, Jenna suggested I read the book White Fragility *by Robin D'Angelou. Jenna gently called me out on something I had said earlier that made her uncomfortable. We then talked about racism. Talking about racism can be uncomfortable for me because I am conscious of my white privilege. Jenna is strong and wise, and so was her teaching in the car that day. At the end she said to me, "Isn't it great that we could talk about race without getting angry?" Yes, it was.*

Each time we met, Jenna was concerned for me as she shared the trauma-based parts of her story. She asked me how I was doing, and what I was going to do to take care of myself after the interview. Jenna is a very compassionate person.

Truth and Reconciliation Calls to Action, Child Welfare

The following five Calls to Action pertain to child welfare and are directly quoted from the 94 Calls to Action established in 2015 by the Truth and Reconciliation Commission of Canada:[9]

Child Welfare

1. We call upon the federal, provincial, territorial, and Aboriginal governments to commit to reducing the number of Aboriginal children in care by:
   1. Monitoring and assessing neglect investigations.
   2. Providing adequate resources to enable Aboriginal communities and child-welfare organizations to keep Aboriginal families together where it is safe to do so, and to keep children in culturally appropriate environments, regardless of where they reside.
   3. Ensuring that social workers and others who conduct child-welfare investigations are properly educated and trained about the history and impacts of residential schools.
   4. Ensuring that social workers and others who conduct child-welfare investigations are properly educated and trained about the potential for Aboriginal communities and families to provide more appropriate solutions to family healing.
   5. Requiring that all child-welfare decision makers consider the impact of the residential school experience on children and their caregivers.
2. We call upon the federal government, in collaboration with the provinces and territories, to prepare and publish annual reports on the number of Aboriginal children (First Nations, Inuit, and Métis)

who are in care, compared with non-Aboriginal children, as well as the reasons for apprehension, the total spending on preventive and care services by child-welfare agencies, and the effectiveness of various interventions.

3. We call upon all levels of government to fully implement Jordan's Principle.

4. We call upon the federal government to enact Aboriginal child-welfare legislation that establishes national standards for Aboriginal child apprehension and custody cases and includes principles that:

　1. Affirm the right of Aboriginal governments to establish and maintain their own child-welfare agencies.

　2. Require all child-welfare agencies and courts to take the residential school legacy into account in their decision making.

3. Establish, as an important priority, a requirement that placements of Aboriginal children into temporary and permanent care be culturally appropriate.

4. We call upon the federal, provincial, territorial, and Aboriginal governments to develop culturally appropriate parenting programs for Aboriginal families.

Acknowledgments

I am humbled by the collaborative act of this book's creation. I am extremely grateful to the participants for their trust, and in awe of their ability to keep overcoming. Sharing a personal story is like giving a most precious gift. I have had the privilege of participants sharing with me their joy, sorrow, anger, questions, and longings. It was a meaningful and intimate experience.

Thank you Andrew Mahon, for your generosity and craft in creating the portraits. You are talented and kind. It was very special to work with you on this project.

Thank you Beatrice Mosionier, for your generosity in writing the foreword. It was serendipitous the day we met at McNally Robinson and you wrote your email address in my copy of *In Search of April Raintree*. I am extremely grateful to you.

Thank you Jackie Traverse for your beautiful cover art that so perfectly embodies the soul of this book.

Thank you to all the people who took the time to meet with me so generously while I was researching and writing, and especially those who introduced me to book participants: Mitch Bourbonniere, Michael Redhead Champagne, Marie Christian, Rhonda Elias-Penner, Trevor Holroyd, Kristy McKlosky, the late Joe McLellan, Clayton Sandy, Jackie Traverse, and Matt Willan.

Thank you Rossbrook House and (now past) Executive Director Phil Chiappetta for sharing your space with me to interview participants.

My thanks to Emily Brownell for your help with the stats, Savannah Szocs for your work on the resource section, and Marie Christian for many small things.

Chi Miigwetch to Auntie Gladys Marinko who agreed to be a listening presence to any participant who wanted a loving community auntie to talk with after a book interview.

A huge thank you to everyone at Great Plains Publications: Mel, Catharina, and Keith for your belief, effort, support, and wisdom. I am grateful as always to Marjorie Anderson my first draft editor, for her keen eye, open mind and compassionate heart.

I gratefully thank my wide group of friends who have supported and encouraged me along the way. You know who you are. A special mention to the early readers of the book: Mitch Bourbonniere, Cathy Finnbogason, Paula Isaak, Carla Loewen, Renate Schulz, and Lori Yarchuk.

Thank you to my family: Paul, Kendra, Mark, Andrew, Brett and Nicole. Your unconditional love and laughter are my oxygen.

AMDG

Resources

CRISIS LINES:

Kids Help Line: 1-800-668-6868

Klinic Community Health Crisis Line: 1-888-322-3019

Klinic Sexual Assault Crisis Line: 1-888-292-7565

Manitoba Association of Women's Shelters Crisis Line: 1-877-977-0007

Manitoba Domestic Violence Crisis Line: 1-877-977-0007

Manitoba Suicide Prevention and Support Line: 1-877-435-7170

First Nations and Inuit Hope for Wellness Help Line: 1-855-242-3310

Ikwe Widdijiitiwin Crisis Line: 1-800-362-3344

Indian Residential School Survivors Crisis Line: 1-866-925-4419

24/7 SAFE SPACES:

Main Street Project Emergency Shelter: 637 Main Street, (204) 982-8229

N'Dinewamak – Our Relatives' Place: 190 Disraeli Freeway, (204) 943-1803

Rossbrook House: 658 Ross Avenue, (204) 949-4090

Salvation Army Centre of Hope: 180 Henry Avenue, (204) 946-9402

Siloam Mission: 300 Princess Street, (204) 956-4344

Tina's Safe Haven – Ndinawemaaganag Endaawaad: 370 Flora Avenue, (204) 417-7233

Velma's House: 154 Sherbrook Street, (204) 560-3007

West End 24-Hour Safe Space: 430 Langside, (204) 333-9681

YRC and Shelter Winnipeg: 159 Mayfair Avenue, (204) 477-1804

CODES:

FA   *Financial Aid Resources*
GC   *Group Counselling*
GS   *General Support Services*
HS   *Shelter/Housing Services*
IC   *Individual Counselling*
IS   *Informational and/or Referral Services*
ICS   *Incarceration Support*
LS   *Legal Services*
MS   *Medical Services*
YP   *Youth Programming*

9 Circles Community Health Centre (MS, IC, GS, IS)
Web: https://ninecircles.ca
Phone: (204) 940-6000
Address: 705 Broadway

Aboriginal Health and Wellness Centre (IS, MS, IC, GC, GS)
Web: https://ahwc.ca/
Phone: (204) 925-3700
Address: Suite 215-181 Higgins Avenue

Alpha House Project (HS, IC, GC)
Web: https://www.alphahouseproject.ca/
Phone: (204) 982-2011

A Woman's Place: NorWest Co-op Community Health (MS, LS, IC, GS, IS, YP)
Web:https://norwestcoop.ca/
program_location/a-womans-place/
Phone: (204) 938-5900
Address: 785 Keewatin Street

Bravestone Centre Inc (GC, IC, IS, GS, HS, YP)
Web: https://bravestonecentre.ca/
Phone: (204) 275-2600

Chez Rachel (HS, IC, GC, GS, IS, YP)
Web: https://chezrachel.ca/
Phone: (204) 925-2550

Clan Mothers Healing Village (HS, IS, IC, GS)
Web: https://clanmothers.ca/

Elizabeth Fry Society of Manitoba (IS, GS, HS, ICS)
Web: https://efsmanitoba.org/
Phone: (204) 589-7335
Address: 544 Selkirk Avenue

Fearless R2W (HS, IS, GS)
Web: https://fearlessr2w.ca/

Fort Garry Women's Resource Centre (IC, GC, LS, GS, IS)
Web: https://fgwrc.ca/
Phone: (204) 477-1123
Address: 1150-A Waverley Street

Futures Forward (FA, IS, GS, YP)
Web: https://www.futuresforward.ca/
Phone: 1-888-395-2135

Heartwood Healing Centre (GC, IC, GS)
Web: https://heartwoodcentre.ca/
Phone: (204) 783-5460
Address: 104 Roslyn Road

Ikwe Widdijiitiwin (HS, IC, GC, GS, IS, YP)
Web: http://www.ikwe.ca/
Shelter Services: 1-800-362-3344

Ka Ni Kanichihk Inc. (GS, IS, YP, IC, GC)
Web: https://www.kanikanichihk.ca/
Phone: (204) 953-5820, (204) 594-6500
Address: 455 McDermot Avenue, 102-765 Main Street

Klinic Community Health (IC, GS, IS, MS)
Web: http://klinic.mb.ca/
Phone: (204) 784-4090
Address: 167 Sherbrook Street

Legal Help Centre (LS, IS, GS)
Web: https://legalhelpcentre.ca/
Phone: (204) 258-3096
Address: 202-393 Portage Avenue

Main Street Project (HS, GC, IC, IS, GS)
Web: https://www.mainstreetproject.ca/
Phone: (204) 982-8229
Address: 637 Main Street

Ma Mawi-Wi-Chi-Itata Centre (GC, IC, YP)
Web: http://www.mamawi.com/
Phone: (204) 925-0300

Manitoba Advocate for Children and Youth (IS, GS, YP)
Web: https://manitobaadvocate.ca/
Phone: (204) 988-7440
Address: 100-346 Portage Avenue

Mount Carmel Clinic (MS, GC, IC, GS, IS, HS, YP)
Web: https://www.mountcarmel.ca/
Phone: (204) 582-2311
Address: 886 Main Street

Ndinawe (HS, IS, GS, YP)
Web: https://ndinawe.ca/
Phone: (204) 417-7233

Neeginan Centre – ACWI (GS, IS, YP)
Web: https://neeginancentre.com/
Phone: (204) 989-6605
Address: 181 Higgins Avenue

New Directions (HS, FA, GS, IS, GC, IC, YP)
Web: https://newdirections.mb.ca/
Phone: (204) 786-7051
Address: 717 Portage Avenue

North End Women's Centre (GC, GS, IC, IS)
Web: http://www.newcentre.org/
Phone: (204) 589-7347
Address: 394 Selkirk Avenue

North Point Douglas Women's Centre (IS, GS, GC, IC)
Web: https://www.npdwc.org/
Phone: (204) 947-0321
Address: 221 Austin Street N

Indigenous Women's Healing Centre (HS, IC, GS, IS)
Web: http://iwhc.ca/north-star-lodge/
Phone: (204) 989-8240
Address: 105 Aikens Street

Our Own Health Centre (MS, IC, IS, GS, FA)
Web: https://www.ourownhealth.ca/
Phone: (204) 691-1600
Address: 230 Osborne Street

Pluri-Elles (Manitoba) Inc. (IC, GS, FA, YP)
Web: http://www.pluri-elles.mb.ca/
Phone: (204) 233-1735
Address: 114-420 Des Meurons Street

Rainbow Resource Centre (IC, GC, GS, IS, YP)
Web: https://www.rainbowresourcecentre.org/
Phone: (204) 474-0212
Address: 170 Scott Street

Resource Assistance for Youth (YP, IS, GS, HS, IC)
Web: https://rayinc.ca/
Phone: (204) 783-5617 ext. 206
Address: 125 Sherbrook Street

Rossbrook House (IS, GS, YP)
Web: https://rossbrookhouse.ca/
Phone: (204) 949-4090
Address: 658 Ross Avenue

Sexual Assault Nurse Examiner (SANE) Program (MS)
Web: https://hsc.mb.ca/emergency/
Phone: (204) 787-2071
Address: 820 Sherbrook Street (Health Sciences Centre)

Sexuality Education Resource Centre (IS, GS, YP)
Web: https://serc.mb.ca/
Phone: (204) 982-7800
Address: 167 Sherbrook Street

Spence Neighbourhood Association (HS, IS, GS, YP)
Web: https://spenceneighbourhood.org/
Phone: (204) 783-5000 ext. 109
Address: 615 Ellice Avenue

Sunshine House (IS, GS)
Web: https://www.sunshinehousewpg.org/
Phone: (204) 783-8565
Address: 646 Logan Avenue

Thrive Community Support Circle (GS, IS, IC, GC, FA, YP)
Web: https://thrivecommunitysupportcircle.com/
Email: resourcecentre@thrivewpg.com
Phone: (204) 772-9091
Address: 555 Spence Street

Voices: Manitoba's Youth in Care Network (FA, IS, GS, YP)
Web: https://voices.mb.ca/
Phone: (204) 982-4956
Address: 3rd Floor, 61 Juno Street

Wahbung Abinoonjiiag Inc. (HS, GC, IC, GS, YP)
Web: http://wahbung.org/
Phone: (204) 925-4610
Address: 225 Dufferin Ave

West Central Women's Resource Centre (HS, GS, IS, YP)
Web: https://wcwrc.ca/
Phone: (204) 774-8975
Address: 640 Ellice Ave

Willow Place Inc. (HS, IC, GC, GS, YP)
Web: https://willowplaceshelter.ca/
Phone: (204) 615-0313 ext. 0

Women's Health Clinic (MS, IC, GC)
Web: https://womenshealthclinic.org/
Phone: (204) 947-1517
Address: 419 Graham Ave., Unit A

Endnotes

1   Transforming Child Welfare Legislation in Manitoba: Opportunities to Improve Outcomes for Children and Youth. Report of the Legislative Review Committee. September 2018, (pg 3-4).

2   Office of the Children's Advocate STRENGTHENING OUR YOUTH: Their Journey to Competence and Independence. A Report on Youth Leaving Manitoba's Child Welfare System -Billie Schibler Children's Advocate (Alice McEwan-Morris November 2006), (pg 54).

3   Brownell M, Chartier M, Au W, MacWilliam L, Schultz J, Guenette W, Valdivia J. *The Educational Outcomes of Children in Care in Manitoba* Winnipeg, MB. Manitoba Centre for Health Policy, June 2015. (pg 85)

4   Brownell M, Chartier M, Au W, MacWilliam L, Schultz J, Guenette W, Valdivia J. *The Educational Outcomes of Children in Care in Manitoba* Winnipeg, MB. Manitoba Centre for Health Policy, June 2015. (pg xii)

5   Office of the Children's Advocate STRENGTHENING OUR YOUTH: Their Journey to Competence and Independence. A Report on Youth Leaving Manitoba's Child Welfare System -Billie Schibler Children's Advocate (Alice McEwan-Morris November 2006), (pg 54).

6   Ibid.

7   Brandon, J. Maes Nino, C., Retzlaff, B., Flett, J., Hepp, B., Shirtliffe, R., & Wiebe, A. (2018). *The Winnipeg Street Census 2018: Final Report.* Winnipeg: Social Planning Council of Winnipeg

8   When Youth Age Out of Care—Bulletin of Time 2 Findings—Deborah Rutman, Carol Hubberstey, April Feduniw & Erinn Brown. March 2006 (pg 17).

9   Truth and Reconciliation Commission of Canada, Truth and Reconciliation Commission of Canada: Calls to Action (2015), https://www2.gov.bc.ca/assets/gov/british-columbians-our- governments/indigenous-people/aboriginal-peoples-documents/calls_to_action_english2.pdf

Index